Praise for *Too Lazy to Work, Too Nervous to Steal*

John Clausen is funny, irreverent and as right on as usual in this essential guide for freelancers. No sugarcoating here—just the truth as only this veteran writer/editor can tell it. It's an anecdote-rich book loaded with information that isn't readily available to writers. I'm going to recommend it to every beginning writing I know and to all freelancers who want to work smart, make more money and still respect themselves in the morning.

> —Bonnie Hearn, author of *Focus Your Writing* and
> *The Freelancer's Rulebook*

I have found that many "how to" books are written by people who never did. Not so in this case. Clausen and the characters he introduces have been there and done that. They know what they are talking about, and everything you need is included. If you don't find several good, money-making ideas for yourself in here, you haven't been paying attention.

> —Jack Edmonston, author of *How to Create More Effective*
> *High-Tech Advertising* and former vice president of IDG

John Clausen, a pro's pro, is a marvelous storyteller. He doesn't just tell; he shows by sharing inspirational stories that support his sage advice.

> —Bud Gardner, coauthor of *Chicken Soup for the Writer's Soul*

Well-paying writing opportunities are everywhere, says John Clausen. I agree. Generously, and with great wit, style and depth of experience, he gives you everything you need to develop the radar to find them, the confidence to demand higher respect and income and the the attitude to stand tall and proudly say, "I'm a writer!" Buy this book.

> —Peter Bowerman, author of *The Well-Fed Writer: Financial*
> *Self-Sufficiency as a Freelance Writer in Six Months or Less*

too lazy
to work,
too nervous
to steal

How to Have a Great Life
As a Freelance Writer

JOHN CLAUSEN

WRITER'S DIGEST BOOKS
CINCINNATI, OHIO
www.writersdigest.com

Visit our Web site at www.writersdigest.com for information on more resources for writers.

To receive a free weekly e-mail newsletter delivering tips and updates about writing and about Writer's Digest products, send and e-mail with "Subscribe Newsletter" in the body of a message to newsletter-request@writersdigest.com, or register directly at our Web site at www.writersdigest.com.

05 04 03 02 01   5 4 3 2 1

Library of Congress Cataloging-in-Publication Data

Clausen, John
    Too lazy to work, too nervous to steal: how to have a great life as a freelance writer /
John Clausen.
        p.   cm.
    Includes index.
    ISBN 0-89879-997-X
    1. Freelance journalism—Vocational guidance. 2. Feature writing—Vocational guidance. I. Title.
PN147. C62   2001
808'.02—dc21   00-066477
                                                                                CIP

Editor: Brad Crawford
Designer: Angela Wilcox
Cover designer: Amber Traven
Production coordinator: Mark Griffin
Cover photo © John Acurso/CORBIS

This book is dedicated to my father,
Morten Clausen,
one of the all-time great storytellers.

Acknowledgments

Jan Latimer-Burch . . . for buying my first freelance piece, thereby making me unfit for regular, gainful employment. Ralph Chavez . . . for telling me that there is no such thing as good writing, only good rewriting. My mother, Doris Clausen . . . for teaching me to love words. Biff Olson . . . for his relentlessly high standards in copyediting. Heidi Storch . . . for her great humor and hard work. Jodi Jill . . . for being my agent, friend and advocate. Jack Heffron, David Borcherding and Brad Crawford . . . for their kindness and professionalism.

About the Author

John Clausen is a twenty-year veteran of the freelance writing business.

If you ask him what his toughest job in the business has been, he'll tell you it was during high school when he ran a single-sheet, hand-operated press for the weekly *Kenmare News* in Kenmare, North Dakota. "The first morning I ran it, I ruined about $50 worth of newsprint . . . at three cents a sheet."

That was in 1966. Since then, John has worked as a reporter on weekly and daily newspapers in Arizona and Kansas, edited several magazines, owned a California-based advertising agency that specialized in direct mail, and taught classes in journalism and advertising. He holds a B.A. in journalism from the University of Arizona, Tucson, and has done graduate work in communications studies at California State University, Sacramento.

A well-known circulation promotion/direct mail writer, John has a client list that includes some of the best-known publications in the world: *The Christian Science Monitor, Billboard* magazine, *The Hollywood Reporter, Farm Journal, San Francisco* magazine, *Federal Computer Week, Carolina Gardener, Keyboard Magazine* and *Yoga Journal.* He has also sold articles to *The New York Daily News Sunday Magazine, Circulation Management, Nation's Business, Law and Order* and other national and regional publications.

John lives in Hendersonville, North Carolina, with his eleven-year-old-son, Pete. He is currently the editor and publisher of Writing for Money (www.writingformoney.com), an online journal for freelance writers.

Table of Contents

Mamas, Don't Let Your Babies Grow Up to Be Wage Slaves

It was between events at a nationally televised rodeo.

The announcer was interviewing a tough little bull rider, asking him the sort of probing, hardball questions we've all come to expect from perky electronic sports journalists. Finally, the young lady asked the cowboy to explain just why he was in the rodeo business.

The cowboy pushed back his hat and said, "Well, I'm too lazy to work, and I'm too nervous to steal."

I genuinely like the sentiment and the self-deprecating delivery, but actually there are few people in the world who work harder at their chosen professions than rodeo cowboys. Holding onto the bull rope with one hand while the bull explodes from the chute was once described to me as the equivalent of grabbing the bumper of a passing Buick at 40 MPH. No question about it, that sort of thing takes some serious conditioning.

As for nervous, all you have to do is get within ten feet of a large, malevolent, incredibly agile, crossbred Brahma bull, and you'll understand the steel nerves these guys must have. Believe it or not, there are parallels between rodeo cowboys and freelance writers.

True, it's unlikely that you're going to have a murderous, one-ton bovine standing on your chest while you're knocking out a few paragraphs. And as a rule, rodeo cowboys dress a lot better than most of us. Big hats, pointy boots, pearly-snapped western shirts and gratuitous physical pain notwithstanding, there are definite similarities in the two jobs. For example, both you and your cowboy counterparts are compensated according to your performance. Some of you will make big bucks. Some of you will not. You both perform in public. Talent is important to both jobs, but guts and determination are what make the real difference. People admire you for what you do, even if they would never, ever have the courage to do it themselves.

Perhaps most important, when you finally get a taste of success at either profession, it is unlikely that you will ever want to give it up. You are your own boss, you take orders from no one, and no one can fire you. You take your own chances (and your own lumps) and go on doing what you love. You may, during difficult economic times, be tempted to give it all up and work at a "real" job, just for the alleged security of it all. Before you do that, ask any downsized former employee from a huge national company (you can find plenty of them in the unemployment line) about the concept of job security.

With this book I intend to help you resist the urge to become a wage slave and to help you take your freelance writing career to a whole new level of income and enjoyment. The simple fact is that almost any writer, even a marginally talented one, can make a living as a freelancer if he or she will approach the profession with a businesslike attitude, positive thinking and a sense of humor and fun.

So pull your metaphorical hat down tight and nod to the boys working the chute. Then brace yourself for a great ride and a great life. I know you can do it.

—John Clausen

What You Want Is Out There

JAY WINCHESTER

For a lot of people, getting "downsized" is a bad thing, but that's not so in Jay Winchester's case. In fact, losing his twenty-two-year telecommunications job might have been the best thing that ever happened to him as a writer.

"I was searching for what I was going to do next," Jay recalls. "Because I was nontechnical [he'd worked for IBM writing manuals and other materials, not as a programmer or technician], I was having trouble finding a job back in that industry. But for some reason I'd always had an interest in writing. . . . Then I found a little publication called *Writing for Money* and started subscribing to that.

"You know, when you're laid off, things can be a little unsettled, and part of the things I'd do to pass my time between job interviews was to kind of surf the TV channels to see what was on. I'd always had an abiding interest in infomercials . . . because there's a transaction that goes on between the viewer and the program. To me, that's an interesting dynamic. Anyway, in the market listings in *Writing for Money* they would always talk about infomercial leads, and they would always say to send a demo reel. Well, I didn't know a demo reel from a pet rock, so I did one of the things that I'd always read you shouldn't do. I called the editor of *Writing for Money* directly.

"I talked to him about infomercials for a little bit and asked him what a writer who had talent but no demo reels could do. He said, 'I don't know. Why don't you do an article on that for me? Then you can find out.'

"So that became a way of making contact with people in the industry. Because of that article, he subsequently assigned me a much larger piece on the infomercial industry. And in the course of doing that, I made contact with an editor of a publication called *Response TV* magazine, which is now called *Response* magazine. I was interviewing that editor for the article, and in the course of the conversation we got to talking about writing. He said I sounded like a person who knew a little bit of what he was talking about . . . and he wanted to give me a couple of assignments.

"One of those assignments was for DRTV in Japan. The infomercial industry is also known as direct response television, which they shorten to DRTV. This was my chance to look into the industry on a more global scale. It was kind of interesting having the interview with the Japanese people. They have a different way of doing business. My intent is not to make fun of anybody in saying this, but the barrier between trying to make them understand the questions I was asking and trying to interpret their answers was a challenge sometimes. That was a cover story for *Response*, one of three I've done for them.

"As a result of doing those pieces for *Response*, I started meeting some of the producers in the business, doing some production-related articles about what goes on in the editing suite. I began to establish some contacts.

"I continued writing for them for a year and a half. That was back in about 1995 or 1996. Then in April of 1998 I got a sort of cryptic note from that first editor I'd interviewed. He said he had a big assignment and was looking for a writer. It involved some people in the infomercial business in Florida not far from where I lived. I made him aware that I was certainly available and certainly interested. I eventually did get the assignment, which was to write an anniversary piece on Kevin and Tim Harrington, two brothers who were active at the time with the Home Shopping Network.

"They were quite famous in the business. At one point, they held the rights to the Ginsu knives, which is probably the infomercial that pops into people's minds when they think about infomercials. They've done a whole long list of 'firsts.' They did an infomercial on a music package—Wolfman Jack Solid Gold Rock and Roll—which was the very first music infomercial. They did a fishing lure called the Flying Lure, which was the first fishing infomercial. They did Color Code Car Wash. They did the Daily Mixer, which was a handheld mixer. They also did one of the first infomercials for Tony Little, the fitness guru. The Tony Little show was for something called "Target Training." It was a three-tape series, and each of the tapes went platinum and at one time held the first, second and third spots on the *Billboard* magazine video sales charts. So you can see that in the industry, these guys were quite famous.

"I had interviewed Tim for a couple other articles, primarily as a background source, but also because he was local. He was very willing to share contacts with me on those stories. In fact, he'd even invited me over to their offices in Clearwater, which is across the bay from where I lived. I sat down with them and spent two or three days with my tape recorder interviewing them and calling people in the industry about them."

When the article came out, the Harringtons were extremely impressed with the job Jay had done. So much so, in fact, that they gave him an office and a computer and offered to teach him the business.

"I got started doing that," Jay says, "and got involved in a couple of projects with them. No scripting or anything, but just kind of helping around the office as best I could . . . using my writing abilities. And I was getting paid. Not a lot of money, but if there is something I'm interested in learning about, something I don't have any experience in, I can usually find a way to lower my rates a little bit. I'm willing to do that. I don't do that all the time, but in this instance I felt that the experience I might get would be worthwhile."

Taking the initiative is one of Jay's trademarks. So, when the Harringtons became involved in another Tony Little project, Jay wrote up a few observations and made them available to the fitness celebrity.

"I was sitting in on a meeting with him," Jay remembers, "and he turned to me and said, 'I just want you to know that I read over the ideas that you have, and I really admire your passion. You and I are connecting on the same level with this, and we'd like you to be involved in the project.' "

The company had already talked about bringing in an experienced infomercial writer to write the show. "I sat there," Jay says, "thinking this will be great. I'll get a chance to work with a very well-known writer. Very successful in the field. And I'll really learn a lot about what I really want to do. As the meeting went on and on, I kept asking when we'd bring this writer in, and they kept pushing the question to the side. I eventually asked it again, and Tim Harrington and Tony looked at each other across the conference table and Tim's response was, 'Well, you know, I don't think she can do anything for us that Jay can't do.' So I got to write the show, which was for me a pretty scary thing at the time.

"I really didn't have very long to write it. We had quite a few discussions, and I had a pretty good idea of what Tony wanted to do. Tony has a unique approach. If you sit down and you're writing grammatically correct sentences and you're making sure that the words are actually words found in the dictionary, you'll run into a little problem. That's just not who he is and what he does. But he does have a style that connects with people. We went through about six incarnations of the script before we actually started shooting."

Jay eventually worked into the company's Web site writing and designing department, where he has helped develop several projects. But through all of this, he never forgets his beginnings as a freelance magazine journalist. "I still write for *Response*," he says, "and I still maintain the contacts I've made all over the world.

"It's funny, you know. Almost everything I've done as a writer has grown out of some assignment I did for *Writing for Money*. I know that any assignment I've ever gotten from them has led to another three or four contacts with editors, just in researching how writers can break into different kinds of writing. What I find is that editors are . . . willing to work with a writer who's willing to work hard to give them what they want. And even if that writer isn't the next Hemingway, that doesn't matter. That's the beauty of it. You have to be able to put sentences together and build paragraphs and from those paragraphs construct a story that fits in line with what the editor has assigned you. They're [the editors] not looking for somebody who's going to go out and say, 'I had a better idea, so I did this instead.' What they want to know is that you're going to get the assignment done the way they want it. You have to build a level of trust with them. You do that, and I think you will be successful.

"A good writer who's willing to work hard and pay attention can take advantage of opportunities and move forward. If money is really what you want to chase, there's a lot of money out there waiting to be chased. If more emotional or creative work is what you want, that's out there, too. I like a nice blend of both, and I'm very content with what I've chosen to pursue. That's the key."

CHAPTER ONE

Making a Great Living as a Freelancer Isn't as Hard as You Might Think!

Not long ago, I read some absolutely frightening advice in one of the writer's trade magazines. The author of the piece, a "full-time" freelancer, said he gets up at 4 A.M. every morning, works twelve hours every weekday and at least eight on Saturday with a couple more hours hammered out on Sunday.

Let's see, that's seventy hours a week multiplied by fifty-two weeks, which makes his annual total amount of time spent writing somewhere around 3,640 hours (give or take a few coffee breaks and maybe twenty minutes to spend with the family on Christmas).

The piece implied that spending any less time than this at one's craft would be almost certain to leave a writer "dead broke."

I would like to say right now, with no apologies, that I do not work that hard.

Furthermore, I think that anyone who does work that hard should be pulling down an annual income similar to that of the CEO of General Motors or RJR Nabisco. Plus benefits and a company car.

In fact, if you think that a six-figure income and a life filled with nothing but work is the definition of success, you might as well quit reading right now. That's not life. Not by my standards.

Here's my short definition of a successful writing career: enough money to pay my bills and live with a certain degree of comfort, enough variety in my assignments and projects to keep me interested and enough time off from writing to allow my mind to relax. If that sounds like a sane way to live and write, then read on and I will tell you how it can be done.

Here—in a nutshell—is *How to Make a Great Living as a Freelance Writer*:

1. Get an attitude.
2. Design a system with which you can live.
3. Find an "anchor client."
4. Understand that marketing is at least half the job.
5. Avoid getting stuck in a single genre.
6. Don't get sloppy.
7. Have some fun.

Let's take a little deeper look at each of these seven main points.

Get an Attitude

A few years ago, I opened a writing seminar with this question: "How many of you are good writers?"

No one answered.

I asked again. Still no answer.

I paced across the room a couple times, cleared my throat and asked again. Finally, a single hand rose timidly out of the crowd.

What is it that inspires such modesty in writers? Maybe it is the fact that every article submitted, every book proposal pushed over the transom, every screenplay treatment dropped on a conference table is an invitation to criticism. Maybe thinking of yourself as a "good" writer sets you up for a bigger fall. Maybe a little foot shuffling and head hanging will protect your delicate feelings.

Get out of that frame of mind immediately. If you don't think of yourself as a good writer, nobody else will either.

Relax, I'm not going to lapse into a touchy-feely discussion of positive thinking or Zen meditation (although I have nothing whatsoever against either).

What I'm saying is this: When someone hires you to write something (anything), they like to think they are hiring the best they can afford. If you show anything but confidence (even if you don't, at the time, possess much), you won't get the job. What's more, if by some miracle you do get the job, a lack of attitude will almost always foster problems in the copy approval, editing or payment cycles of the transaction.

One of my former clients, an East Coast technical publisher, is a case in point. When we first began negotiating my fee, I told him he would have to pay 50 percent up front on each project. He said that it was "no problem." After about ten days, my mailbox and I were still waiting. I called his office and found out that he was in Europe and had forgotten to sign a check for me before he left. "OK," I told his assistant. "Tell him he'll have to find someone else to do the project."

He called me about a week later, apologized and asked me what it would take to get me to do the job. I told him he needed to make a check for $5,000 appear on my doorstep the next day. It showed up bright and early, and I did the job with no problems. I had earned his respect. Perhaps more to the point, that year I earned about $20,000 in writing fees from his company. I am convinced that I only landed this client because I didn't allow him or his assistant to jerk me around with tales (true or not) of unsigned checks and trips to the Continent.

I don't want to sound overly adversarial here, but you have to create the image that the client needs you more than you need the client. If you lose that edge, your business (and don't kid yourself, if you are a freelancer, you are in business) relationships will be filled with late payments, chiseled fees, unreasonable copy changes and dwindling revenue.

This doesn't mean that you have to insist that every word you write is golden and not subject to editing or revision. The client is paying the bill and, therefore, the client gets to have what he or she wants. But don't be obsequious. Insist on a professional relationship. Go on the record with your observations, predictions or objections. If a patient argues with a doctor, he'll probably be asked to find a different doctor. If a client berates her attorney, she will likely be invited to hunt up a new attorney. That's the attitude for success as a freelance writer.

Be a pro and believe that what you're writing is worth at least as much as you are being paid.

Design a System With Which You Can Live

When I first started freelancing, I was lucky enough to be unemployed. I wasn't exactly living under bridges, but believe me, I didn't have to spend a lot of time agonizing over the security that I would be giving up.

For the employed writer, however, the thought of kissing the old paycheck good-bye and actually trying to feed a family by freelancing is a scary, scary thing. The starving freelancer image is probably exacerbated by the fact that a lot of start-up freelancers don't get too far before they are forced to scurry back to the security of a regular job.

The leading cause of freelance failure is, in my experience, the lack of a realistic system. If you are to succeed, you'll need to take yourself through a thorough reality check. Take a candid look at your financial situation. If you have no savings, credit cards at their outer limits, three kids in college, house payments that you can just barely make and no other income to support your family . . . well, maybe you are going to have to make some adjustments.

Don't expect your freelance career to immediately replace your pay-check. Talk to your spouse, and make sure you have some moral and psychological support. You will need it. You'll probably also need to make some plans to reduce your monthly overhead. Set aside as much money as you possibly can before you make the move to full-time free-lancing. Nothing will erode your confidence and destroy your attitude quicker than being broke. Later, we'll talk about ways to speed up cash flow, but for now, please realize that money can be a big problem if you aren't prepared for life after the paycheck.

You'll also have to prepare yourself for life after the supervisor. You are the boss now. A lot of new freelancers have trouble with that. They actually miss being told what to do. Or maybe they miss the structure. Or maybe they simply miss "going to work" in the morning.

If that's the case with you, I suggest that you set your alarm clock, get up at your regular time, throw on a tie and "go to work," even if the commute is only three or four feet into the den or spare bedroom. Take regular coffee breaks and lunch hours. Give yourself a quota or a list of things you have to do in a day. Have staff meetings with yourself. Do whatever it takes to make you feel like you're on the job, because that's what it is—your job.

Another critical piece of your freelance "system" is the handling of your money. Since I don't enjoy and am not particularly good at bookkeeping, I have enlisted the help of a CPA. It was one of the best investments I ever made. If you like to balance your checkbook yourself and understand the tax code, however, you might want to do without some of the bookkeeping help. Whichever you decide, keep in mind that the time you spend bookkeeping could probably be more profitably spent writing or plotting your personal marketing strategies.

Since you will probably experience "dry spells" during your free-lancing career, you will have to learn to put something aside during flush periods. OK, so this sounds a little simplistic. Gosh, everybody knows that, right? Maybe so, but when you're sitting there with a check for $5,000 in your hand it can be difficult to remember that part of it has to go to pay quarterly taxes, feed the retirement fund or bolster the kids' college funds. This may be *the single most important part of your system*, so don't blow it. Learn to handle the money. That alone may not make you a total freelance success, but it will keep you from being a total freelance disaster. My advice: Find a CPA who has worked with self-employed people and understands the "feast or famine" aspects of freelancing. Together you can work out a money-handling system.

Find an "Anchor Client"

When you sit down with your CPA, there's a good chance that he or she will tell you that you need to smooth out your cash flow. The best way I know to do this is to get what I call an "anchor client."

The next time you are in the local mall, look at the stores instead of the merchandise. You will almost certainly see among the shops and boutiques at least one large department or discount store. This is what the mall owner considers an "anchor tenant," a tenant who provides a large chunk of rent each month. The mall may not be able to survive with just that tenant, but it will pay a large portion of its overhead with the revenue from the anchor tenant.

It is precisely the same with a freelance "anchor client." The client could be almost anyone. When I first started, there was a local advertising agency that used my copywriting. Later, I had a regular public relations client. Others have included a book publisher in Virginia and a direct-mail agency in Boston. Some of you may have magazines that buy your stuff regularly. That's great, although it is usually the commercial client that keeps me in Legos and lager.

I know a relatively new-to-the-business freelancer in California who used his former careers in real estate and engineering to land a large civil engineering firm as an anchor client. Incidentally, he tells me that when he first began freelancing, his income fell from the $175,000 per year he had earned in real estate to about $30,000. Thanks in large part to his anchor client, that annual income had recently climbed back up to approximately $85,000.

Networking (if you'll pardon a rather shopworn phrase) is a great way to expand your markets and land the all-important anchor client.

I know a West Coast freelancer, a specialist in motorcycle, car and gun magazines, who broke into the European market when a friend asked him to help out with an overflow of assignments from a British motorcycle magazine. He did a great job on the assignment, and one hundred issues later, he's still working with that British magazine, as well as with several other overseas specialty magazines. Even better, the same freelance friend who gave him the original break continues to call him with overflow assignments. Another freelancer in Florida told me that for every story he does he'll make contacts for three or four more stories or writing assignments. If he were interviewing Billy Crystal for *People* magazine, you can be sure part of the time would be spent talking about what the comedian looks for in a screenwriter. He's not one to let an opportunity go untapped, and neither should you.

Don't be shy.

Ask your freelance colleagues to swap contacts with you. I was at a friend's apartment one afternoon when I noticed that he was working on an assignment for a national book publishing company. I asked him for the contact person, sent in my clips and ended up doing a couple dozen fairly lucrative projects for them. My friend didn't mind passing the information along to me—especially since he'd gotten the contact's name and number the same way I had.

Sometimes networking can have a weird, down-the-road effect. More than a decade ago I spent about a year working on a screenplay and living in a Manhattan loft surrounded by a bunch of genuinely crazed Latvian artists and filmmakers. As far as I remember, I never made a nickel writing for any of them, but I kept in touch over the years. One day not long ago I got a call. One of them was putting together a video for an industrial client and needed a script written. So now I'm a few dollars richer and know far more that I ever wanted to know about those shiny machines that pump the filling into jelly donuts. As my friend the motorcycle rider says, "I'll write just about anything that has a check on the other end."

Don't overlook the value of a little personal public relations campaign.

A good client or a fruitful networking pal is worth a little special treatment. One year I sent signed, numbered prints as client gifts. Another year I sent out a dozen or so crystal balls. The point is to make sure the client knows you appreciate his or her business. And let those generous souls who give you new contacts and overflow work know how much you value the tips.

Gifts and cheap flattery aside, the best way to keep an anchor client is to give that client your best work. Never blow a deadline; always do your best work. Try hard to fit your schedule to your client's.

However, no matter how hard you try, you can't expect your anchor clients to stay around forever. They tend to fade for a variety of reasons, usually having nothing to do with your hard work and talent. Sometimes they'll decide to go in-house. Maybe they'll fall victim to bad economic times. Maybe a new CEO will have his own person in mind to replace you. Strive heroically to keep them, but always keep your eyes open for potential anchor clients.

Understand That Marketing Is at Least Half the Job

Whenever I think of marketing, I always think of a sign I saw in Sacramento, California, a few years ago. The sign, which listed the services available from a local agency, read "Advertising, Public Relations and Marketing."

This was, according to my definition, like saying, "Fords, Chevrolets and Cars." In other words, everything you do to promote yourself and your writing career can be considered marketing. It doesn't matter whether it's public relations, advertising, taking an editor to lunch, joining the local writers group, getting a new haircut, washing your car, designing your business cards and letterhead or working on anything else you do to get noticed favorably by prospective word buyers.

Go at this task as if your livelihood depended on it—because it does.

And remember that there are a lot of places to sell writing. You don't have to be content with just selling and reselling magazine articles. Explore the markets (more about markets later on in this book).

Don't waste time. I know that I confessed earlier to being somewhat less than a workaholic. That does not, however, mean that I advocate total sloth. Keep busy during your writing time. Your job is to turn your wits and words into cash. If you have some down time on one job, make sure you have some other projects to go after. Sell some greeting card copy (it won't buy you a new Porsche, but it may help you keep up the payments on the heap you already own). Put together an advertising copywriting portfolio. Show your clips to a reputable public relations firm. Study technical writing. There are practically no limits to the number of people who will hire you to do their writing for them.

You just have to make yourself available to them.

Advertise yourself. If you want to write guest editorials and brochure copy for attorneys, then you should advertise in legal journals or in the kinds of publications lawyers read. The same is true if you want to write for physicians, clergymen, school boards, political candidates and just about every other kind of business. (In the case of politicians, always get the money up front!)

You should also practice what is known as "guerrilla" marketing. By that I mean marketing that costs you little or no hard cash and pays a relatively healthy return. Here's a good example from a very successful freelancer who plies her trade in the Boston area. She had been hired to write a product brochure for a local company. Like any good freelancer, she did her job promptly and professionally. The client was very happy and gladly paid her fee.

That would have been the end of it had she not been a good guerrilla marketer. During the course of the job, she made it a point to talk with her clients about their business and their various marketing plans. At one point, they asked her if she knew anyone who wrote newsletters. A simple "I can do that" gained her a job that lasted for nearly a year and a half.

Her husband, also a freelancer, makes it a policy to let his clients know what he's up to at all times. He sends out samples of the work he's done and maintains a regular schedule for checking in with old clients. His intent is to make sure they don't forget about him when it comes time to request bids. He also wants them to know about all of the writing services he offers. "One of the worst things that can happen to a freelancer," he says, "is to have your clients think of you as someone who only writes brochures, or only writes speeches, or whatever. Personally, I'll write just about anything, and I want my clients to realize that. I don't want to miss a chance to bid on any kind of writing job."

While you're out there scrambling for assignments, you should also be keeping your eye on the *big money*.

Just about anything you write has some kind of big money potential. It may take a little tweaking or even some fairly extensive rewriting, but there is money to be made if you know what sells and who's buying it. That piece you wrote for the local paper on the local bachelor rodeo cowboy who bakes fancy wedding cakes might look good to the Sunday *Los Angeles Times Magazine*. The only difference between the local story and the *LA Times* story may be a little refocusing and several thousand dollars. Think large. Somebody has to sell to the big guys; it might as well be you.

Above all, spend at least half your time looking for new markets or developing ways to expand the ones you already have.

Avoid Getting Stuck in a Single Genre

It's easy to start thinking of yourself exclusively as a magazine freelancer, or a speech writer, or an ad copywriter.

Try to avoid such prejudices.

I make most of my income as a direct mail copywriter, specializing in magazine circulation promotion. This can pay anywhere from $3,000 to $20,000 per project, depending upon your experience and the relative depth of your clients' pockets. I advertise my services in several trade journals and speak at various circulation-oriented seminars whenever I get the chance. I look forward eagerly to my next direct mail assignment and to the resulting surge in my income.

But that doesn't mean I won't do a magazine article, or script a video, or write an ad campaign, or write a chapter of a children's book, or put together a services brochure. I've done all of those things (and more) and been well paid for them. There is no reason why you can't do the same.

Consider yourself a writer for hire. Period. As long as it doesn't conflict with your personal, professional code of ethics or violate your moral standards (writing child-directed tobacco ads, for example), you should be prepared to write practically anything for anybody.

There are literally millions of dollars out there waiting to be distributed among writers who are willing and able to write what needs to be written.

Don't Get Sloppy

It would be pretty easy to say "always do your best" and leave it at that. But that really doesn't communicate the serious financial consequences of sloppy writing.

Let me, therefore, give you a graphic example.

Several years ago, I had an anchor client, one of my best. My monthly income from this company ranged anywhere from $1,500 to $7,500. There was virtually no overhead on my end, and they paid cash in advance. I had a long, friendly relationship with the company and a steady flow of work—a freelancer's dream.

Then one day, I got a three-project assignment from them. I accepted the job, even though there was a serious illness in my family and my attention (not to mention my time) was being directed away from writing. As a result, I ended up writing the last of the projects after midnight, fighting a 9 A.M. deadline.

Normally, if I work that late, I leave the piece on my desk until I have a chance to review it. That night I did not. I faxed it hot out of my printer without so much as a second thought. The first two jobs had gone well, and I assumed that this one would, too.

The next morning I read the copy and recognized it for the gibberish it was. But it was too late. The client had been forced to rewrite the piece in-house. I offered all manner of restitution, but the damage had been done. I've never done another job for that client.

My point is this: Your reputation as a writer rides on every piece you write. Never, never, never turn in sloppy work. If there is something keeping you from doing top-notch work, then it's better to explain to your client what's happening and regretfully turn down the job. Believe me, it's easier to explain why you can't take a job than it is to explain why you didn't do the job right.

Have Some Fun

At the beginning of this diatribe, I mentioned my definition of success as it pertains to freelance writing: enough money, a pleasing variety of work and enough time away from writing.

Don't overlook that last concept. Grinding out copy is fine when the deadline is bearing down on you. Hard work is good for you and for your bank account, but don't forget to have some fun along the way.

Take some time off when you need it, or when someone needs you. Spend some time with your family. Take a walk. Go fishing. If you are a successful, mortgage-paying, grocery-buying freelance writer, you've done something remarkable with your life. You turn words into money. The whole world envies you. You deserve to take some pleasure in life.

My friend who dumped his real estate and engineering career to become a freelance writer puts it this way: "I took a hundred-thousand-dollar pay cut, but I'm enjoying life 100 percent more."

Not many people can say that. May you be one of them.

Jane

AAA

Cancun —
Oct. 4 - 8 —

$50 spa coupon

Cancun Palace — $1121.50
1087.00

includes airfare

Adventura — $1144.50
~~1091~~ 1110.00

— Jamaica —

Beaches Negril — $1863.50

Ochos Rios — $1783.50

"Think Less and Do More."

DONNA BOETIG

Take one look at the cover of Donna Boetig's book, *Feminine Wiles: Creative Techniques for Writing Women's Feature Stories That Sell,* and you'll understand how she's able to sell to top women's magazines.

The subheads say it all: *39 Things Editors Like From Writers, Generate Ideas That Intrigue, Get Intimate With Your Readers, Why Gushing Doesn't Sell,* and my personal favorite, *Stark-Naked Interviews—Getting a Woman to Bare Her Soul.*

Donna has always been drawn to freelance writing—even in 1972 when she worked as a teacher in Miami, facing forty-six non-English-speaking third and fourth graders from Cuba. And even later when she was a full-time mom.

Donna, who holds a bachelor's degree in journalism and a master's degree in writing, was working as a staff writer for the *Baltimore Sun* when the notion of freelancing moved from the back of her head to a more prominent position. It was a particularly dry assignment that pushed her over the top.

"I know this sounds terrible," she says, "but I was so totally bored to tears. I was thinking that there must be something I can do besides write this story for the *Sun.* I thought there must be some way to tweak what I was doing for my day job and unload it."

Thanks to her annual purchase of *Writer's Market,* she was able to turn the information she collected for the *Sun's* story on local government into a story-and-photography assignment for the official magazine published by a national civic organization.

She picked up $500 for her trouble, not a bad payday, especially considering that she had accumulated the information while being paid as a reporter. Not only that, but she also sold the editor on a handful of additional pieces based on the same interviews and information.

Of course, nothing lasts forever. The editor who had been so enthused about Donna's work was eventually replaced. "Just as I couldn't do anything wrong for the old editor," she recalls, "I couldn't do anything right for the new editor. No matter what I suggested, nothing jived."

Nevertheless, the freelance bug had infected her. "I guess it seemed so terribly creative to me," she says. "I was hooked after that initial experience."

Since then she's written and sold articles on a staggering array of topics. There was the Annapolis crab feast and the fireworks factory explosion. And who could forget the Catholic nuns who sued their bishop, or the inmate mothers with newborn babies? Then there was the single dad nurturing his two desperately ill sons, and a whole parade of dramatic, amusing or touching stories that have appeared in an equally staggering array of publications. A short list of her clients includes *Family Circle*, *Woman's Day*, *McCall's*, *Reader's Digest*, *The Optimist*, *The Rotarian* and *Catholic Digest*.

Over the years Donna has developed an effective, if somewhat unconventional attitude when it comes to finding new work. "What I tell people over and over again," she explains, "is 'think less and do more.' Yes, you do have to do your homework and really have a feel for the market and what's out there. But I can think of so many stories that were published that if I had given them more thought I wouldn't have even suggested the stories. For instance, I wrote a story a couple years ago for *Sesame Street Parents* magazine. It was called "Only, Not Lonely," and it was based on the premise that only children can grow up to be just as 'with it' and just as emotionally healthy as children with multiple siblings. Well, if I had looked in the *Reader's Guide to Periodic Literature* I would never have suggested such a story [because of the large number of articles already written on the topic]."

An odd contradiction exists in the writers guidelines provided by a lot of magazines, she says. "One way they're telling you to really fit the idea to the publication, but then, in another way, they're saying that editors want something fresh and frisky that they have not seen somewhere else."

She also cautions against overselling your proposition. "I have a friend who calls herself the Queen of the Query. The problem is that she is able to do a wonderful job, but then sometimes she has had problems actually executing the article, getting it finished.

"I think that the best advice I could give a freelancer right now would be to find something that you can give an editor that no one else can. This can be easier said than done. It could be something from your private life. For instance, one of my friends broke into the *Ladies' Home Journal* by writing about her father, who remarried a few months after her mother died. That was a story I couldn't have written because it was her personal story. Sometimes it can be something you find in a small publication in your own town or in your alumni magazine. It's going to be the idea that's going to sell."

It may be due to that early training as a teacher, but Donna has discovered that teaching others to write is as fulfilling and profitable for her as actually writing and selling stories.

She got started in the seminar business when a friend showed her a pamphlet for a writing workshop. She had been teaching an adult education class on how to get published. She did a little quick math and discovered that the workshop leader was out-earning her at a ratio of about ten to one . . . for imparting basically the same information. "I was looking at this," she remembers, "and thinking you know I really could do this. So just on a whim I wrote a letter and sent [the workshop leader] some clips."

The workshop leader liked her clips and was intrigued by her background, which by then included teaching, contract writing, journalism, corporate writing and an impressive education. They struck a deal that is still in effect. She tours the country giving writing advice in sold-out workshops to folks interested in magazine feature writing. As of this writing, she's booked up eighteen months in advance.

Donna takes a typical mom-turned-freelancer view on writing and her lucrative pay: "It puts my kids through Ivy League schools."

CHAPTER TWO

Take What's Yours

Many freelancers—myself included—feel an occasional urge to give up our chosen field and get an actual job.

This often occurs about the same time a fat phone bill or credit card dunning notice shows up in a mailbox that is supposed to contain a check that has been "in the mail" for more than sixty days. One can feel a bit uncertain when facing the harsh reality of the "famine" part of the freelancer's "feast or famine" business world. The temptation to chuck it all and let somebody else worry about making those quarterly tax payments can be very strong.

But you must resist.

Do more marketing; take a hard look at your overhead and the way you're running the show. Treat writing like a business. Make a solid business plan, acquire the equipment you need, pay attention to details and keep your eye on the practical aspects of freelancing: earning as much money in as short a period of time as possible (while still maintaining your integrity, of course).

Practice the diligence that any entrepreneur would apply in maintaining a small business, but make sure you don't analyze yourself into inaction. And, most of all, recognize the great position in which your own God-given talents have landed you.

While on a trip through upstate New York, I once found myself talking about life and ethics with a college student from one of the finer East Coast colleges. He was smart, articulate and passionately committed to an intellectual life.

He was also unemployed.

I asked him if he'd ever considered writing for a living. He brightened and trotted off to find a writing sample from one of his college classes. When he returned, he handed me a stack of handwritten essays and roughly typed manuscripts. I looked them over and told him that with a little preparation and self-marketing he could probably be making $40,000 or more a year as a freelance writer.

He shook his head and told me that his skills were not of a high enough caliber to allow him to actually be paid for writing. He was sending his stuff mainly to underground publications and a small journal owned by a friend.

This kind of thing just drives me nuts.

He was wasting his talent and severely limiting his potential for writing success simply because he lacked the confidence to step up to the plate and take a bit of a risk. And, really, the risk was almost nonexistent. He was already unemployed, had a great command of the language and had no family to support. But still he was looking for "a job."

Jobs are good in some ways, I suppose. We certainly hear enough about them during election years. And some people simply do not have the mental agility and self-discipline to work for themselves.

But think for a moment what a "job" really is. Your salary is a limit on how much you can earn. Your efforts are certainly worth more than you are being paid for them. (Would your employer be willing to pay you for them if he weren't planning to sell them at a profit?) You are often forced to accept the decisions and directives of someone not nearly as smart or as experienced as you are.

And, perhaps worst of all, you will almost always be required to show up at a given place and stay there doing as you're told for a given amount of time—even if you can clearly see that your time would be better spent in some other place pursuing some other activity.

Now I ask you, is that any way to live? Of course not!

When you freelance, you formulate your own plans, set your own hours, make your own decisions and are allowed to make as much money as possible. There are no limits on your compensation, other than those determined by your own talents, drive and abilities.

Is that any way to live? You bet it is.

So, if you're ever feeling ready to trade your freelance career for corporate suits and false safety, I would just like to say—"Don't do it!" Do what you need to do to keep freelancing in your life. Dream your dreams, make your plans and follow through.

If you're a freelancer, work hard, enjoy your work and be brave. No one has a better job than you do.

CHAPTER THREE

A Straw in the Mouth— and Other Affairs of the Freelance Life

Back in the late 1970s when I was fresh out of college, I landed a job as a general assignment reporter for a small daily newspaper in Kansas. It was a great paper staffed by solid reporters and edited by some exceptional editors. I learned a lot there. One of the things I learned was how to be in five or six places at one time.

On the second Tuesday of each month, the surrounding small towns all held their various town meetings, sewer board meetings, etc. My job was to cover all of these meetings and turn in a two- or three-inch story on each of them the following day. It would have been impossible to attend each of the functions, so I was forced to rely on phone interviews. I'd go to one or two and sometimes even three of the meetings in person, but that left at least four without my journalistic presence. Each month I'd switch around the ones I'd attend and the ones I'd call about. In order to pull this off, you have to be a little bit intimidating. The people you're calling on the phone have to believe that if they lie to you or blow you off you will rain trouble down upon them. I remember one city official from a little town calling me one morning to report that some relatively harmless but officially unacceptable bacteria had been discovered in the town's drinking water supply.

"I didn't want to call you," he admitted, "but I figured you'd find it out anyway." Smart man.

In addition to these stories, I covered the agriculture beat, filled in on the cop beat, wrote obituaries, covered charity drives like United Way and picked up whatever other assignments hit my desk. On top of this, I was expected to turn in regular "enterprise" pieces, which were basically feature stories that I ginned up on my own. This made for a lot of interviewing, a lot of reporting and a lot of writing. I'm not complaining, please understand. This was great training. You learn to think fast when the managing editor is standing over you screaming, "Fifteen minutes! Wrap it up!"

It was during this time that I developed the "straw in the mouth lead," a technique that I've used successfully ever since. Put simply, the lead contains two actions followed by an observation. Here's an example: "Jim Bob Chambers put a fresh straw in his mouth, pushed his sweaty tractor cap back on his head and said, 'If I ever won that million-dollar lottery, I reckon I'd just keep farming 'til it was gone.' Here's another example: "Game warden Joe Pile cranked the wheel of his pickup truck hard to the left, slammed on his brakes and said, 'Just look down there, all them boys spittin' and scratchin' and they don't even know we're up here watchin.' "

Obviously, just about any feature story can start this way. I won't say that I used it every time, but I did use it often—especially when I could feel the hot breath of the editor on my neck. It's actually a pretty good word picture that puts your reader right into the situation, sort of like the opening to a movie. Done right, it can subtly foreshadow what the story is about. It also forces you to observe your interviewee more carefully. I used to mark my notebook with a small X every time I heard something that could be used for a straw-in-the-mouth lead. It never failed me, and I never got a complaint from any of the editors, even though I'm sure they noticed a certain similarity in my stories.

No doubt other journalists and writers have developed similar techniques and practices. The following tips and suggestions don't necessarily deal with techniques in writing, but they do give you some idea of the things I've done over the years to make my life less complicated and more productive.

If you are a freelance journalist or a book author, one of the first and best pieces of advice I can give you is to get a transcribing machine and hire somebody to run it for you. The machine I have cost about $350, if I remember correctly. I pay the young lady who runs it a modest hourly fee. This is about the best money I've ever spent. I also have a little Radio Shack voice-activated tape recorder that hooks up to the phone. I tape the interviews, turn them over to Sara and by the end of the day (or sooner) I have a written, on-disk record of the complete interview. I don't have to take notes like a madman and I don't have to suffer through the interviews again. Don't be intimidated by the price of the machine. If you get a good one, it will last for years and cost you only pennies for each use. Hiring help is also a little scary, but I think it's well worth the effort and the expense. A hired assistant can do a lot of things besides transcribe your tapes. She or he can help you maintain a solid, ongoing marketing effort, sending out query letters or new business pitches while you write. She can answer your phone, get the mail, keep your calendar and do all of the other things large and small that keep you from doing what you're paid to do—writing. Consult a good CPA about setting up your payroll. He or she might also be able to help you set your assistant up as an independent contractor, thereby eliminating a lot of payroll paperwork and expense. But even if you have to actually take your assistant on as an employee, it's still a good idea. You're in business, and you will find that good employees don't cost you money, they make you money.

A good assistant can be particularly helpful by compiling and maintaining a customer database. I know a freelance travel writer, Lynn Seldon, Jr., who is a master at this task. He never goes anywhere unless he has multiple assignments. He gets a lot of the assignments by working his database. I bought a story from him when I was editing *Writing for Money*. It really had nothing to do with a travel destination; it was more of a piece about a certain aspect of travel writing. Nevertheless, every time Lynn got a trip together, I'd get a little postcard asking me if I needed anything from that area of the world. I never bought a travel piece from him, but when it came time to assign a larger story on the art and practice of travel writing, Lynn was the guy I went to, simply because he had kept his name in front of me so consistently. I'm sure other editors were similarly inclined to hire him. They must have been. He tells me that his income has risen consistently every year since he started freelancing. That kind of success is not an accident.

Sometimes I've received query letters written on plain paper with no letterhead or logo or anything to tell me that this person is in the business of freelancing. Perhaps it reflects on my shallow-mindedness, but I immediately form a prejudice against the writer. As an editor, I expect to deal with professionals, and I expect to see certain businesslike things. I want to see a business card that I can stash in case I ever want to use this person again. I want to see a modest letterhead that gives me all the necessary contact information. I expect the letter to arrive in an envelope with a preprinted return address and my address typed cleanly and correctly. This tells me that the person I'm about to deal with is a professional who is likely to be around in the future. Not only does this kind of presentation increase your chances of successfully selling your work, it also makes life easier for you. You don't have to do as much work on your queries and new business pitches, so you have more time to write and earn money.

While we're on the subject of query letters, let's take a moment to consider your clippings and writing samples. Until a year or two ago, I was sending out color copies of copywriting jobs I'd done and maintaining a file of clippings to be photocopied and mailed when an editor or creative director wanted to see what I'd done in the past. This was quite time-consuming and even a little expensive. This problem, like so many others these days, was solved by the Internet.

I have a friend and partner who collaborates with me (my copy, his design) on commercial jobs: direct mail, ads, brochures, etc. He's also an extraordinarily gifted Web designer. So we teamed up on a Web-based portfolio page. Prospective clients can click on www.copy-design .com and immediately see our portfolio, our list of past clients and our contact information. We also use the page to deliver color proofs, which has proven very popular with clients who are in a hurry to get their projects approved and shipped to the printer. In fact, I've been told that we've been awarded some jobs almost exclusively because of the Web site.

That particular site is strictly for our circulation promotion magazine clients, but a similar site could easily be adapted for use by a freelance magazine journalist. In fact, if you'd like to investigate further, I'd suggest you go to our site and click on my partner's contact information.

I probably don't have to tell you this next tip, but I'm going to anyway just in case you may have been in a cave for the last decade or so. Here it is: Get as good a computer as you can possibly afford. It will make your writing easier, your research more complete and your business life a great deal more tolerable. A freelance writer without a Web site is at a disadvantage. A freelance writer without e-mail and Internet access is almost out of business. Like I said, get a good computer—and don't be afraid to buy a new one once in a while. When you stack up what they can do for you, computers are incredibly cheap.

The same thing goes for the other machines and equipment you'll use as a freelancer. I have a pretty good Minolta camera, complete with a handful of useful lenses. If you plan to sell photos with your articles, go to the local community college and take some classes on photographic techniques and lighting. Good photos can seriously improve your sales performance.

Probably the best piece of equipment I own is my office chair. This is a $1,000 chair. (Relax. I got it at a huge discount because it was a floor model.) If you're a busy freelancer, you'll be spending a lot of time in your office chair. Getting a good, ergonomically designed one can actually save you money in medical expenses and lost time. This is not something you should take lightly. Creating a good place to work is extremely important to your success. I recently moved my office from a windowless corner to a room with a whole wall of glass that looks out onto a small well-traveled walkway. The increase in sunlight alone was worth the move. This is not just my opinion, by the way. There have been many studies on the effects of sunlight on creativity and productivity, two things you'll need as a freelance writer.

One last recommendation: Take a nap every day.

I'm certain some people do not consider falling asleep at work a good success-oriented practice. They are wrong. One of the best things I do for myself is a thirty-minute, post-lunch siesta on the couch in my office. I wake up refreshed and ready to work. I have no doubt that a little down time increases the quality of my writing. Plus, it makes me feel like a free man. How many wage slaves out there can put their world on hold for a half-hour and simply recharge their batteries? Not many, I'll bet. When I had the couch delivered to my office, one of the delivery guys asked me what I needed it for. When I told him I figured on taking a nap on it that very afternoon, a look of awe mixed with envy shown in his eyes. "You've really made it," he said, "if you can take a nap in the middle of the afternoon." I had to agree with him. It's one of the things that make me feel privileged to be doing the kind of work I do and living the kind of life I have, a sign of success. I heartily recommend it. One caveat, though: Try not to make your nap much longer than thirty minutes or you may wake up groggier than you were when you crashed. If you need more than half an hour to replenish your energy level then you probably ought to be getting more sleep at night.

OK, let's review. Here, in a nutshell, are my tips for success and a good life as a freelance writer: Buy the best equipment you can afford. Hire good, capable people to help you. Make your workspace as comfortable and healthy as possible. And take a nap every day. Doesn't sound that hard, does it?

"Find Something That Moves You. Then Write."

D I A N E   R H O A D E S

Every once in a while I run into somebody who is just having way too much fun in life.

Diane Rhoades is one of those lucky people. Spend any time talking to her and you'll see what I mean. A burst of song here, a playful little dance routine there. All the while carrying on a perfectly logical conversation. If some people march to the beat of a different drum, Diane Rhoades is fox-trotting to a whole different orchestra.

A lifelong writer and artist, Diane moved from New York City to a small farm in the mountains of North Carolina. The move opened up a whole new world for her and her daughter, Casey. It also set the stage for Diane to write and sell her first book, *Garden Crafts for Kids: 50 Great Reasons to Get Your Hands Dirty*.

"When I first moved here from Brooklyn, it was amazing to have land, and it was amazing to garden. I didn't have a clue what I was doing. My first garden was in complete shade by the time June came around. I started when the leaves were not on the trees.

"One of the most exciting things I did," she recalls, "was make a bean teepee for Casey. I put a whole bunch of saplings together and wired them around and planted seeds by it. It was so much fun. We had goats and a pig and chickens—the setting was really right to play in the garden. In a way, there was an alchemy to all of this that was beyond me or anything I planned in particular.

"Casey and her friends loved the bean teepee. We had a party there one time on the hill. That was the first time we found the wild strawberries. The kids were having so much fun, and of all the things we could have spent money on, the most exciting thing during that whole party was [getting to play in] the bean teepees. I had several of them, like a little village. What came out of that whole experience with the kids and the garden was my impulse to just write about it. Mostly when I write about something, it's because I had an experience that was so inspiring or so fun that I just have the urge to share it.

"So I wrote my first article about gardens and brought it to *What's Happening* magazine. The editor loved it. It was summertime and there were lots of grandparents with grandchildren and other people who had kids with them for the summer. They're not used to the company of kids, didn't really know what to do with them. So the editor asked me to write a weekly column about things to do with kids in Hendersonville. The column dealt with art and activities and gardening and even things kids could do to make some money. One of the printing companies in town donated packets of cards and envelopes for the kids to draw on and create greeting cards. A store called Honeysuckle Hollow offered to buy them, so the kids were very encouraged. I was very into it—and it paid. And then it was really nice to see my name in print."

Diane didn't make a whole lot on those columns, she recalls, but writing them did lead to a much larger opportunity.

"The big thing that came out of it was a book deal. My editor at *What's Happening* magazine was friends with one of the editors at Altamont Press in Asheville. Altamont was looking for someone to do a gardening book for kids. Without hesitation, [the editor at *What's Happening*] told her, 'I have the person for you.'

"That was such a good recommendation for me. I met with the editors and showed them my articles. I signed a contract and I was on. It was the first time I'd done a book—a real prize for me because I couldn't have picked a better topic to write about. I was already fluent in the joy of gardening. But I still had to brush up on facts, because after gardening for years, I still didn't know, technically, what I was doing. But I was really happy with what I was doing; it was a real adventure for me to get educated. I made a strict schedule for myself, and for the most part I kept on it. I got up earlier. I put a computer in my attic and worked up there. Nobody else was allowed on the computer. Only book stuff went on in that little attic.

"It wasn't all easy, though. I was very new to the computer and once I lost my introduction, my first twenty-five pages. My daughter has never seen me behave like that in her life—cursing, flipping out, throwing things. It was a very passionate enterprise to take this book on. I kind of ran it by themes and projects. Whether I spent the day actually familiarizing myself with the topic or whether I actually wrote about it, it was all very real for me."

The whole project took her about nine months, she says, during which time she took her gardening to a whole new level.

"I kept my garden in impeccable shape," Diane says, "because every now and then the photographers would come out. My garden had to look great all the time. It was a fairly intensive nine months. I held a full-time job. I was a mother. I was cooking. I was also getting married then. It's so ironic that the wedding and the book's deadline ended up being the same week. It was neck and neck with madness. But during that little window of time while I was researching and interviewing I got to meet amazing people. It opened me up to so many people. . . . It was a very valuable experience."

One of the people she met, by the way was a "wonderfully eccentric" worm rancher (operator of one of the nation's largest worm spreads), who introduced her to Herman, a 16-inch pet worm.

Enhancing the experience, of course, was good old-fashioned money. "They gave me $3,000 up front to do the book," she says. "As a single mother, that translated into all kinds of wonderful things. And then once the book came out, it was a great boost to my self-esteem. I've always considered myself fairly 'alternative.' This, though, was something that I absolutely delivered as fluently as I could, as passionately as I could, as clearly as I could—and it was very well received. It brought up my sense that this was my culture, this is my beautiful planet. I kept all of the clippings from reviews. The best one I got was from the *School Library Journal*. They gave me four stars, and they said that if you were going to buy just one book this year, buy this one.

"My royalties were big, and I was going to book signings and having a lot of fun with it. And, oh my God, I had no idea what a ham I was. I absolutely loved being this person who had written a book. All these kids would show up. Back in my hometown, all the bookstores carried it. It was really nice to walk into bookstores and find my book. I was such a weirdo. Every time I went through a store that had my book, I said, 'Excuse me, can I sign it?' I was just so happy to have delivered something in the world that can go on and on without me. I still am happy about that."

Diane plans to write another book soon, although she isn't sure what the topic will be. Probably not gardening. "I think it's going to be short stories that involve being in nature. I have a bunch of short stories already written and some I still think about putting down on paper. Like once when I was collecting eggs in the dark and reached in and found a big black snake. I relocated her and kind of became friends with the snake. For a New York City girl that was pretty different."

I asked Diane for some advice for writers contemplating a book project. "The biggest thing," she told me, "is to find a relationship, a connection that is absolutely fluid and fluent. [The writing] will move. Then the book delivers itself. I think it's real work to sit down and write a book. No matter how wonderfully connected I am to gardening, there are times when it's really work to write. But find a subject. Have something that just in and of itself moves you. Then write."

CHAPTER FOUR

What's the Big Idea?

If you have one strong idea, you can't help repeating it and embroidering it. Sometimes I think that authors should write one book and then be put in a gas chamber. — JOHN P. MARQUAND

I was going to use this space to advance the notion that a freelance writer's time is most wisely spent querying large, well-paying magazines.

The premise was to be that it takes just as much time and effort to put together a good, low-paying story as it does to produce one with a memorable payday. So why not go for the bigger, better deal?

It's hard to argue with that.

The audacity to ask for big paychecks is one of the best tools a freelancer can develop. One of the finest freelance magazine writers in the country is Leo Banks (see more about Leo elsewhere in this book), a friend of mine who lives in Tucson, Arizona. He once turned in a story to a national travel magazine that ran about twice as long as the assignment had called for.

This vexed the managing editor, mostly because my friend gets paid by the word. After listening to the editor scream and rant for a while, Leo said, "Sure it's long, but it's a good story, and it ought to be that long."

The editor-in-chief agreed with him and told the managing editor to pay up.

Trust me, this approach will not work for just anybody. My Arizona friend is blessed with icy nerves and a tough Boston accent. Plus, he is a great writer, and I have no doubt that the piece needed to be the length it was.

So, OK, let's all work on developing our self-esteem and negotiating skills.

But let's talk about one other very important component of the successful freelance sale—the Big Idea. If you can gin up a seriously tasty Big Idea, your chances of a big payday increase exponentially.

Here's an example, also from Arizona.

When I was going to college at the University of Arizona, there was a small number of students who made at least some of their living by selling freelance stories.

The grand champion of all these folks (based on the dollar amount of a single freelance sale) was a young woman whose writing and reporting skills were far from the top of the class. She won the unofficial competition (and my undying admiration) in one swoop with a story about the contraceptive sponge, a dainty device researched and developed (at least in some part) at the University of Arizona.

How she stumbled onto the story I never heard. I do know that she used the piece as a class project and then promptly sold it to one of the major women's magazines. I don't remember which magazine, but I do remember the dollar amount—$1,500. (Perhaps not a fortune by today's standards, but those were mid-seventies dollars, and we were impoverished students). That put her about $1,200 ahead of the closest competition and earned her the title. She told me later that the magazine that bought the piece almost completely rewrote it.

So, my point here is that writing and negotiating skills are very important, but it's the Big Idea that brings in the major money. Unfortunately, Big Ideas do not surrender themselves to you voluntarily. You have to hunt them up. There are a handful of really good places to look, but first you have to know what your quarry looks like.

A genuine Big Idea has to be timely and must affect a lot of people, thereby making it appealing to magazines with large circulations and, hence, larger freelance budgets. A new contraceptive device qualifies, as do radical new surgical procedures, cures for common-but-serious diseases, breakthrough technology (cold fusion, cars that run on seawater, etc.), interviews with reclusive celebrities (show me your verifiable interview with J.D. Salinger and I can pretty much guarantee you a major payday).

Universities are usually pretty good Big Idea hunting grounds. Call all the departments at your local college or university and tell them you're a freelance journalist. Ask to be put on their press release mailing list. Get to know the professors who are working on interesting projects. Do the same thing with teaching hospitals and large companies that do a lot of research and development.

But don't stop there. Work your sources as if you were a reporter on a regular beat. Call the people in charge and let them know you are interested in what they're doing. Make sure they understand that you're looking for stories with national and international appeal. If you keep in frequent (once a month or so) contact with your potential sources, they are unlikely to forget you when they have something interesting to report. But don't depend on them to recognize the newsworthiness of what they're working on. When you talk to them, make sure you thoroughly understand what they're doing and take time to analyze the information for potential article topics.

Go to the library and ask to see the *Directory of Associations*. Analyze the associations to find the ones that might harbor Big Ideas from time to time. Get on their mailing lists. If you see a lot of potential in an association, go to one of its conventions. Some of them may be a complete waste of time from a news peg point of view. Some of them may be hard to tolerate. (You haven't really lived until you've been locked in an Opryland banquet hall with 850 slightly tipsy auctioneers.) Don't become discouraged. As the old saying goes, "You have to kiss a lot of frogs to find a prince."

The more information that flows over your desk, the more Big Ideas you will find. And keep your wits about you when you read. The Big Idea can come from anywhere. The Arizona writer I mentioned earlier is a master at capturing the Big Idea. One time he was reading movie ads and it occurred to him that the quotes from critics may have been taken out of context. He did a little research and came up with a great story that showed just how deceptive Hollywood ad writers actually were. He sold the piece all over the country.

And speaking of Hollywood, keep in mind that the movie, television, video and cable TV industries are eating up material at a staggering pace. Just about any story that qualifies as a Big Idea could also have a screenplay, stage play or TV show concept hidden in it. And if ever there were a business that could use some help in the Big Ideas department, it would be the film industry. The Internet is another great source of ideas. Keep in mind, though, that just about everybody has access to this technical marvel. Finding sources beyond the Web is probably a good idea.

Journalism and entertainment aren't the only places where the Big Idea lives. Successful advertising copy absolutely relies on the Big Idea. A lot of books, both fiction and nonfiction, began as a Big Idea. I met a writer a few years ago who had landed a $400,000 advance to write a book with the son of a legendary movie star. He had no more than finished that job than he landed another, this one to ghostwrite the memoirs for a popular situation comedy actor. He was always open to the Big Idea. He'd drop everything, jump on a plane and go all the way across the country on the chance that he could grab an opportunity.

Actually, maybe the Big Idea really isn't an idea at all. Maybe it's more like an attitude or a frame of mind that sets you up to take advantage of opportunities that present themselves. Part of that is alertness. Another part is intelligence. But the biggest part, I think, is the courage to see yourself as someone with something significant to offer the world.

When a writer has that kind of courage and confidence, he or she will look at the world differently. Fear of failure dissolves, as does fear of success. Successful freelance writers don't get bogged down in their anxieties. They recognize the anxieties for what they are and take steps to get past them. I've always said that, for me, action kills angst. If I'm worried about a big project or a difficult interview, the only way to break it down and get on with it is to—get on with it. Like a lot of writers, I've let myself become intimidated by the idea that I swap words for bucks (sometimes pretty big bucks, as a matter of fact). It's such an extraordinary way to make a living that it seems almost absurd that I get to do it. The only way for me to overcome that feeling is to start hunting for the Big Idea, whether it's a new junk mail project, a book proposal or whatever.

I can't tell you how long it will take you to find your own Big Idea. But I can tell you that you will find it if you keep your eyes and ears tuned, conquer your reluctance to ask for big money and refuse to give up.

CHAPTER FIVE

Jimmy the Newsstand Guy Goes Horizontal

I've always known that Jimmy the Newsstand Guy was a sharp operator, but it took a really, really good jumbo hotdog to reveal just how resourceful he is.

Jimmy's family has operated a newsstand in my town for at least half a century. He grew up selling "Co' Colas" and moon pies and copies of just about every Southeastern newspaper you ever heard of. Not only that, the newsstand has always generously offered transplanted Yankees a chance to buy "questionable" publications such as *The New York Times* and *The Wall Street Journal*. This I consider to be very open-minded, given the fact that a lot of my neighbors are still waiting faithfully, if somewhat impatiently, for the Confederacy to rise again.

The newsstand has always been pretty hard to miss, situated right next to Smokey's Barber Shop on the main drag through town. And it's only one storefront away from the huge Dogwood parking lot, which serves downtown during the week and takes the overflow from the First Baptist Church on Sundays.

That location has served Jimmy well over the years, giving him a virtual monopoly on the selling of journalism and snacks in the downtown section of the little North Carolina mountain town where I now live.

You want a *Charlotte Observer*? Go see Jimmy. Interested in an *Atlanta Constitution*? Jimmy's the man. Dying for a can of sugar-free Cheerwine? It's right over there next to the Vernor's (an evolved form of ginger ale, for the edification of you uninitiated Yankees) just on the other side of the motorcycle magazines but not quite as far as the computer publications. Take a look at that new issue of *George* while you're there.

Whenever local authors self-publish a book, usually a treatise on some aspect of mountain lore or a biography of some local celebrity or other, Jimmy is always more than happy to put their work in front of the public. Did I also mention that Jimmy's the guy to see if you want to have somebody cater a nice pit-style barbecue or a pig-pickin' in your backyard?

Since his establishment is only a half-block from my office, I run into Jimmy quite often. One fine, clear morning not long ago, I stopped at Jimmy's place to feed my Cheerwine habit and shoot the breeze.

Something was afoot.

Commercial kitchen equipment, well worn but sparklingly clean, was bunched up in the right rear corner of the store, and Jimmy's perpetual grin was a little wider. It seems that one day Jimmy noticed that the section of the store just behind the comic book department wasn't really pulling its weight. It was just kind of sitting there sucking up overhead dollars, which offended Jimmy greatly.

On the same day, he had gone to lunch at a local eatery (one that sold newspapers in its waiting area, he indignantly explained) and came home enraged that "you can't get a sandwich in this town for less than six bucks." In that moment, Jimmy's Take-Out Sandwiches was born— barbecue pork and chicken sandwiches and platters, jumbo or regular, and of course, those great jumbo hotdogs full of juice and God knows what else.

And none of it had a price tag of more than two or three bucks. Once in a while, just out of a need for retail mischief, Jimmy will roll his prices back to mere pennies. He's also been known to celebrate his birthday by selling RC Colas and hotdogs for exactly what they'd sold for on the day he came kicking and screaming into the world. He mounts all of these price campaigns with a wicked gleam in his eye and a total disregard for the objections of his fellow food service professionals. Challenge him on the way he runs his business, and he'll come out from behind the counter and walk out the door. He'll look up at the sign and say, "Yep, that's still my name up there."

More than anything else, Jimmy's little enterprise is an example of niche marketing from which we all can benefit—especially those of us stuck in the vertical spiral that can infect a freelance writer's marketing efforts. Jimmy's sandwich corner is a triumph of what I call Horizontal Thinking.

I've talked to scores of freelance writers whose main business effort is directed at writing and selling more articles. The more enlightened of us try to sell the same article or at least the same information to as many buyers as possible. That's great. But couldn't we do more?

Take a look around your own store, much the same as my pal Jimmy did, and see if there aren't a few opportunities for Horizontal Thinking lying around gathering dust. My bet is you'll see plenty.

I've found that my skills as an interviewer are useful in many businesses other than journalism. As journalists, we are used to asking and re-asking important questions until the answers stack up logically and all the loose ends are tied up neatly. You would be surprised and appalled at how many business meetings adjourn without that happening.

You have to be careful how you try to break into this sort of thing. You can't very well waltz up to a local captain of industry and announce you are available—for a nominal fee—to save him from making a fool of himself in his next meeting.

Inserting yourself into the business community may be as simple as attending a merchants association meeting. Maybe you'll have to print a stack of flyers advertising your services as a business communications consultant or a marketing adviser. List your services: press releases, public relations, speech writing or whatever.

Spend some time at chamber of commerce functions. Write guest editorials on business topics for the local paper. Keep your eyes open for opportunities. Let your friends and acquaintances know you are open for business.

I am currently involved in an infomercial project simply because I introduced a gadget inventor to an acquaintance who happens to be in the direct response television business. I stuck around to see if I could help put the thing together. The original deal fell through, but we're still working on getting the thing to market. If we do get everything moving forward there should be a fairly good payday in it for me. If we fail, I will at least have gained some experience in the infomercial business.

You have to keep your ears tuned to opportunity. I landed another marketing job when a local pet store owner told me about some kind of natural, vegetable-based cream that restored his hair. I was skeptical at first, but then I saw pictures of him before and after. He had definitely grown a bunch of new hair, so I thought I'd give him some assistance. Mostly I'm writing ad copy and press release stuff. I'm also helping him find a shop that can make wholesale quantities of aquarium stands. Some of this may not seem like a job for a writer, but all of it uses my skills as an interviewer and an information gatherer.

Several years ago, I read a story on some Indians in South America who were making waterproof hats from the leaves of local vegetation.

A few phone calls later I was the middleman between the native manu-facturers and the buying public in Northern California. I called my company (long since defunct and dismantled) The Blue Smoke and Rabbit Tracks Trading Company. Again, it wasn't journalism, but it did use my writing and information skills. We didn't sell very many hats, I'm afraid. But at least I got some interesting experience—and I still have my own palm hat, which is still pretty much waterproof.

The process of retooling and reselling your journalistic abilities doesn't have to be difficult. In fact, in can be a lot of fun. My pal Jimmy didn't do much to promote his sandwich business. He just shoved a few flyers under doors one evening, hung a couple of signs at his newsstand and chatted a lot with loyal customers. I don't really work that hard at selling business communications, either. I just keep it in mind when I'm making the everyday contacts of life.

Just remember this: Everybody out there has something to sell, and as a skilled communicator, you can help him or her sell it more effi-ciently or more profitably. That can be worth a lot of money.

Late-Breaking Jimmy News

Since I first wrote about Jimmy and his business endeavors, he has followed up on yet another shrewd observation. Poring over his accounts one day, he noted that the newsstand was making a slender fraction of what the pig-pickin' and backyard barbecue business was pulling down. With a bold (some say heartless) stroke worthy of a Bill Gates or an Andrew Carnegie, Jimmy shut down the newsstand that had been in his family for more than half a century. The pig barbecue business would now enjoy his full attention and folks would have to get their weekly copy of *The New York Times* elsewhere. People complained bitterly, he told me, but that doesn't seem to bother him in the least. His name, after all, is still on the sign.

Like any good businessperson, he weighed his options, made his decision and took action. I saw him shortly after he'd closed the store. He was trying to figure out a way to wedge a soda machine through the door into the old store. He figured people would still buy drinks even if they couldn't get the latest pro wrestling magazine or a Sunday paper. "It's probably going to be a gold mine for me," he said. The man is a monument to the art of Horizontal Thinking.

CHAPTER SIX

Taking Care of Business

Over the years, I've spent a lot of time admonishing my fellow writers to treat freelance writing as a small business. When I mount this particular soapbox, most of my writer friends fidget from foot to foot and get a glazed look in their eyes. I suppose this resistance springs at least partly from the fact that the term "small business" doesn't sound as romantic as "freelance writer." People apparently prefer to think of writers as artists rather than businesspeople. The fact remains, however, that writing on a freelance basis is very nearly the same as running any small service company.

You can apply the same business practices and principles to both. The risks and pitfalls are very similar. The commitment required is the same in both. And the potential rewards in terms of self-direction and unlimited earning potential can be very enticing. Nevertheless, people don't seem to take seriously the image of the freelancer as businessperson. This was made apparent to me when I was editing *Writing for Money*, a newsletter for freelance writers, a few years ago. One of my larger tasks was to call on editors, publishers, agency creative directors and anyone else who might represent a possible market for freelance writing. I'd introduce myself and explain that I was with a publication called *Writing for Money* and that I wanted to talk to them about their freelance needs. I'd say that 75 percent of the editors I spoke to started our conversation by saying something like, "Writing for money? Hey, I didn't know that was possible."

I'd generally ignore the comment and get right down to what I wanted. The phone bills in those days were astronomical, and I didn't want to waste any more time than necessary. Since those days, I've purchased *Writing for Money* and made it into an online journal for freelance writers (www.writingformoney.com). Because we use e-mail, we don't do much phone contact work anymore. Hence, I don't get to hear that comment as much as I once did, but it still comes up.

Well, I'm here to say—once and for all—that, yes, it is possible to write for money. It's even possible to write for considerable amounts of money. Thousands and thousands of dollars. Maybe even millions.

There is virtually no limit other than your own abilities and ambition and drive.

Just because your opportunities are limitless, don't make the mistake of thinking it will be a simple matter to gain riches through writing. You have to work at it. You have to have a solid plan and stick to it. The best thing you can do at the outset of your freelance career is the same thing you should do at the beginning of any business launch: Write a business plan.

This can be as simple or as complicated as you wish to make it. When I bought *Writing for Money*, I wrote a sixteen-page business plan that included a title page, an executive summary and a mission statement. I also added a company overview, market research, promotional strategies, an analysis of the competition, a list of strategic alliances, a discussion of possible follow-up publications, a risk/opportunity analysis, a management team roster and various exhibits. It took me quite a while to write the original and even longer to modify and improve it. The final product reposes in my safe-deposit box. I dig it out once in a while to make sure I'm on track or at least proceeding in the general direction I intended when I wrote it. I don't stick to it as religiously as I thought I would, simply because "stuff happens" in business and you have to be flexible. It's a valuable asset, though. Writing it forced me to focus on my writing as a business enterprise. This, in turn, led me to make certain decisions and act upon them.

The same opportunity presents itself to you as a freelance writer. A good business plan—and it certainly doesn't have to be as elaborate as the *Writing for Money* plan I just described—can mean the difference between perpetual struggle and glorious success.

A smart marketing guy once told a friend of mine that there were really only four simple elements to any business plan. As a professional consultant, he never told his clients how simple it was to create their business and marketing plans. He and his colleagues would dress up the four elements with impressive charts, complicated surveys, graphs and tons of business jargon. That was all just "eye wash" though. The real purpose of any plan they created was to answer these main four questions:

1. What do I want?
2. What do I have to offer?
3. Who would buy what I have to offer?
4. How do I reach the people who want to buy what I have to offer?

I once spent a fine spring weekend in South Florida talking to writers at a workshop about their writing careers and their plans for promoting themselves. I was fascinated to see that almost none of them had any long- or short-range plans for promoting themselves. I asked at one session for a show of hands to see how many people wanted to write magazine articles. Almost every hand shot up. Then I asked how many of them had query letters out to publishers. Maybe three hands went up. I found this most puzzling. Several of them later told me that they weren't really certain what I meant by query letters. To be fair, I have to admit that a lot of them were fiction writers who were just sort of dipping their toes into the pool of nonfiction freelancing. They hadn't had any experience but were interested in making more money as writers.

To illustrate my talk, I asked for a volunteer from the audience. A very charming woman in the first row said she would be willing to have the workshop attendees and me put together a rudimentary business plan for her writing career. Midway through the session, people were calling out suggestions from all over the room. By the end of the ninety minutes, she had networked with one travel writer and jotted down enough ideas to keep her busy for the following three months. What follows here is basically the same treatment using a fictitious forty-six-year-old beginning freelance writer named Walter Jones. He currently works in middle management for a medium-sized home-building company in Northern California. The questions we'll be asking and answering will be the same ones you can use to build your own freelance writing business plan.

Question #1: What Do I Want?

The first and most obvious question to ask Walter: How much money does he want to make? People tend to be a bit modest when asked this question. Perhaps they don't want to appear greedy. Nevertheless, this is the time to be bold, to set your sights high. Let's say that Walter is currently making $47,000 per year plus benefits as a middle manager at the home-building company. He'll probably lose at least $15,000 of that to the federal government as income tax and another $10,000 in various other taxes and levies that are just part of life here in the United States. So now we're dealing with an after-tax income of about $22,000. If he has a good benefit package, we can add another $8,000 to that in savings on health insurance, dental, retirement plans, etc. So now we're dealing with an income of $30,000, from which Walter has to pay his monthly bills, save for the kids' college, build a retirement nest egg and go to the movies once in a while.

As a freelancer, he will have to pay for this—taxes, expenses, savings and all—from the proceeds of his writing. Taking all of that into consideration, Walter bravely announces that he can do everything he needs with an annual income of $70,000. We pat Walter affectionately on the head and tell him he needs to rethink his goal. Seventy thousand dollars minus $40,000 in state, local and federal taxes will leave $30,000. Subtract from that his health insurance premium, groceries, car payments, mortgage payments, etc., and it becomes obvious that Walter's $70,000 will be stretched pretty thin. If he wants to live a hand-to-mouth existence then he might as well continue working for the home builder.

However, if he really wants to be a freelance writer and live his dream, he needs to set his sights a good deal higher. Let's give him an annual income goal of $150,000, with a goal to increase each year's income by $50,000 over the following five years. How much that leaves him to spend is a matter for a CPA and depends a lot on how wisely he can handle his money. But if he doesn't go nuts with credit cards or develop a serious substance abuse habit, he can probably live pretty well on that $150,000.

To achieve this goal, Walter is going to have to make an average of $12,500 per month as a writer. That's $3,125 per week or approximately $450 per day. That's each day and each month, all year long. Sounds like a lot, doesn't it—especially if Walter was considering writing magazine articles for $300 apiece and taking a week to research and write each of them. Clearly, Walter is going to have to find some new profit centers if he is to make his goal. We'll talk about that later, but for right now let's settle on Walter's money goal: $150,000 per year.

If all Walter needs is that impressive sum of money to bring him happiness and fulfillment, we'd already be done with this section of the business plan. But surely he wants more than mere money? We ask him what else he wants and Walter confesses that he wants to travel, he wants to work at home in a nice office, he wants to spend more time with his children and he wants to have enough time to try his hand at clay sculpting. Way to go, Walter. That sounds like a great set of goals to me. Let's jot them down so that we can refer to them easily. Do the same thing with your own goals.

Goals for Walter Jones:
1. $150,000 per year
2. Travel opportunities
3. A nice home office
4. More time with family
5. Study clay sculpting

Question #2: What Do I Have to Offer?

Now that we have Walter's goals firmly in mind, the next step is to figure out what on earth Walter has to offer that will command that sort of income. This is a very important part of the freelance plan. It is critical that we explore Walter's assets (and your own) in a thorough, creative way. Anything that can be used to his advantage must be discovered.

Let's look at Walter from these individual standpoints and discuss how they can be exploited to help him meet his goals (feel free to come up with more on your own):

1. Education
2. Special skills
3. Experience
4. Hobbies
5. Physique
6. Personality
7. Age
8. Friends/acquaintances

Education is a good place to start. In high school, Walter was a second-string quarterback and ran cross country. He has a bachelor's degree in English that has never earned him a nickel. He has an MBA from a relatively unknown non-Ivy-League state college. He has also attended continuing education classes in Spanish, bricklaying and personnel management. He took the continuing education classes because he thought they would help him gain promotions in the home-building business. So far, he hasn't used any of the skills he acquired through the classes.

So what does all of this mean in terms of making money as a freelancer? To begin with, Walter can put together a pretty good resume for pitching commercial writing accounts. He holds the MBA, which implies that he understands business practices and, more important, puts him on a level that is perhaps a bit higher than some of the business-people he will be pitching. Even if his degree isn't from a name college, he still has the initials after his name, and that is very impressive to a lot of people. It also means that he may be able to pick up some part-time work teaching writing at a community college. Most of them require at least a master's degree of some kind. His English degree will also help him land that kind of work. In general, the more education you can claim, the better you're going to look to people buying freelance. His training in business administration will also help him when it comes to running the books for his writing business. And, of course, let's not overlook the fact that training in English language and literature can actually make him a better writer.

The Spanish classes will help him a lot, especially if he can legiti-mately claim to be bilingual. That alone will open up a lot of writing opportunities in both journalism and commercial writing. The country is becoming increasingly Hispanic, and writers who move easily from English to Spanish are at a tremendous advantage. We're also glad to see the bricklaying classes because that puts him in touch with "work-ingman" issues and sets him up to do how-to articles. And not just about bricklaying. If you can talk the talk and walk the walk as a bricklayer you're also going to be able to relate to general contractors and other tradespeople about their public relations needs, advertising materials and other services you can provide. More life experience almost always means better writing and better interviewing (necessary in journalism and just about all other forms of writing). I've seen this firsthand. I grew up working on a farm in North Dakota, drove trucks in Arizona, worked in construction, sold mobile home anchors, installed awnings, worked as a handyman and chauffeur and did lots of other jobs before I settled on writing as a profession. Since then, as a journalist or commercial copywriter, I have talked comfortably with farmers, grain buyers, con-tractors, home builders, salespeople and people from all walks of life. If you can relate to people on a personal experience level, you'll get much better information than a less-experienced writer could get. I remember a grain elevator manager in Kansas telling me I was the only reporter he'd ever met who knew that wheat weighed 60 pounds to the bushel. He turned into a great, willing source of information. I landed a $900-per-month newsletter-writing job largely on my experience as a con-struction worker. Not only did it help me get the job, my experience in the field helped me do the job more quickly and, hence, more profitably. A magazine in Arizona assigned me an investigative piece on the mobile home industry mostly because I had worked in that business a few years earlier. My experience got me the assignment, and it helped me get straight information—because a lot of the guys I was interviewing were guys I had worked with. They couldn't lie to me because I'd been on the inside of the business, and I knew what was going on.

The same holds true for Walter. Even his limited high school athletic career can help him. As a former cross-country runner, he can more easily understand and write about the world of running. That's a huge market for freelance writers. If he's still running, that's even better.

Walter's special skills, he says, include typing and a fairly thorough knowledge of computer-related issues. He can handle a calculator like a CPA and took piano lessons for seven years as a child. He is also pretty handy on a mountain bike and knows how to brew some decent homemade stout, which he calls "The Dark Maria" after an old girlfriend from his college days.

Take a few moments now and think about how Walter can turn these special skills to his advantage as a freelancer. Typing and computer knowledge are pretty obvious, as are his calculator skills. I'd say that his years at the piano would probably yield some knowledge or appreciation of music—even if he hated every minute of this childhood experience. Biking is a market almost as big as running, so that could also help a lot. The stout brewing puts him in position to write articles for beermaking magazines, advertising and public relations for breweries and equipment manufacturers. Just about any experience you've accumulated can become a writing asset down the road.

A couple of decades ago I spent six months or so traveling with a carnival. I made a little money working in one of the joints and another $3,000 when I sold the article. But the real money came later when I pitched *Amusement Business* magazine to write direct mail ad copy for their circulation promotion. They were very pleased to learn that I knew the difference between a hanky-pank joint and a flat store. I've done a lot of work for them over the years and we always end up talking about my old days on the road. The money is good—and so is the reminiscing.

Your hobbies work for you much as your past experiences do. A passion for flying model airplanes can translate into magazine assignments, commercial writing jobs, etc. Walter's interest in clay sculpture probably positions him better than the next guy when it comes to interviewing artists or putting together brochures for a hobby trade show or a hobby manufacturer.

Walter's physique can also be a writer's asset. We can assume from his interest in biking and his early years of running that he is probably in better-than-average shape. This is important if he's planning on doing some adventure travel writing, a growing field of freelancing that is also a lot of fun. Good cardiovascular health and a strong immune system are pretty much required for adventure travel. As one writer told me, "It's not a good idea to get sick in Africa." Nor is it a good idea to trek in Nepal if you can't survive walking uphill in the very thin air that one finds at high elevations.

Walter's age is also a factor in his writing career. As a middle-aged man, he has a certain built-in credibility when it comes to some kinds of writing. Business clients are, as a rule, more comfortable talking to a writer who has some gray hair. The same thing is true of some of the people Walter will meet when he's conducting interviews for book projects or magazine articles. Age implies wisdom and experience—and in some cases there is truth to that. Of course, in some other areas being middle-aged or older is not necessarily an asset. The film and television industries, for example, are said to discriminate against older writers. Don't take this as a written-in-stone rule. Just be aware that you may run into situations where your age (young or old) may become a factor. I don't want you to worry too much about this, at any rate. Great writing and spectacular results will overcome almost any prejudice your client may be harboring.

Walter's friends and acquaintances will become extremely valuable as he plots his freelance career. You never know when a past friendship will come in handy. I had a job covering a speech by the famous Israeli general and statesman Moshe Dayan at the University of Arizona auditorium. Through circumstances beyond my control, I arrived late and wasn't able to push my way up to the press gallery. I happened to sit down next to a guy I'd worked with in the construction business. He was from a prominent Jewish family in Tucson and had, to my delight, just returned from a trip to Israel where he had actually had lunch with then-Prime Minister Yitzhak Rabin. I was able to give my story an added dimension simply because I'd happened to sit next to an old friend. Another old friend of mine is a well-known Houston psychologist who works in family counseling. I've called on her and several other old friends many times over the years to give a story a more national flavor.

When you're writing your own business plan, spend some time thinking about the people you know and how they might fit in as sources for articles or as contacts for commercial writing assignments.

Question #3: Who Would Buy What I Have to Offer?

Walter may already be closer to a client than he thinks he is. If he's careful to leave his home-building job on good terms, he may be able to turn his old employer into a new client. Perhaps he can get together with a graphic designer and pitch the home-building company on a company newsletter or on some advertising work. Who would know the company's requirements better than Walter? Nearly every business in his city (or any other city for that matter) has a use for brochures, direct mail solicitation, sales materials, press releases and other business enhancements. But he shouldn't stop there. Every business, trade or profession in this country has at least one trade magazine, and those magazines are usually hungry for well-written articles on current topics in their fields. Often these articles can be sold and resold many times over. Maybe the CEO of his old company would hire Walter to write speeches or to ghostwrite a book. Ghostwriting for celebrities and business leaders can be quite profitable. Lots of people in business and entertainment feel they need to have "authored" a book. It's good for their image. Usually, they don't have the time, the ambition or the writing skills to produce one. The same goes for guest editorials in the local paper, president's messages in annual reports (not to mention the annual report itself as a great writing assignment) and just about any other form of business-related writing. One caution: A lot of business clients can be difficult in the editing process. Some of them are frustrated editors who insist on making arbitrary copy changes that really have no effect on the potency of the writing. Others pass the material around to colleagues (who often know little or nothing about writing) and dither over conflicting suggestions. And once in a while you hit a real professional who says, "You're the expert. Here's what I want to accomplish," and then leaves you alone. Obviously, you want to cultivate the latter category. A thorough interview before you begin writing can sidestep a lot of problems. Most businesspeople know what they want to accomplish and can easily identify the strong points of their products or services. Your job is to turn their knowledge into compelling copy that sells their company.

Motivational speakers often hire ghostwriters to turn their taped presentations into books to be sold at their seminars and workshops. Not long before starting this book, I finished ghostwriting/editing one for a gentleman from the Chicago area. He'd first tried to write the book, a print version of his taped seminar, all by himself. When that didn't work out, he hired a man who claimed to specialize in ghostwriting for speakers. That didn't pan out to his satisfaction so he called me. I'd done some promotional writing for his self-improvement tape series, and I'd mentioned to him once that I could do other sorts of writing as well. We settled on a price, and a few months later the book was completed. He mentioned me in the book as his "editor" and promised to give me a good recommendation. That, along with the fairly large money I charged him, made the book project an enjoyable one—plus the fact that he was a genuinely nice guy who didn't mind paying a fair price for what he needed. I still hear from him once in a while when he has some small marketing job. I'm waiting for him to want another book.

With Walter's experience in athletic pursuits, he should be able to approach a whole list of "jock" magazines: running, biking, paddling and other physical fitness-related publications. Then, after he's made his mark as an outdoor sports freelancer, he can approach manufacturers, event planners, retailers and others involved with running or paddling or biking or whatever. The important thing is to think horizontally, not vertically. Vertical thinking dictates that, if you're making money selling magazine articles, the way to make more money is simply to write *more* articles. Certainly, selling more articles will increase your income, but is that enough? Remember that we're looking for $150,000 per year to make Walter a happy guy. Horizontal thinking says that while more articles would be good, there must be something exploitable in the knowledge you collect as a freelancer. These profit centers may or may not be all that closely related to journalism.

For example, suppose Walter is going to a beer-making festival in Roanoke, Virginia (which is, by the way, a lovely town). His assignment is to write a story for *Brewmaster Quarterly* on a contest the festival is sponsoring. The magazine also wants a sidebar profile on one of the more prominent brewers scheduled to give private and group lessons in beer making. With those assignments in hand, Walter approaches a travel magazine (because he heard there was a beautiful, endangered waterfall near the festival grounds) for a "destination" story assignment. That waterfall angle may also find a home with an environmental magazine. In Walter's case, he could probably get some kind of article assign-ment dealing with the craft of brewing as a small business. His MBA should help him get some attention on that angle.

Once in the gate at the festival he needs to keep his eyes peeled for more opportunities. I'd recommend that he carry his microcassette tape recorder and plenty of batteries. He should do the interviews imme-diately and have them transcribed when he gets home. The object here is to gather as much usable information as possible. No potential story subject should be allowed to escape. That goes for stories that he will write as soon as he gets home, as well as those that have a little more "shelf life." By that I mean articles that can be sold over and over in other markets, or that can be refurbished slightly and sold as completely new.

Here are some examples: Talk to the guy teaching the seminar about the best kind of equipment, pick up a couple of recipes and see what the content of the beer is (maybe it will turn out to be good for you). Ask the experts what kind of food goes best with home brew. Find out how much the home brew costs per liter and compare that to the price of commercially produced beer. Get some information on how to buy beer-making equipment. Find out the basic steps that go into organ-izing a beer festival. Ask one of the experts how to put on a blind beer tasting. You get the idea.

This information is the raw material for Walter's writing factory. He should pick up everything he can—even if it doesn't obviously relate to the article at hand. There is no such thing as too much information. Later, he can sort it out and write the stories. He should also make sure he has contact information on everybody he talks to.

Know and Protect Your Rights

Negotiating the rights to your writing can be one of your most important tasks as a freelancer—and one of the most confusing.

Publishers—and I include myself in this group—want to get as much as they can for the money they spend. Nothing personal—that's just business. And you should respond in a businesslike fashion. You should get as much as you can for your writing. Accomplishing that is largely a matter of realizing just what rights you're selling and what you can reasonably expect to receive for them.

Writer's Market has an excellent section ("The Business of Writing") that deals with contracts, agreements, subsidiary rights, copyright law and the kinds of rights normally sold or retained by writers. I recommend it highly.

I hasten to point out that I'm not a lawyer and that any legal questions you may have should be posed to someone who has passed the bar exam in your state. That said, however, I will point out that the following are, in general, the types of rights with which you'll be dealing as a freelance writer:

• **First serial rights.** This means that you're giving the publication in question the right to publish your article, essay, etc., for the first time. After that happens, you retain all other rights. Sometimes this is modified to first North American serial rights, which is the same except that the agreement is limited to publishing in North America only.

• **One-time rights.** This is a generic term that could include any type of nonexclusive rights to publish your writing. If a work is being sold for the first time, its rights are almost always identified as first rights, so one-time rights usually refers to reprints, whether in print or online.

• **Second serial rights.** These could also be called reprint rights. Also nonexclusive, these rights are, in my opinion, very important because they represent potential income with little or no extra effort on your part.

• **All rights.** It's not hard to understand what this means. You sell all rights and walk away from any future income from the work in question. Don't do this unless you're being paid a *lot* of money or have another very good reason (charity, personal interest in the topic, etc.) for doing so.

• **Electronic rights.** This is an extremely volatile area of law with bitter disputes and court cases all over the place. Jonathan Tasini and other writers won a landmark case in this area in

September of 1999 against *The New York Times* and other data-base aggregators of writers' works. Until the Second U.S. Circuit Court of Appeals delivered that verdict, the defendants, or any publisher, could sell previously contracted works to data-base aggregators as "revisions" of collective works without further compensation for the writers. The ruling bars publishers in the Second Circuit from selling online and electronic rights to aggregators without authors' permission, but no doubt it will influence interpretation of the law in other regions. To track the latest developments in electronic rights, I suggest you visit some of the Internet sites devoted to protecting writers' rights. This includes http://www.asja.org, maintained by the American Society of Journalists and Authors, as well as http://www.nwu.org from the National Writers Union. Because the Web is a continuous medium, you should also specify in any rights negotiations how long your work can remain on a site. Whatever the rights, make sure you charge enough for your work. The labor involved in writing an article for a Web site is not much different than for a magazine $.40 to a $1.50/word at profitable commercial publications), but, overall, Web sites tend to pay less because there are so many start-ups and the business model is unproven.

• **Subsidiary, dramatic, television and motion picture rights.** These rights cover the use of your writing in movies, TV, audio-tapes and other media. If you don't think these are important, consider that the John Travolta movie *Urban Cowboy*, which grossed millions, started out as a magazine article.

Along with his tape recorder, Walter should carry a good camera with a "portrait" lens and semi-wide-angle lens. Any good camera store can help select the camera. All he needs to do is tell the camera expert what he intends to do, which is take portrait shots to go along with interviews and wider-angle shots of the event itself. We're assuming that Walter is bright enough to talk to the magazine's photo editor for tips on what they like to run. We also hope that Walter doesn't sell "all rights" to this material unless he is getting an obscene amount of money for the articles. If he sells only the first North American serial rights, which most magazines accept, he can then put together a catalog of stories to sell to Sunday supplement magazines at metro dailies across the country. They generally won't care if he's selling the stuff elsewhere as long as the circulation areas of the papers don't overlap. If he can pull this off and sell twelve newspapers at $75 per article, he's added a quick $900 to his bottom line with no additional overhead and very little time invested. A little rewriting and the home brew inventory of stories could find markets in city magazines ("Organize Your Own Octoberfest Beer Tasting"). Or how about trade magazines for event organizers ("10 Essential Steps for Organizing a Local Festival") or men's magazines ("Why Hot Babes Dig Home-Brewed Beer") or women's magazines ("Make Your Man a Home-Brewed Beer—He'll Love You for It!"). The market is almost limitless when you approach the information as raw material.

Walter might also consider handing out his "advertising copywriter" card to the manufacturers' representatives and booth operators that inevitably crowd such get-togethers. If he notices that the festival is lacking in promotion, he can approach the person in charge and offer his services in the future. Of course, it's not a good idea to just waltz up to the head guy and tell him you think his festival stinks. It's best to approach him or her as someone doing a story on one or more aspects of the festival. Name the magazine you're working for and mention that you also have assignments from other publications. Directors and organizers of events know the value of good publicity and will usually be more than happy to cooperate with you. Eventually, you will find an opening in the conversation to make your pitch for your business-related writing services. Be sure you have ample promotional material to leave with the prospect.

In addition to the special interest magazines and journals that may need Walter's services, there are also book publishers with specific needs. He's probably well set up to do recipe books, for example, or books on computers and technology. He could probably get a green light on, say, a recipe book specifically for men. Call it *The Single Dad's Guide to Good Eating and Eventual Survival.* Or maybe *10 Great Dishes That Even a Man Can Cook.* Or *A Dozen Easy Dishes That Impress Women.*

Walter's background in business and his educational credentials could also get him some respect from publishers of business-related books. Since he has children, maybe a book on raising children in the Internet age or raising children to be independent of credit card debt (a book I could use for myself). And, of course, if he's computer-hip enough, Walter can probably find a niche in the computer book business. With a little self-training, reading and creative Internet surfing, Walter can probably set himself up as a Web site writer. There are tons of Web sites out there, and many (if not most) could use some help with writing. E-mail promotions are becoming increasingly popular, but a lot of people are missing their goals because they simply do not know how to write effective e-mail copy. There's plenty of information about such writing. It's simply a matter of Walter taking time to brush up on the finer points and then making a pitch to someone who needs his help.

Whether you're writing magazine articles, books, advertising copy, computer manuals, Web sites, e-mail messages, junk mail or whatever, there's always another market for your repackaged and resold information. The secret to making money from your writing is to keep your eyes open for new ways to get the most use out of the information and experience you have collected.

Question #4: How Do I Reach the People Who Want to Buy What I Have to Offer?

OK, so we've figured out what Walter wants, discovered what he has to sell and identified who might be willing to give him dollars for words. Now the fun begins. Now we have to figure out how to reach Walter's market—and reach it in a way that will cause $150,000 per year to find its way into Walter's bank account.

This is the same step Walter would take if he were opening a frozen yogurt store or a gas station or a clothing boutique. A business needs to find the most efficient way to attract paying customers. We're going to suggest to Walter that he exploit the following list:

1. Personal contacts
2. Professional contacts
3. Personal Web site
4. Web searches
5. Tickler file
6. Advertising
7. Cold calls
8. Public relations
9. Referrals
10. Mailing lists

Personal Contacts

Since Walter, like many beginning freelancers, probably doesn't have a ton of promotional money to get him started, let's begin with one of the best and least expensive ways to let people know that he's opened his writing store. He's going to tell his friends and ask them to tell their friends.

Just about every week in the little town where I live and work, a new business opens. I almost never hear about it through an ad in the paper or a radio spot or even a TV commercial. I usually hear about it from a friend. As I write this, a friend of mine is on the way to my office to take me to a new sushi bar he and his girlfriend found. On the way to the restaurant, we'll probably talk about some new movie they saw or a TV series they find amusing. As a carpenter and home builder, Matt has almost nothing to do with the writing business, but last year he sent me a pretty good client. The guy walked into my office one day and said he'd heard I might be able to help him with some writing and marketing consultation. It works both ways. Any time I hear people talking about builders or carpenters or home-improvement work, I tell them I know a good man for the job.

You never know when you're going to stumble upon a writing job or a person who knows somebody who needs a writing job done. Without being boring about it, Walter should let everybody he meets know that he is a freelance writer who is accepting new clients. This will undoubtedly lead to some interesting conversations, and it may well lead to some lucrative work.

Not long ago, I was talking to a friend of mine who happens to be an inventor. He was thinking out loud about ways to market some senior-citizen-oriented physical therapy products. One of the things he was considering was an eight-page newsletter to be delivered free to places like Sun City, Arizona, and other retirement communities. He'd already contacted the management at a number of these places and gotten a tentative go-ahead on the project. He just didn't want to take on the extra work of writing, designing and producing the newsletter. In the middle of stoking up his omnipresent pipe, he looked at me and said, "Hey, you're a writer. You could do this for me." Right on the spot he offered me a contract publishing job that involved some fairly heavy dough. Unfortunately, I had way too much on my plate at the time, so I had to turn him down. I did, however, turn him on to a graphic designer-writer team in a neighboring town. There's a pretty good chance they'll strike a deal—all because somebody knew somebody who needed some writing done.

There's something about being a writer that makes nonwriters want to see you succeed. Maybe they just want to be able to say they know a successful writer. Perhaps they just want to know that it's possible for a normal, mortal human being to make a living writing. Whatever the cause, Walter (and you) should exploit the phenomenon for all it's worth.

Professional Contacts

Let's not forget to exploit Walter's professional contacts, too. There's no reason why Walter's CPA, for example, shouldn't send him clients. His attorney probably knows somebody in need of some writing help. Everybody he does business with has a vested interest in seeing him make money. The more money he generates, the more he will have to spend on accounting, legal services, printing, mailing lists, etc. Even his landlord and his cleaning lady have a stake in his success.

It's not hard to put your professional contacts to work for you. A handful of business cards and a modest lunch on your tab are a good start. A capabilities brochure describing your commercial copywriting services can be a handy thing to leave with professional people. You might also tell your CPA or attorney that you will give them a courtesy discount on their writing work. I make it abundantly clear to everybody I trade with that I'm in the writing business and would appreciate greatly any work they send me. If a printer recommends me to a new client, for example, I will almost certainly give that printer my next letterhead or my next promotional mailing to print. It's really quite remarkable how much people appreciate a little reward or loyalty. We're all in business, and we're all looking for more business. Networking with your professional contacts can be an effective, inexpensive way to generate more work and more dollars.

Personal Web Site

Before we go much further, let's talk about the value of putting together a Web site for Walter. In this Internet age, it goes without saying that Walter will have to have all of the usual business tools: a good computer, color printer, e-mail, telephone, fax, Federal Express (or similar service) account, maybe a scanner, business cards, letterhead and possibly a capabilities brochure. Adding a Web site to Walter's list is also a good idea.

His site can serve as a portfolio for articles he's done. When he e-mails a query letter to an editor, he can include a "clickable" URL to give the editor instant access to his clippings and resume. This is, of course, much quicker and more efficient than sending the usual hard copy clippings and paper resume. It also establishes Walter as a cutting-edge kind of freelancer who would probably be easy to work with and edit.

If Walter follows our advice and adds commercial copywriting to his repertoire, the Web site will be a handy way to deliver proofs to his clients. My artist friend and I collaborate on dozens of "junk mail" projects over a year's time. I pass the copy to him via e-mail. Then he puts the copy into design and posts the proofs on our Web site so I can edit and approve them. Once we're happy with them, we e-mail the client and let him or her know that the proofs are on the site. The proofs are usually password protected so our client's competition can't get at them. This gives our clients a chance to look over our portfolio, which is right there on the site. They also have an opportunity to see our client list and read the testimonials we've scattered throughout the site. The biggest benefit to our clients, though, is the speed with which they can see and approve the proofs. If we can shave a couple of days off their schedule and get their proofs to the printer earlier simply because we have better technology than our competitor—well, that's just another reason to hire us for future projects.

A Web site for a generalist writer like Walter should include some basic elements. His portfolio should be there, and it should be divided into categories: articles he's written, advertising copy and commercial copywriting he's done, Web sites (complete with hyperlinks) he's written and/or designed, public relations projects for which he's been hired (show the press releases or whatever and include clips showing the results), books he's either authored or ghostwritten, speeches he's produced, TV and radio spots he's done, etc. All this does a couple good things for Walter. First, it positions him as a guy who can write anything that needs to be written. It's easy for a writer to get typecast as someone who writes brochures or does radio spots or churns out good press releases. If Walter's clients go to view their proof and see all that he's done, they are less likely to forget him when the next big job shows up. Second, putting together a Web site portfolio forces Walter to pay attention to his clip file and work samples. If he looks at his site one day and sees that it's a little weak in terms of video scripts, for example, then he'll probably make a bigger effort to get that kind of work, if for no other reason than to keep the site looking complete. As a result, he could very well find more lucrative work and find himself a handful of green rectangles closer to that $150,000 goal.

By the way, building your own Web site isn't that difficult. I have a partner who is extremely hip on such things so it hasn't been necessary for me to learn this skill. If you don't have that luxury, don't worry. There are tons of software packages out there to help you get started and tons of books on the subject. Hey, maybe you could put together your writer's Web site and then write a "how-to" piece about the experience. Or maybe you could advertise your Web site-building services to other writers.

Web Searches

While Walter is contemplating building his own Web site, let's also encourage him to use the Internet to search for work. There is an astonishing number of writer-related Web sites out there. Some are quite good; some are a waste of time. Sorting out the good from the bad is largely a matter of putting in some time surfing. My colleagues and I at *Writing for Money* (www.writingformoney.com) find new sites almost daily. *Writer's Digest* has some good information at www.writersdigest.com. Probably the best bet is to use a good search engine and simply see what's out there. When you find something that looks like it fits your skills and ambitions, send the editor (or whomever) an e-mail inviting him or her to have a look at your portfolio on the Web.

When you're out there surfing, don't limit yourself to magazines and book publishers. For someone with business skills and credentials like Walter's, for example, there are other places to search. You might try typing "graphic designers" in the search box and then offering your copywriting services to the people you discover there. A search of Fortune 500 companies (or some other index of large, well-heeled corporations) might turn up a flock of corporate communications officers in need of copywriting. When you're approaching potential corporate clients, it's a good idea to hook up with a competent graphic designer. That way you can offer either copywriting by itself or a full service that takes their project from copy through final art. You're not going to have a huge positive response to this kind of query, but don't let that discourage you. These companies often have enormous promotional budgets and are more interested in results than in haggling with you over price. I had one firm call me on a Wednesday to ask me to show up for a meeting in Boston on the following Friday. I told them I'd go if it was a done deal, but I wasn't flying up there for an audition. They said, OK, the job was mine. Just get there Friday. I flew to Boston on Thursday night, stayed in a snappy hotel (at the company's expense), ate a very nice dinner (also on my benefactors) and the next morning attended an hour-and-a-half meeting that could easily have been conducted on the phone. To this particular company, the couple thousand bucks it cost them to have me there (vs. the five bucks for a conference call) was insignificant. This may seem profoundly wasteful to you and me (and Walter), but try not to struggle too much with such issues. These companies make huge profits and expect to pay market price or more for consulting help. Just do your best, take the money and, if they ask you back on another job—raise your rates. And keep surfing the Net for more prospects. If you close one out of a hundred you're doing phenomenally well.

Tickler File

While Walter is making all of these inquiries and queries and sorties into the world of commercial copywriting, it could be easy for him to get a bit disorganized. There are a number of ways to deal with this. One way, which I admit is hopelessly old fashioned and low tech, is called a "tickler" file. Basically, it's a large file with a slot for each day of the year. Say, for example, that Walter calls Mr. Jones of the Rock Solid Manufacturing Company. Jones says he is indeed interested in a copywriter for his annual report, but he isn't ready to award the job just yet. Call back in three months, he says. OK, so Walter finds a date about two and a half months from today and puts a note to himself in the tickler file. He continues recording his promises and leads in this same manner all year. Every morning he looks in his file and his memory is "tickled" to do what he's suppose to do on that day. Clients are usually very impressed when a writer calls them back on the appointed day. This also gives the writer a viable reason to call on that day. Walter is not just pestering Mr. Jones. He's calling him back as Jones requested. This also can help Walter avoid forgetting deadlines, blowing off interviews and all sorts of other embarrassing mishaps.

Of course, all of this can be handled electronically with any number of devices and software packages. Just about all of them work—if you use them. Walter will need to find a system that works for him and stick with it. A system that also keeps track of his revenue stream is even better. Periodically, he will need to check his income against a calendar and see how the quest for $150K per year is going. Doing this often enough will help him determine which writing opportunities he should pursue more vigorously and which ones he should be ducking.

Advertising

When I lived in New York City, I had a friend who worked for a type-design company. They were heavily involved in the Madison Avenue advertising industry. Every time I'd stop by to see my friend I'd notice a small sign in the waiting room. I don't remember the copy exactly but it was something like this:

> A man will get up from his advertised bed in the morning, take off his advertised pajamas, shower using advertised soap, dry off with an advertised towel and put on his advertised cloth-ing. He'll eat advertised breakfast cereal soaked in advertised milk and wash it all down with a cup of advertised coffee. Then he'll drive his advertised car to work where he works on advertised office equipment and eats lunch at an advertised restaurant. Then he'll look at his ledger books and decide that he can't afford to advertise his business—after which he goes broke and advertises his business for sale. Why is that?

My apologies to whoever wrote the original sign. I'm sure I've com-pletely misquoted it. However, the point is well taken. Any business that hopes to survive—including Walter's freelance writing business—has to let its customers know where and how to find them. For freelance writers, especially those just starting out, advertising can seem like a daunting expense. Let's try to avoid this attitude. Advertising done correctly and effectively is not an expense—it's a tool to dramatically increase your income. To be sure, you have to plan carefully and execute effectively. You have to study the available media and settle on one that doesn't waste your bucks. For example, I wouldn't recommend ad-vertising your copywriting services via a TV spot. Sure, you may reach some potential customers, but you'll pay to reach a lot of folks who couldn't use your services even if they wanted to, which they probably don't.

I used to advertise in a trade journal that served magazine publishers and circulation directors. I arranged a work-trade situation wherein I wrote and designed some of their sales materials in exchange for a quarter-page ad offering my circulation promotion (read: junk mail) services. The magazine in question finally was sold and then discontinued, but while it was publishing I used to get at least one serious call per week from that ad. I'd say that I closed about two-thirds of them. It was a gold mine of great leads. After they went out of business, I tried a couple other similar trade magazines, but the expense of actually buying the ad (as opposed to trading for it) made it a "swap buck" operation that really got me nowhere. I bought a list of circulation directors and started sending them letters suggesting that they visit our Web site (www.copy-design.com) and look over our portfolio. I included a bounce-back card. (That's a self-addressed-stamped card with a check-off list of our services. They fill it out and return it if they'd like to be contacted.) So far the cards haven't been as successful as that earlier advertisement, but they've certainly paid for themselves and more.

Advertising his services in the local yellow pages may work well for Walter if he intends to pursue local business. He can also get a list of businesses in the area from the chamber of commerce. A little time at the word processor and a few stamps could scare up some interesting hometown work.

If he intends to work on a more national or regional level, Walter will need to do a bit of research. A few phone calls can produce a lot of information on the various trade magazines. Be aware, however, that these people sell advertising for a living. They are not vitally interested in making sure that folks like you and Walter get the most bang for their buck. They want to sell space in their publications. Period. You'll have to ask some pointed questions before you can make an informed decision. Ask what their magazine's CPM is. That means cost per thousand. Say you're thinking of spending $1,000 on a trade magazine ad. One magazine offers you a full-page ad for that $1,000. Another says you can have a quarter page ad for that amount. Short decision-making process, right? You go with the full-page ad, right? Not necessarily. Ask them for their independently audited circulation numbers and then figure out how much it will cost you for every thousand qualified people who receive this magazine and will, you hope, read your ad. If the full-page ad is shown to just a thousand subscribers (and make sure they show you an audit report verifying their claims), for $1,000 you might want to consider the quarter-page ad (which is still pretty prominent) that will be shown to forty thousand people for that same $1,000. The same holds true for ads in a classified section, buyer's guide or any other advertising vehicle. It's all about getting the largest number of qualified people to see your message at the most efficient price. Be ruthless with these salespeople. There are few things as depressing as shelling out $4,000 for an ad that pulled a single $100 job—and believe me, the magazine will have no inclination to refund your dough for an ad that didn't work.

OK, now that Walter has made his media buy, he'll have to decide what to put in the ad. This is pretty darn crucial in any advertisement, but it's even more important when you consider that Walter is advertising his ability to put together potent, compelling language. If his ad doesn't live up to that—well, he's sunk.

There are many books on the topic of ad copywriting. I recommend anything ever written by Herschell Gordon Lewis. The man is a genius in my opinion. A representative sampling of his works includes:

- *Herschell Gordon Lewis on the Art of Writing Copy* (Prentice-Hall)
- *Direct Mail Copy That Sells!* (Prentice-Hall)
- *How to Make Your Advertising Twice as Effective at Half the Cost* (Prentice-Hall)
- *How to Write Powerful Fund Raising Letters* (Pluribus Press)
- *How to Handle Your Own Public Relations* (Nelson-Hall)
- *The Businessman's Guide to Advertising & Sales Promotion* (McGraw-Hill)
- *More Than You Ever Wanted to Know About Mail Order Advertising* (Prentice-Hall)
- *How to Write Powerful Catalog Copy* (Bonus Books)

I also recommend that you take a look at the late David Ogilvy's *Confessions of an Advertising Man* (Atheneum) and *Ogilvy on Advertising* (Vintage Books). Both are full of top-notch information and great reading.

If I could impart one solid, unbreakable rule for advertising Walter's services, it would be that your advertising must always answer the reader's question: "What's in it for me?" Potential big spenders won't care a whit about your background and accomplishments unless you can somehow convince them that they will benefit handsomely because you've been what you've been and done what you've done. In general, clients like to know that they're getting your best price, your best work and your best results. They look at your advertising the same way you and Walter look at the CPM at those trade magazines. They want to make money by hiring you. If they see results, or even potential results, they will hire you time and again.

I once heard a marketing expert say that the secret to success in business is to actually care more about the success of your clients or customers than you do about your own. This can be hard to accomplish, but what a great concept. Note that he said you must "actually" care more about your clients than about yourself. He's not telling you to fake it or to use some kind of slick language to give that impression. He's telling you (and Walter) to throw yourself into the task of improving your client's lot in life. This is wonderful advice—not only in writing but in any business, in any life situation.

Cold Calls

I remember a tremendously successful salesman who worked for a radio station in Sacramento, California, a few years ago. This guy made thousands and thousands of dollars for himself and his employer simply by working the telephones. He was the undisputed king of cold calling. Unlike the other salespeople, he almost never left the office; in fact, I hardly ever saw him without a phone pasted to his ear. Then one day a new manager decided that this guy should be out pounding the pavement like the rest of the sales force. The phone-efficient salesman tried it for a couple of days and then got on the phone and got himself a new job with another station where the manager was bright enough to leave him alone.

Not everybody has what it takes to use the telephone to gin up new business. In fact, most of us would rather take a beating with a garden rake than spend our days making cold calls. No doubt you've had the pleasure of chatting with that annoying fellow who calls you at dinnertime. He wants to sell you a bass fishing magazine and you want to finish your mashed potatoes. The intrusive and aggressively commercial nature of these calls has probably prejudiced us all to some extent. That, however, is not the kind of call we're going to encourage Walter to make.

Walter is not going to buy a list of phone numbers and just randomly start calling. Instead, he's going to watch the newspaper for developments in the local business scene. Companies that seem to be on the move, managers who are getting promoted, just about any activity in local business could warrant a cold call. When he calls, he needs to have a specific angle in mind. Just getting a busy prospective client on the phone can be tough, so he should avoid just asking if the prospect needs any writing. Instead, he can say that he'd just read about [the promotion or whatever] and thought it might be a good time for Mr. Prospect to write a guest editorial in the paper. When the guy confesses that he is a lousy writer, Walter can say, with a chuckle, "Well . . . that's why I called you. I write that kind of thing all the time and it would be really easy to put one together for you. You'd just have to tell me what points you want to make about [the topic that Walter is suggesting] and I'll put the whole thing together." It will help, of course, if Walter has written a few guest editorials or business columns himself.

Be aware that not every call will result in a sale. In fact, hardly any of them will hit pay dirt. This can be discouraging, but it's important to keep a positive attitude. Cold calls can have an accumulative effect. The guy you've called may not want to buy, but he may run into some-body the next day or the next week who is looking for just that kind of service. After each cold call Walter (and you) should follow up with a brief thanks-for-taking-time-to-talk-to-me-I-really-appreciate-your-help letter and a business card. The letter is easy to boilerplate and shouldn't take too much time or effort. Then put the address in your computer's address book and make a note in the tickler file to give the guy another call later on in the year. Again, when you call him, have an angle (different from the first one) that's tied to something current in the life of the prospect or his company. Eventually, this kind of diligent effort will pay off—sometimes very handsomely.

Public Relations
There's an old saying that goes, "Nothing succeeds like success."

There is a lot of truth in that. Most people, particularly those in business, want to associate with people they think are successful. If Walter (and you) can promote an image of success for himself, his efforts to sell his writing will be much more effective. The question is, of course, how to go about this.

Here's a short list of things Walter can do to help himself foster a favorable image, particularly when it comes to writing for local business clients.

1. Personal press releases
2. Public speaking
3. Local writing
4. Charity work and events
5. Teaching classes
6. Tutoring

All of these steps are fairly easy for Walter to take and are highly effective . . . if he keeps at them. A good personal public relations program is a cumulative thing. If you consistently put out a PR effort, you will reap the benefits. How rich those benefits are depends on how diligent and how lucky you are. Personally, I think diligence is the more important of the two. As Woody Allen once said, "Ninety percent of success is just showing up." Don't expect that every bit of PR you put out is going to find fertile ground. Just know that some of it will, and the more you put out, the more good it will do for you.

Personal Press Releases
It's sometimes difficult to get freelance writers and other noble-minded folks to talk or write about their own accomplishments. It seems immodest, I suppose. We're taught at an early age that bragging is an unattractive activity. It's far more comfortable to have other people sing of our considerable virtues. We're going to ask Walter to get over this. Promotion is not bragging. Promotion is marketing. Marketing is good, especially if Walter is serious about that $150K annual goal.

One of the easiest and most effective ways to promote yourself as a writer is the personal press release. Newspapers and other media are set up to accept press releases. They expect to receive them. Actually, when I was in the newspaper business I looked forward to getting a good press release. By "good press release" I mean one that the editor or reporter can read and understand quickly—and one that is appropriate for the media outlet to which it was sent. Make sure that the subject of your press release can be understood within the five to fifteen seconds it will command the editor's or reporter's attention. When I worked in the city magazine business, I was often asked to speak to journalism classes. Mostly, the students in these classes wanted to know how to get editors to notice them and their ideas. To illustrate the sheer volume of press releases with which an editor must deal, I would save one week's worth in a cardboard box. At the beginning of the class, I'd dump the contents of the box onto the desk in front of me. Usually the press releases not only covered the desk but also overflowed onto the floor. And that was not even including the dozens of query letters I'd get. Interestingly, about 90 percent of the press releases and at least half the queries were inappropriate for my publication.

I'm certain that the volume of mail and paperwork arriving on the desks of editors, creative directors and other word buyers hasn't slowed since those days. In fact, it's probably increased with the addition of e-mail and voice mail. Thus, Walter will have to be even more clever if he is to get his message across.

He can start by making a database of media contacts, complete with all contact information and any hints he can find regarding what the individual media folks like to print or air. This isn't too hard to round up, but it can be a little time-consuming to maintain. Nevertheless, it is very important to keep your media list up to date. It's hard to sell an editor or creative director on your value as a freelancer if you've gotten his or her name wrong. This is so important that we're going to recommend a bimonthly update. If Walter doesn't have enough time to do this, we're going to suggest that he hire an assistant to take care of such things. Either way, maintaining an accurate media list is crucial to the success of a personal PR program.

OK, now we know where Walter will send his press releases. But what will he send? Content is vitally important, of course, but keep in mind that we're looking for a cumulative effect. If you send a press release to the local paper regarding a writing job you've been hired to perform, you may assume that the newspaper will be interested in the client you sign up next week. Actually, they may well choose to ignore your second press release, simply because you've had recent exposure and they don't want to be seen as a cheerleading organization for you (or anybody). Don't let this bother you. Keep sending the press releases. Picture the editor who receives all of these well-written, well-timed press releases. Walter's (and your) steady stream of press releases will likely accomplish a few things. First, the editor may well decide to print some of them, which will result in your exposure as a successful, expert writer who is in big demand. Second, the volume of information on you and your writing business will position you as an expert source on business writing (or whatever other kind of writing you've been promoting for yourself). Thus, when the editor is looking for someone to quote regarding business writing, etc., she will think of you and send a reporter

your way, which will also enhance your position in the business community. Third, when the editor is talking to people in the business community, someone may ask her about professional writers in the area. Who's
she going to recommend—you or somebody she knows nothing about?
You know the answer to that question.

We've talked mostly about press releases to local newspapers, but
don't overlook other media outlets. You probably won't get much airtime for your press releases sent to TV stations, for example, but at some
point the assignment editor is going to need a national story localized,
and he could decide that you're a local expert on business communications or whatever. And don't forget the national trade press. Say, for
instance, that Walter lands a project writing direct mail copy for a mail-
order company in Omaha. That press release is likely to find a home in
the local press in his hometown and possibly in Omaha as well. But let's
not stop there. There's a trade journal for just about every activity,
profession and pastime in the country. I know of one company in Southern California that publishes about 140 separate and distinct journals.
Maybe Walter's press release will work for a direct marketing magazine
or a mail-order trade publication. Maybe the editor of one of these
journals needs an expert source, just like the local newspaper editor did.
If so, Walter may be on his way to being quoted in a magazine that
helps hundreds (maybe thousands) of word buyers decide whose words
they are going to buy.

One caution about frequent press releases: Be sure they have a
legitimate news "peg" and are not simply rehashing your old accomplishments. Few things irritate editors or reporters as much as wasting
their time.

Public Speaking

I read somewhere that speaking in public is the number one fear in
America, more dreaded, in fact, than death itself. This extreme reluctance represents an opportunity for folks like Walter and you. Good,
willing speakers are in high demand. With his writing skills, Walter
should have no trouble putting together a recyclable speech on the
importance of concise communications in the business world. I'd recommend that he study some really good, classic speeches (anything by Dr.
Martin Luther King, Jr., for example) before signing up for the speaking
tour, but once he has his "stump speech" down pat there's no reason
he shouldn't accept all invitations.

A simple boilerplate letter to civic groups, corporations, etc., offering his services and detailing his qualifications should give Walter all the speaking engagements he can handle. He should also put together a portable set of props, charts or whatever he needs to illustrate his talks. It's also a good idea to bring along his capabilities brochure, business cards and other promotional materials he might have. People love to come away from a seminar or speech or workshop with something in their hands. If Walter (or you) has written a book, a copy should also be at the speech venue along with a credit card machine and order forms for the book. And please, let's not forget to put out a press release to the local paper saying that Walter (or you) will be speaking at the appointed time and location.

Local Writing

I'm not a huge fan of writing for local newspapers as a source of revenue. Most of them pay in the neighborhood of $35 to $50 for a piece that could take days, even weeks, to research and write. In that same time period, a handy writer can put together a lot of lucrative commercial writing assignments and generate paydays in the thousands of dollars. Fifty dollars or several thousand bucks—it's a short decision-making process for most of us. However, there is some value to having your byline appear locally.

This is particularly true in the case of guest editorials and columns in the paper. Such exposure, again, helps position you as a media expert, someone who knows how to get noticed. It doesn't take a quantum leap of logic for your prospective PR clients, for example, to assume you can also help them get their opinions and observations published locally. It's a great boon for a local attorney, for example, to have a pithy article on some point of law appear under his or her byline. I once ghostwrote an op-ed piece for a Northern California advertising executive on the proper way for doctors to advertise. This was back when doctors were just beginning to give themselves permission to market their practices via advertising and public relations. After the article came out, the advertising executive's agency picked up a very profitable ophthalmology practice. I know of several other professionals who have hired professional writers to ghost their op-ed pieces. It's great publicity for them because it carries the tacit endorsement of the publication in which it appears (something no ad can ever do) and puts their issues in front of the people in a balanced, dignified fashion. A lot of physicians still balk at paying someone to build ads for them, but very few will turn down a chance to wax expert in front of a willing audience of newspaper readers. The more they see your writing in the op-ed pages, the more they are likely to hire you to put them there, too.

The same holds true for writing in a more journalistic vein. Every time your byline appears over a feature story or a news piece or a local magazine story, your value as a media consultant goes up. Every time you appear in a radio or TV news story you move closer to being a highly paid media star yourself. I've seen it happen. I've mentioned this before, but I feel it bears repeating: Make sure you separate your public relations writing from your journalism. Your clients have to understand the difference between an objective news story and an opinion piece.

Charity Work and Events

This may seem a bit mercenary, but one of my mottoes is: "You can do well by doing good."

By this I mean that participating in charity events, performing charity work and donating money or materials to charities will pay you a tangible dividend—not to mention the emotional and spiritual rewards that one might expect. Let me give you an example. While driving to my office a year or so ago, I was feeling pretty sorry for myself thanks to a temporary summer slump in the junk mail business. Cash flow was down, bills continued to arrive and I was a tad worried. On the way into town (I lived, as I do now, in a cabin in the mountains of North Carolina), I passed a farmers market. It was an extremely hot and humid day and the market had a bunch of iced-down watermelons for sale by the road. Huge melons, as big as beach balls and very tempting. I bought four of them, loaded them in the back of my vehicle and drove down to the local rescue mission where the melons were received with great enthusiasm. The whole thing made me feel pretty good, too. That morning, as I sat stewing over those bills, I heard the mail chute bang on the front door. In flew an envelope containing $3,500. It was money I had earned, to be sure, but I hadn't expected it for another six weeks or so. The same sort of thing has happened to me countless times. The more money and time I give away, the more money and success I get in return. No one can tell me that the "give" is not related to the "get." Try it yourself—I promise you it will work. Open yourself up to it. Give without fear or hesitation. And feel good about accepting the rewards that

follow. It's part of the Big System, if you ask me—and we should partici-
pate willingly.

Charity work also carries with it more traditional rewards as well.
Say, for example, that you offer to write a press release (as I have) for
a charity fashion show to benefit the local domestic violence shelter.
The people who volunteer in these things are usually very well connected locally. A couple of bank presidents, a local hospital official and
a very well-thought-of retired businesswoman all participated in the
fashion show about which I wrote. All of these people either need writing services themselves or know somebody who does. You position yourself as an expert, a good-hearted person and an associate of important
folks. You may not get paid for your initial efforts, but who do you think
that bank president and that hospital official will look to when he or
she wants a press release done or a brochure written or an annual report
edited?

Teaching Classes

Few things in life have given me as much pleasure as teaching writing to
people who truly want to learn. I always meet wonderfully experienced,
multitalented, genuinely interesting human beings every time I get in
front of a class. One of my favorites was Les, a retired federal magistrate
I met while teaching an extension class for the local community college.
During the course of the two-weekend class, Les and the other students
talked about projects they would like to work on. Les told us that he'd
found more than three hundred love letters he'd written to his late wife
during World War II. He thought they'd make a nice article. I told him
I thought they'd make a nice book. A couple of years later, *Dear Betty:
Letters to a War Bride* saw print. It was a rare privilege to read the book
and to know its author.

Teaching writing puts you in front of the public in much the same
way as public speaking. You're an authority. You're helping people understand the difficult but fascinating task of writing well. You may not
discover an author in your class, but there's a good chance you could
discover a client or someone who knows a client. As in all personal
public relations efforts, success is a matter of persistence.

Tutoring

Tutoring is, of course, a form of teaching. But it really takes on a larger
life if you let it. I tutor for the local literacy council, and I've truly

enjoyed getting to know the gentleman I'm helping. Let's not lose sight of the fact that as writers it behooves us to encourage people to read well. There are other, more subtle rewards in store for you when you take on a project like this.

Suppose Walter volunteers to help someone pass a GED test or learn to read to his children at night. It's a great feeling to do this, but it's also a large commitment requiring organization, scheduling, several hours a month and even a little frustration when the learning process bogs down, which it almost certainly will. Tutoring hours can get in the way of work and recreational plans. I've skipped my weekly poker game a couple times to honor my tutoring commitment. I've turned down after-work cocktails with prospective clients to make sure I didn't miss the meeting time.

The fact is, I don't know if I'll ever get any kind of monetary return from tutoring. I certainly don't expect it. But working with my student gives me a feeling of belonging, of contribution, and that's not a bad thing for a writer to have in his emotional bank account. I write more confidently when I feel good about myself and, if the truth be told, I've picked up a few points of grammar that I'd obviously forgotten, simply because I had to explain them to my student.

One last thing about tutoring: Every time I mention my tutoring activities to a colleague or client I always get the same response. A raised eyebrow and an expression of admiration for being a good guy. That's something Walter, you, me and everybody else on the planet can use.

Referrals

Most marketing professionals will tell you that the best advertising is word of mouth. Basically, that means that satisfied customers often tell their friends and associates about a person or company that's done a good job for them. So how do people like you, me and Walter get a word-of-mouth campaign going? This can be difficult, mainly because most people are more likely to voice their opinions when they are angry or dissatisfied with goods or services. If they think you've done a good job, they will happily pay you and then forget about it.

So, how does Walter get his clients to give him good referrals and word-of-mouth advertising? He just has to ask. That builder friend I mentioned earlier has a refreshingly candid way of getting referrals. Anytime someone tells my friend that he has done a good job—and that's pretty often because he is a phenomenally talented carpenter/builder—

he gets the person's name and permission to pass along the favorable comments. Every few weeks he runs a modest advertisement with the headline: "Looking for a reliable contractor?" and a handful of quotes from his happy clients. His phone rings off the hook.

You can do the same thing. I'm sure you've shown copy or a story to some lucky word buyer and had that person enthuse over the quality of your work. When that happens, say something like, "Hey, I'm glad you liked that. I wonder if you'd mind being interviewed for some self-promotional work I'm doing." Then whip out your tape recorder and do a quick question and answer on the work you've done for this person, the results he or she has experienced and what it all means to the interviewee. Let the person go on about himself a bit. Remember, you're gathering raw material here. Sure, your main purpose is to get enough info for a testimonial to be used in your own promotional material, but wouldn't it be great to discover some other bit of information that might grow up and become a story (or part of a story) on its own? The more information you have, the more money you are likely to earn.

So now you have a handful of testimonials. But how are you going to use them? Look at such bits of self-serving information as spices to sprinkle around in your promotional brochure or your portfolio Web site. Advertising experts will tell you that well-done testimonials are extremely strong. Don't be afraid to use them liberally.

Of course, testimonials aren't exactly the same thing as referrals. A referral is when one of your happy current clients recommends you to a potential new client. This is great stuff and should be encouraged as much as possible. At the very least, the referring client should get a phone call or letter thanking him or her for the referral. Perhaps a nice gift would be in order if the referral results in a large jolt of income. A few years ago, I used to lift weights with a guy who owned a small janitorial service. One day at the gym, I told him I'd heard one of my corporate clients was looking for a new cleaning service for some buildings they owned. I gave him the number and forgot about it completely. The next week, my friend came into the gym all smiles and said that he'd doubled his business by acquiring this one client. He also called me out to his van and gave me a shiny new 12-gauge Wingmaster pump shotgun as a token of his appreciation. I was flabbergasted by his gratitude and by his gift. After that, there wasn't a chance I'd have recommended anyone else for a similar opening.

The same thing works with people who refer writing work to you. If the job they send you brings in $500 and you spend $50 taking them to dinner—well, you've paid a lousy 10 percent commission. Be as generous and as creative as you can be. If my janitor friend had given me the cash equivalent of the cost of the shotgun I would have certainly appreciated it, but there was something really spectacular about receiving the shotgun.

I won't presume to tell you what you should give your referring clients, but do give them something even if it's just a nice phone call. They are, after all, putting money in your pocket.

Mailing Lists

A good mailing list can be invaluable to a freelance writing business. I've used mailing lists for years and have enjoyed results from nearly nothing to wildly successful. Choosing an effective list is a genuine skill. Finding the right group of names is crucial to the success of any mailing campaign. In publishing, careers have been made or lost on the basis of this one task.

List acquisition is only slightly less important to Walter and you as freelance writers. Seriously, you probably won't lose your job (since you're self-employed) if you make a bad choice of lists, but you can waste an appalling amount of money mailing your message to a bad or inappropriate list. A mailing campaign, complete with postage, printing, list rental and handling charges can be quite pricey. If you spend $1,000 and bring in $10,000 you are a hero. If those numbers are reversed you're a doofus—and a poorer one at that.

I recommend going to a reputable list broker for mailing lists. And I wouldn't want you or Walter to waste your money on e-mail lists that weren't "opt-in" lists. This means that the e-mail addressee has authorized the use of his address and is at least vaguely interested in hearing about certain products and services. Try to narrow the list as much as possible. If you're looking for work in the corporate world, try to ferret out names and addresses of corporate communications directors. If you're shopping in the advertising business, ask for a list of creative directors or vice presidents of creative services. You can narrow the list of magazine editors and book publishers the same way. Be sure you have a firm idea of whom you want to reach and how much money you have to spend on the mailing or e-mailing before you call the list broker. Those are two of the first questions he or she will ask you.

One other thing to consider when you're mailing or e-mailing your promotional efforts: Your mailing could be phenomenally compelling.

That sounds like a really good thing, doesn't it? But maybe it isn't. In fact, a giant response can cause some serious troubles. Say Walter puts out a thousand e-mails to corporate communications directors, magazine editors and advertising agency creative directors. He invites them to look over his Internet portfolio site. They do—and 15 percent (probably way higher than real life, but I'm trying to make a point here) of them are so impressed with Walter's writing that they ask him to do some work for them. That's 150 new jobs, and Walter is going to be a very busy lad. He might not even get half the work done. The point, of course, is to be careful with this potent medium. Test a small mailing first. If you get a huge percentage of response on a small universe of names, you will be busy but you won't be completely swamped. Gradually increase the number of addresses until you're pretty sure you're feeling the top of your ability to deliver the goods.

Reaching Your Financial Goal

Now that Walter has gotten his promotional activities under way, let's take another look at his money goal. How on earth is he going to translate all of these possibilities and potential profit centers into $150,000 per year? The fact is, he may or may not get it done in the first year. As we discussed earlier, he's going to have to take a sort of integrated approach. If he researches and writes magazine articles, he's going to have to work hard to resell them. If he scores with an average of one out of ten query letters and his average payment for an article is $350, he'll need to have no fewer than twenty letters in front of editors each working day. He can take a bit of pressure off that number by reselling articles, conducting (for pay) writing workshops, writing advertising copy and producing collateral material.

Add to that the occasional TV commercial, radio spot, ghostwriting job and any of the other profit centers we've talked about, and Walter may well be on his way. It's crucially important that he keep a record of his earnings and refer to it weekly. This will let him know if he needs to step on the gas in the marketing department or get busy cranking out work for which he's already contracted.

Most of all, Walter, and anyone else hoping to make a good living in the world of freelance writing, must continue to think of writing as a business—an incredibly satisfying, amusing, fulfilling business. Sure, clients must be served and schedules must be kept. The bottom line must be monitored. But through it all, remember to have some fun.

Waiting for Your Empty Vessel to Come In

ED GOLDMAN

Ed Goldman is a master communicator, a guy who knows how to use words to get what he wants.

Take, for instance, the letter he wrote to me when I was the managing editor of *Sacramento Magazine*. Apparently we were considerably overdue with a payment for one of the many excellent articles Ed had contributed over the years. The letter, polished and polite as any I've ever read, asked us to define our payment policy. Was it "upon acceptance, upon publication or upon death of author"? We paid his bill the next day.

Ed got his start as a freelancer, for local newspapers, during his high school days (1965–1968). His first magazine sale came in 1970—a piece about low riders for the Sunday supplement of the *Long Beach Press-Telegram*, a metropolitan daily newspaper for which he worked as a reporter. Basically, Ed says, he stood around for a few hours listening to guys talking about their cars and their lives. "I asked a couple of questions," he explains, "then went back to the newspaper office and wrote a largely bogus piece about them."

Ed's modesty aside, the piece must not have been all that bogus. The article generated a flood of reader correspondence and prompted the paper to ask the nineteen-year-old writer to put together some more magazine work.

"I ended up writing seven or eight pieces for the paper's magazine, *Southland Sunday*," Ed says. "There was a wonderful reporter at the *Press-Telegram*, a man named Stan Leppard. He was a cop reporter, but he also freelanced to those allegedly true/remarkably virile adventure and crime magazines—the kind that always had guys on the cover with squinty eyes, leathery skin, world-weary expressions and unhealthful tattoos. I doubt that Stan ever wrote basic freelance pieces, like 'Weekend Getaways for Two,' but if he did, they would have been called something like 'Escaping From Bahrain on a Budget' or 'How to Tell Your Cellmate No and Really Mean It.'

"Stan never wrote anything remotely recreational. What he would do was take some of the stories he had been covering at the *Press-Telegram* and add some facts that might not have been appropriate for a family newspaper. And then he'd turn them into pretty good fare for the true-crime-and-adventure market. He was getting at that time six or seven hundred dollars per magazine. That was real good dough back then. I was intrigued by the money, so I started sending out query letters.

"In 1981 I sold a piece to *TV Guide*. I was so used to getting my manuscripts back a few weeks after I'd sent them that this kind of took me by surprise. My wife and I had come back from a vacation and found a very thin envelope from *TV Guide*. I was infuriated as I picked it up. I thought they hadn't even returned my manuscript when they sent my rejection letter. Then I opened the envelope and saw something I rarely had seen—an acceptance slip and a check for $750, which I thought was pretty nice. It made me think that my wife and I should go out of town more often, because I was starting to realize that I made my best freelance sales while I was gone. It's sort of the writer's equivalent of the watched pot that never boils. A watched mailbox never holds the check you're waiting for."

Another of Ed's memorable sales came from the famed Lawrence Livermore National Laboratory. "They paid me to write a piece about their tech transfer program for *California Manufacturer* magazine. In essence, the national lab bought advertorial space in the magazine and hired me as a freelance writer to come in and write the piece. It was a great check, but it was also a terrific experience because it got me into a whole other field of writing. I wouldn't call it technical writing, but it was taking highly technical information and trying to translate it into recognizable English.

"If there's any advice that I would give any freelance writer it's to be as agile as possible. Be a generalist. Read all kinds of things, and don't think that you can't write science articles because you once got a D in science, as I most certainly did—and let me tell you, I *worked* for that D. I've since written a number of science articles. You're not writing as an expert in science. You're writing as a reporter, and I think that's an important thing to keep in mind. I do a lot of freelance writing the same way you might cram for a final."

It takes a special talent for a freelancer to be able to gather all that technical, scientific information, use it and then keep it from cluttering up the mind. "I've met wonderful people and learned amazing things that I've tended to forget all about a few weeks later," Ed says. "I don't just clear the decks after a story: I completely clear my *mind*. I apparently have this amazing facility to become a completely empty vessel. I suppose others might call that being superficial and this should explain why I rarely speak with others about it."

Ed also has a reputation for fearlessly asking interviewees to explain themselves in plain language. Once, a real estate section editor from the *Los Angeles Times* sent Ed to a conference of economists. "I had never done any of that kind of work before. My aptitude for economics was similar to my aptitude for science—which is to say, nonexistent. I went to the conference, and the people there might as well have been speaking Martian for all I knew. And they went on and on and on. What I did manage to pick up was that they weren't actually expressing any real opinions on what the economy was going to do. There's an old joke that goes, 'If you laid the world's economists end to end, they still wouldn't reach a conclusion,' and that certainly appeared to be the case here. So I went up to the most verbose guy on the panel and said, 'I am absolutely lost. I have got to figure out what you guys are saying.' He was about to dismiss me, but he made the tactical error of asking me who I was covering the story for, and I said the *Los Angeles Times*. Suddenly, I couldn't shake the guy for the rest of the afternoon. I think he took me back to the cave people counting out rocks. I filed the story after really sweating over it and vowed never to try to do that again. But the *Times* ran it verbatim and said I was going to cover all the economics conferences related to real estate from then on. I started reading everything I could about economics; before long, I could balance a checkbook with the best of them."

Just about every freelance writer has a favorite rejection letter story. Ed's involves a book he wrote and sent to an editor at a major publishing house. The book, a comic novel about city government, found an enthusiastic supporter in this editor. He sent it on to the main office where the decision to buy would be made. "Then months and months and months went by," Ed recalls. "During that time we'd met for lunch a few times. Finally, he said, 'They're not sure they want to do a comic novel right now, but why don't you think about writing a funny book about business?'"

This was all the encouragement Ed needed. He put together an outline for a book he intended to call either *'Til Debt Do Us Part* or *How to Incorporate Your Dog and Other Solid Business Tips*.

"[The editor] took it. Said he loved it. Sent it to New York, and again months and months passed. After nine months—literally—the New York editors called him back and said, 'You know, we think this might be a little passé now. Maybe it would have been good about nine months ago.' "

The book finally sold to a small publisher in California and sold well in Sacramento, Los Angeles and Kansas City. He followed it up with another book, this one titled *On Goldman Pond*. "If your name is Goldman," Ed says, "you probably have a copy. Outside of that market, though, it didn't sell very well."

Other Goldman books—as yet unpublished—are *Fear of Frying* (a humorous cookbook), *Every Little Breeze Seems to Whisper Disease* (set in a large hospital) and *Shocked and Deeply Saddened* (the adventures of a battling public information officer for a large metro California city). He is currently completing a comic novel set in the world of California real estate, *Soaring Ceilings*. He also works in radio and television, public relations, advertising and just about any other form of writing that involves a client and a check in that (now) unwatched mailbox.

Ed's wife, Jane, is a freelance writer herself, with a degree in magazine journalism from Northwestern University and sales to *People, Mc-Call's* and *Glamour*. They maintain separate offices within a large home in one of Sacramento's more fashionable sections.

"It's been great," Ed says. "The one thing everybody who owns a business wants is a trustworthy partner. Well, I've got one—my wife. We've been married for twenty-two years. She's my best editor and I'm her best editor. We have completely different styles and approaches to writing, which is good—we read each other's pieces without any preconceived notions. The only questions are: (1) does it work, and (2) who's going to set the table?"

CHAPTER SEVEN

Breaking and Entering

In the early 1980s, I spent a year knocking around New York City looking for writing work and just generally misbehaving. It was a splendid time to be in the city. Not only that, I was perfectly set up to enjoy myself. I had not yet taken my first ill-advised trip down the aisle. I had no children to support and no home to keep up. No credit card companies were after me for payment. The IRS had no particular interest in me, and I had a pocket full of greenbacks from a couple of fairly major freelance sales. Plus, I was living rent-free at a buddy's 2,500-square-foot loft in fashionable Chelsea (on Eighteenth Street between Fifth and Sixth). Actually, it was the building where they filmed the Dustin Hoffman/Bill Murray movie, *Tootsie*. I should hasten to point out that while Dusty and Bill and I did not hang out together at the time, I did once get to say, "Excuse me" and step past them at the door to the elevator.

Most of my writing time was spent banging out a screenplay (which remains unsold to this day) on an old manual Royal typewriter that I'd picked up for $25. Life was good. Write in the morning and entertain myself in Manhattan the rest of the day.

Of course, even an arrangement as thrifty as mine still required some income. I did a little temporary work for an architect who was restoring the Fulton Fish Market. I did a little freelancing for McGraw-Hill's doomed Product Information Network, and I hustled a few freelance jobs for the *New York Daily News Sunday Magazine* and a few other places.

Being only a few blocks from Madison Avenue, I figured I owed it to myself to take a stab at advertising work. Some serious money was available, according to a pal who worked at a type shop that catered to some of the larger agencies in town.

So, laden with visions of pointy cars and big nights on the town, I typed up a resume and looked through the *NY Times* want ads. Immediately, I found a likely looking employer (right on Madison Avenue, no less) and called them up for an interview. Come on down with your "book," the creative director's assistant told me. I wasn't totally clear what he meant by a "book," but I showed up at the appointed hour with my resume and the only legitimate example of my copywriting, an ad I'd written for a radio station in Sacramento, California. I still say it was a pretty clever ad, featuring an attractive young lady who could hit a baseball out of the local ballpark and drove a fancy convertible car, the radio in which was always tuned to the station in question.

The agency was housed in an incredibly small space with a tiny waiting room crowded with young men and women clutching large leatherette briefcases. The guy who interviewed me described the agency and its clients, among them a very popular designer jeans company and a bunch of other solid New York City accounts.

After he'd finished introducing himself and the company, the interviewer asked to see my book, by which he meant a portfolio—just as I'd suspected all along. When I handed him my solitary piece of advertising work, he stared at it for a moment and then looked up. "How much did you have in mind for a salary?" he wanted to know.

Well, I like to feel the top in this kind of negotiation so I told him I could come on board for "around $40,000 a year."

That's when the interview began to break down. Just as the words "$40,000 a year" left my mouth, a brass button sort of exploded (don't ask me why; the jacket fit me perfectly) off my navy blazer. It flew through the air and landed in my loafer, which I had been sort of dangling nonchalantly off my foot. As I was digging the fugitive button out I happened to look up at my host. He was staring at me, eyes bulging and the veins in his neck standing out nicely against the collar of his well-starched, blue button-down dress shirt. For a moment, I thought he was going to come over the desk and throttle me. Apparently, I'd overestimated my marketability somewhat.

He calmed down quickly though, a talent he'd no doubt had to develop in his stress-filled job. Gently handing me back my "portfolio," he quietly told me that he was pretty sure he could hire just about any of the applicants waiting in his lobby for about $800 a month, just for a chance to get into the business. He also pointed out that each of those applicants had thick books full of work they'd either had published or worked up on speculation just for this interview. The salary situation did not seem to me to be a wise proposition in a city where, at the time, a tiny apartment could cost $1,200 a month (or more), and none of the markets was giving away free groceries. I asked him how this could be, and he said, "Lots of roommates."

I expect I looked a bit crestfallen. As I shuffled out of his office, brass button in hand, he put his arm around my shoulder and told me that I needed to hook up with a graphic designer and put together a lot of sample work. He also gave me another good piece of advice. He said that when this graphic designer and I were deciding what to put in this speculative portfolio, we should study the agencies we wanted to pitch and come up with ads for products or services similar to the ones their clients provided. Do not, he pointed out, try to rewrite or redesign the ads that the agency has already done. Our chances of dazzling them with our insight would be statistically insignificant compared to the very real chance that we'd be trashing the work of the person or persons interviewing us.

It was the first time I'd ever realized that there was a certain science to breaking into a new line of writing. It was a lesson that has profited me greatly in the years since that interview. For one thing, I always check the buttons on my sports coat and I never wear loafers when I'm facing a potential client. Seriously, though, a bit of research and preparation can vastly improve your chances when you're expanding your writing business. What follows in this chapter are some of my observations on the craft of breaking into new writing markets.

Breaking Into the Magazine Market

Establishing yourself in any new writing genre is mostly a matter of research and persistence. In that respect, magazine writing is no different from any other kind of writing.

Your first step should be introspective. Think about what kind of writing you wish to do. Are you intrigued by travel writing, or would you prefer to write personality profiles? Maybe you'd like to take a run at sports writing or try your hand at the women's magazine market. There are many ways to go. There are hundreds of viable magazine markets: general interest, special interest, women's, men's, sports, professional trade magazines, technical publications and many others. A good place to start is your local newsstand or the magazine section at the local library. Work your way through the shelves and see what tickles your interest. You'll be astounded at the number and variety of publications available. I once heard comedian George Carlin say that in this country if more than three people are doing the same thing at the same time somebody will publish a magazine about it. He has a point.

Once you narrow the field to a handful of magazine genres, take some time to pick out the specific magazines for which you would like to write. Buy some back issues of each so you can study content and style. Look for their Web sites. You'll find a great variety in the way magazines maintain their Internet pages. Some will practically give the editorial content away online. Others just toss something up on the Net, include some online subscription pages and leave it at that. I think magazine Web sites are extremely valuable in that they allow you to research the publication without spending a lot of money. If the site is well maintained, you'll also be able to see what the publisher and the editors think their magazine is all about. Note the Web site address and any e-mail contact information for the editors. Pick up contact information for the circulation director or manager; they sometimes buy writing services for their promotional efforts.

When you have complete contact information, start a file for each magazine you intend to approach. Include sample copies of the magazines, the contact information you've accumulated and a list of story ideas you'd like to pursue with them. These story ideas should come from studying back issues and, of course, from your own fertile imagination. If you see that the women's magazine you've targeted likes to do holiday theme issues or physical fitness sections or whatever, use that information to plan your story suggestions.

Once you have a list of stories you'd like to do for your targeted publications, compose a query letter to each of the editors. If you are unfamiliar with query letters, I suggest that you look through *How to Write Attention-Grabbing Query & Cover Letters*, by John Wood. Put simply, your letter should pique the interest of the editor in respect to the story you wish to write and lay out your qualifications to write the piece. Please remember that this letter is about the story—not about you. Any information about yourself should be there only to convince the editor to hire *you* to write this story. Any query letter that begins, "I am a . . ." or "I am writing because . . ." or "My name is . . ." will probably fail. No doubt there are exceptions to that rule. I remember buying one article about a chocolate factory from a very talented writer whose letter began (if I remember correctly), "I am a shameless chocoholic and I need your help." Words to that effect, anyway. The letter worked because the personal information she gave me actually had to do with the story she wanted to write. She didn't dwell on herself, and she wrote very cleverly.

When you're writing your query letters, think of them in the same light as the junk mail you receive in your own mailbox. You probably pitch most of it in the round file without reading more than the outer envelope, right? Why is that? Two reasons: You get a lot of mail and you don't want to waste time on stuff that isn't important. And, what you did read did not convince you that the sender had something you could use. That's why you see words like "Yours *free!*" and "Send No Money" and "Money-back Guarantee" on the outer envelopes that carry these commercial messages. I write a lot of junk mail (sorry about that), and I know that these words increase response. In this form of writing (which is quite similar in a lot of ways to query letter writing), copywriters like me aspire to net responses of one or two percent. In other words, we're happy if two people out of one hundred recipients actually spend money on the product (in my case, magazine subscriptions) that we're pitching. If I could consistently put together direct mail pitches that netted out, say, four percent, I would be living in a castle somewhere, enjoying fine wine and getting gout from my lavish lifestyle.

Consider that goal for your own efforts. You write one hundred query letters and you get four jobs. Say those jobs bring you an initial fee of $350 apiece. You make $1,400, plus whatever you can make reselling them in Europe or to magazines that buy second rights. Actually, you'll probably have a much higher percentage of sales from your hundred letters. Nevertheless, you will have to keep a lot of query letters in the system if you intend to make some serious money.

It's really that simple. The better the ideas you have and the more editors you solicit, the more money you make. Don't let this volume waver, and don't get discouraged by the rejections you will no doubt receive. If you have a hundred queries in the mail, you're a lot more likely to score and a lot less likely to worry about the fate of any individual pitch. Write and mail ten queries per day to start with. If that doesn't bring you success, send more.

Once you start getting positive responses from editors, make sure they stay aware of you. Avoid getting distracted by other projects. While I was writing this chapter, I got a call from a former client. She said she had been trying to get in touch with me to write a $10,000 project for her. I was appalled that she'd been forced to hunt me up for the job. She hadn't even put the work out to bid because she only wanted me to do the writing. Clients like these should not have to search for you;

you should be right there whenever they want you. Don't let it happen with your magazine editors, either. They are your valued clients. They have money to spend on you. Keep them up to speed on what you're doing and what you'd like to do for them.

OK, so now you've got all of these magazine editors interested in you. How do you keep them interested? Simple: Do great work, and do it with as little pain and hassle as possible for the editors. Bend over backwards to accommodate their needs. I've been on both sides of the editor's desk, and I know professional freelancers are scarce. If you want to be treated well by editors, make yourself as valuable as possible.

Having said all of the preceding, however, I should also point out that you need to be firm in your negotiations with editors—particularly after you've established yourself as a professional. Be aware of the rights you're selling. If you sell all rights, for example, your revenue stream for that particular piece will dry up. If you sell first North American serial rights, which a lot of magazines prefer, you will be delayed in selling the piece again in the United States and Canada, but you'll be free to peddle it in Europe and anywhere else in the world. Don't be intimidated by foreign markets. Editors need content for their magazines no matter where their offices are.

Breaking Into Public Relations Writing

I've heard many veteran reporters say that if the newspaper business ever became unbearable, they could always turn to public relations writing. This is usually said in a tone that implies the switch from journalist to publicist entails nothing more strenuous than a massive lowering of standards and a willingness to accept tons of money for "doing lunch."

This is patent nonsense, of course. Writing for public relations is as demanding as any other kind of freelance writing—perhaps more so. For starters, you are not simply reporting the news and letting the chips fall where they may. You are writing for effect. You are attempting, through your writing, to make your client more successful. You have to put together story ideas and articles that do more than find a sympathetic editor. You have to come up with ideas and writing that please your client and still get recognized as a legitimate news or feature story. This can be more difficult than you anticipated.

It's best to approach the selling of your PR services as though you were a media consultant rather than a writer. That way, your experience as a reporter or freelance journalist becomes an asset rather than a liability. That's right, a liability. A lot of businesspeople have a profound distrust for anyone in the press, even freelancers. If they think you're more interested in journalism than in business, you won't get the job. They're much more likely to hire you if they think they're hiring an insider with major contacts. This does not mean that you have to kiss your journalistic ethics good-bye the day you sign up as a PR writer. It simply means that you will have to be conscious of your clients' attitudes and prejudices and work within them. Your value to your client is your experience in the world of assignment editors and hostile reporters. Your job is to help your client present his or her information to a sometimes skeptical audience of journalists. It's not your job to lie on behalf of your client or to mislead the press. If your client asks you to do anything unethical, you really have to decline. If the client persists, find a new client.

Clear, concise, accurate writing will benefit your client more than anything else. Your writing skills will be most important when you are putting together press releases. This standby of the PR field attempts to do the same thing as a query letter—entice the editor. Make sure your information is correct and verifiable. Your headline has to attract attention and reveal what the story is all about. The information in the first paragraph must stand alone. In journalism this is called the inverted pyramid. In other words, the information in your press release begins with the most important and descends in importance. Here's an example of a press release I did for a local car dealership:

For Immediate Release   Contact: Frank McGlashan
March 4, 2000   Telephone: (828) 555-5555

Hunter Chevrolet Names Randy McCrory
1999 Salesman of the Year

Hendersonville, NC—Randy McCrory has been named 1999 Salesman of the Year at Hunter Chevrolet, Volvo, Subaru and Hyundai.

Mr. McCrory, whose track record in customer satisfaction and sales volume prompted the award, is a retired mechanical engineer who worked for DuPont for twenty-two years.

His training in corporate management has helped him as an automobile salesman. "I try to keep a positive attitude with the objective of helping people," he said. "It's very easy for me to be professional with people because I have a professional background.

"I wasn't sure at first if I wanted to get into the car business, but then I interviewed at Hunter, and I came away impressed with the way they did business. Now I'd have to say that back in 1965 when I was starting college, if I'd known what I know now I probably would have skipped college and gone right into the car business. I love the business; it's the most fun I've ever had. Interesting people, never dull . . . no two sales are ever the same. Plus, I think I've helped a lot of people."

His customers apparently agree. Fully 50 percent of his sales come from referrals and repeat customers. "I work very hard," he said. "I try to be very diligent and take this as my own personal business."

Diligence is definitely the key to success, he explained. "I do a huge amount of follow-up. I have a file on every car I've ever sold. I communicate with my customers at least eight times during the year, mostly through telephone calls and follow-up mailings."

Mr. McCrory has two grown children and three grandchildren. He lives in Maggie Valley at the Ketner Inn & Farm, a bed and breakfast inn he bought in 1995.

Hunter Chevrolet, Volvo, Subaru and Hyundai, located at 9999 Acme Highway, offers new and used cars, service on all makes and models, a parts store, a body shop and a tire outlet. Mr. McCrory can be reached at (828) 555-5555.

-30-

Note that the headline and the first paragraph tell the important parts of the story, while the rest of the piece fills in background and offers the client a chance to utter a few self-serving lines about customer service and the secret of his success. The -30- at the end is just a convention of newspaper people. It signifies "the end" and can also be expressed as ###.

Very little of a press release like this one will see publication. Editors will cut from the bottom and fit the piece into whatever space or format they feel is appropriate. Sometimes they don't print it at all. To over-come that problem, my client will sometimes buy advertising space and run his releases the way he wants them. Since this is considerably more expensive than sending out a press release, he does it sparingly and only when something at his dealership merits more elaborate exposure.

As a PR practitioner, you will also be called upon to write speeches, set up interviews, plan and execute events, plan overall media strategy and generally advise your client in the ways of the press.

PR services get sold much the same as any other service. You have to make it happen. If you're working alone, you'll have to be the sales force, the writer, the media consultant and the janitor.

In my opinion, the best way to break into PR writing is to hire yourself first. Put together a media plan for your own company. If you can make yourself well known, there's a pretty good chance you can do the same for other clients. But how will you go about this?

First, place yourself as far as you can into the local circle of movers and shakers. Attend charity functions. Volunteer to help stage events and promotions for nonprofit organizations. Write guest editorials in the paper every chance you get. Write local news and feature stories even if they pay poorly. Getting your byline in front of the public is the important thing. Cultivate relationships with media folks. Let them know you're opening a PR shop and ask them how you can help them.

Figure out what companies you want to work for and go after their business. Make no secret of it. If you run into the CEO of your target company, let him or her know how much you admire the work they do and how much you would appreciate an opportunity to help them publi-cize that good work. Make sure you have your business cards handy. Attend networking parties and chamber of commerce functions.

Whenever you land a new client, make sure you send out a press release to publicize your new business relationship. You'll have to get permission from your client, of course, before you send out the release. Most will be flattered that you consider their business newsworthy. Oth-ers may consider the press release just that much more publicity for them. You should encourage that line of thinking. Be aware, though, that a small number of your clients may consider their public relations efforts to be covert and ask you to refrain from publicizing your deal with them.

Most of all, be ready when you get the telephone call (and you will) from a potentially big client. Go to the meeting with a professional attitude. You're not there with your hat in your hand. You're there to help these people achieve better media relations. You are more valuable to them than you may imagine.

And one last thing: Make sure you charge enough. This goes beyond mere avarice. People in business, especially the people at the top of the local food chain, are used to dealing with people of means. They are not going to respect you if you come with a low-ball offer. Dream big. These folks have money and are willing to spend it lavishly if they think they are getting the best available. As a general range for projects such as press releases, catalog copywriting or event promotions, PR freelancers can earn $25 to $60/hour. Ad copywriting can bring $50 to $100/hour.

Of course, it's a fine thing to say "feel the top" and "charge enough," but how does a freelancer go about finding out what the top really is? I'm reminded of the *Austin Powers* film where Dr. Evil, who has been freeze-dried since the sixties, tells his minions that he is planning to hold the world ransom for "one million dollars." His minions squirm and finally tell him that his legitimate businesses are making billions all by themselves.

The trick, whether you are Dr. Evil or just a freelancer trying to maximize profits, is to find out what the going rate is and then nudge it up just a bit. You can do this in a covert fashion by calling up an ad agency and asking what they charge for copywriting. Or you can be up-front about the whole thing and simply call other copywriters and ask what they charge. People will usually help you if you ask them nicely.

You might also consider joining the local advertising and public relations club. Almost every city has one. They get together, talk about ad and PR issues and usually hold an annual awards dinner. Get to know your fellow copy scribes, and pretty soon you'll be swapping war stories and pricing info. You might even get some overflow work passed your way.

Once you've established your rates, make sure you keep track of the time you spend and the money you net. Don't be afraid to raise your prices if you're doing good work, the client is happy and you have plenty of assignments. Be proud of what you do—proud enough so that you don't feel awkward asking for fair compensation. You're providing a great service to somebody who can't do the work for himself. That's worth some money.

Breaking Into Commercial Copywriting

If you're trying to break into the commercial writing field from a journalism background, you'll probably be a bit frustrated by clients who demand to see samples of your work before they bestow any dollars on you. Unfortunately, you probably don't have the kind of samples your potential client expects to see: brochures, direct mail packages, advertising copy, etc.

Don't give up. There is a way around this problem. You must, however, do some things to enhance your position.

First, remember that your client is buying what is called "business-to-business" writing, not journalism. Unless the articles in your clip file have to do with advertising techniques or some other nuts-and-bolts marketing information, they aren't going to dazzle your average corporate executive. So what's it going to take to get into the commercial writing business?

Creating a Commercial Portfolio

Let's say you want to write advertising copy for a local agency. As I mentioned earlier in this chapter, the first thing you need is a portfolio of ads you've worked on. You've never written an ad before, you say? Well, unless you have a close relative in the agency's upper management, you'll have to find some way to fill that portfolio before you approach the creative director.

Doing It for Free

There are those in the copywriting fraternity who will tell you that the best way to acquire samples is to find someone (friend, relative, local retailer) who needs some advertising copy written and offer to do the work for free.

I consider this to be a big mistake. Here's why:

1. I don't think you should give away now what you are planning to sell later.
2. It takes a long time to get a good sample. You have to deal with client approval, publication schedules, etc. Plus you have the same responsibilities as the person who gets paid for writing ads.
3. When you work for free, you risk having your client (and anyone else who happens to be in on the project) get the idea that you can be had, that you don't consider your work to be worth much.

Advertising can be a tough racket. You don't want to start out with a reputation as a wimp.

That said, I won't claim that the "writing for free" approach will never succeed. Clearly, writing for free will work in some cases (guest editorial, nonprofit volunteer work, etc., as I've mentioned before), but if your writing benefits a commercial enterprise, you should be getting paid—and paid well.

Creating Spec Ads

In my experience, a far more effective tactic is to follow the suggestion of the creative director I mentioned in the beginning of this diatribe: Find a sympathetic graphic artist who is willing to work with you on a portfolio of spec ads. Many self-employed artists are in the same position as you—looking for work. If you have a particular agency in mind, find out whom they represent and put together spec ads for similar products or services. This will allow you to get your portfolio filled quicker. It will also let you show the agency's creative director ads to which he or she can relate. And it will demonstrate your initiative and your ability to research.

Please note that I am not advocating any kind of deceit here. Whatever you do, don't try to pass these ads off as samples of published work. Aside from the obvious moral considerations, you probably wouldn't get away with it. Instead, explain to the creative director that you have studied copywriting, that you've followed the work his or her agency has done for its clients and that you would like to share some ideas you've developed with your artist.

Most creative directors whom I've known will be happy (if they can do it at their convenience) to look over your work. By the way, an agency can be a good place to polish your skills. You get to bounce ideas off other writers, somebody else handles most of the face-to-face encounters with the client, and you will build a network for future work.

Things to Do Before You Say Yes

Once your bulging portfolio is in order and on the desks of creative directors everywhere, you're going to have to learn to prepare for and deal with the possibility of success.

Freelance writers are generally a well-focused group. We write dazzling query letters, we do endless research, we take copious notes, we conduct piercing interviews, we suffer and moan at the keyboard. All of this effort and emotion serves one simple end—to get some editor or creative director or copy chief or whomever to say yes.

Consequently, by the time we get to the point of hearing (or reading) that wonderful word, we can be so wrung out from the process that we'll agree to almost any deal. The fact is, however, that money (and just about any other part of the deal) is almost always negotiable. It may be a little scary to risk that "yes" by asking a few probing questions, but such bravery will often pay off handsomely.

So, with that in mind, the following are a few things to think about before you make the sale and sign on the dotted line.

Payment Options

First of all, how will you get paid? Is it a flat-fee, by-the-word, or by-the-hour situation? Each arrangement has its advantages and disadvantages. Earlier in this book, I described an Arizona-based writer I know who, when asked to write a 1,300-word piece at about 50 cents per word, turned in about 3,000 words. The editor went semiballistic, but finally agreed that the article was well worth the extra words—and the extra money. Not all editors are that circumspect, however, and I don't recommend this tactic unless (1) you have a truly magnificent article, and (2) you know the editor very, very well. It also helps if you know that the magazine has deep pockets. I don't recommend this tactic—at all—when you're dealing with creative directors or other commercial writing accounts. It will kill your chances of success.

I personally prefer the flat-fee, by-the-project method of billing for commercial writing. I know fairly well how long a certain piece of direct mail or ad copy or whatever will take me to write, so a flat-fee arrangement means I won't have to keep a log of hours spent. I also insist on getting a 50 percent deposit up front, which is difficult if you're working by the hour. After a few jobs, you should be able to work out just which system is right for you.

I would, however, avoid letting your customer tie your pay to performance. In commercial writing, there are many details (mailing list selection, media buying, graphic design, timing, the client's sometimes unreasonable demands, etc.) that affect performance. The same is true of other commercial writing projects. There are many factors involved in achieving success. Writing is the only one over which the writer can exert some control. You don't control the other factors, so why should you gamble that they are being handled competently? That's not to say I would not accept a performance-related bonus above and beyond the base pay.

Reimbursable Expenses

You should also find out up front if you will be reimbursed for your expenses. These could include telephone, travel, lodging, bribes to third world officials, or any number of other unforeseen bites out of your bottom line. In other words, make sure you can afford to do the work before you sign on the dotted line.

If your customer isn't going to pay expenses, then you need to be very careful that you will be paid enough to cover your expenses and maintain a reasonable profit. If you're freelancing as a journalist, multiple sales can often put your efforts into the black, if you haven't sold off all of your subsidiary rights. In the case of commercial writing, however, the client will almost always buy all rights, so make sure you can survive on that first sale.

Ancillary Sales

Another way to add profit to your writing is to consider selling some ancillary products. Maybe you can put together some photos or illustrations. If you're writing about your customer's clients, you might want to write up your notes and sell those separately. Your client might pay to hear what his or her clients are saying about the company beyond what you selected for the brochure, annual report or press release. I know a California freelancer who once sold (to a scout from the *Tonight Show*, no less) the notes he took while writing a feature story on a local "character." The scout wanted the notes gratis, but our hero held out for fair compensation. And it paid off; he made a few extra bucks even though the object of his article never made it to Johnny's couch.

Some writers tell me they set a specific number of rewrites and revisions they will include with their bid. Any additional work, after those revisions have been spent, will be billed at an hourly rate. I suppose this is a good deal if you have a nitpicky client who likes to see copywriters squirm. However, I prefer to include all necessary revisions in the base price. It seems to me that the client is paying for a completed product, not for the process by which that product is produced. If the brochure is worth $5,000, then that's all the client should have to pay, no matter how much effort it takes on your part. Billing for revisions gives the whole deal a sort of open-ended feel that I wouldn't appreciate if I were the client.

Of course, that doesn't mean you should cave in every time you are challenged on a copy point. You are a professional hired to do a professional job. You deserve professional courtesy and a working environment free of petty harassment and game playing. With my 50 percent deposit up front, if the client becomes too obstreperous, I can always fire him or her and back away with at least some compensation. It's worth noting that, in the last twenty years, I've never had to do that.

So, my basic point is this: Whether you're writing magazine pieces, press releases or handling any other freelance assignment, make sure both you and your client understand the ground rules completely—and that you can live with those rules.

"I Wasn't Going to Stop Until I Had One Published."

HARLAN COBEN

For a guy who is awash in mystery and intrigue, Harlan Coben is a remarkably open fellow. The author of the critically acclaimed Myron Bolitar mystery series, Harlan has no doubt had a fair share of recognition. He's won the Edgar Award, the Shamus Award and the Anthony Award. *Publishers Weekly* declared one of his books the "Best of the Year." His books sell increasingly well with each new one published.

One might speculate that a man of his rapidly acquired reputation (the Bolitar series debuted in 1995) could develop something of a celebrity attitude. Nothing could be further from the truth. Harlan remains the friendly, wisecracking, self-deprecating lad he was before his books started moving to the eye-level shelves at bookstores. He is also extremely candid when discussing the road to success in the mystery-writing field. Like many of the very best writers in the genre, he isn't afraid to help others do well. "I think it was Lawrence Block," he remembers, "who said, 'No one has to fail so that I can succeed.' I think that ought to be the mantra for all writers. It's absolutely true. If I have a book out at the same time as Robert Parker or whomever and his book is really good, that's probably going to encourage you to read more mysteries. If I read a book that I really love and really get into it, the first thing I want to do is read something just like it or something that's in the same mode. In a sense, the whole boat does lift together and sink together."

I asked Harlan how he made the transition from working in the travel industry to making his living as a mystery novelist. "It's a ridiculously long and complicated tale," he says. "I was trying to write and work at the same time. I think that's the way to do it. I don't really recommend anybody quit their job unless they really have a hell of a good safety net, which I did. [His wife, Anne, is a pediatrician.] You'll always find the time to write. If it would take you a year to write a book if you're doing it full time, it might take you fourteen months to write it if you're also working. There's a hibernation period in there where the story has to sit in your brain, no matter how much time you have to write it."

Deadlines, he tells us, are our friends—no matter how painful they might be. "I like having deadlines," he says. "I think that's really important. For some reason, if the book is four hundred pages long, let's say, in manuscript form, and it takes me nine months to write it, by the end of eight months I may have two hundred pages done. In the last month I'll write two hundred pages. I finish books writing forty to fifty pages a day. I finished one called *Fade Away* on January 27 an hour and a half before the Super Bowl started. Coincidence? I don't think so. When you're starting out, of course, you have to set your own deadlines."

His rapidly increasing success notwithstanding, Harlan didn't always know what he wanted to do. "I was a political science major, which is a euphemism for 'I have absolutely no idea what I want to do with my life.' You know, whenever I sit on a writers panel there's always the one guy who says, 'I always knew I wanted to be a writer. When I was four years old, my friends would gather around me in the playground and I would regale them with pirate tales.' I never buy that. I was a college senior when I decided I was going to write. My dream was to one day have a book published. I didn't care if it sold any copies. I didn't care if it was hardcover, paperback, or whatever. I just wanted to have a novel published. Of course, as soon as that happens you realize that it's a fairly empty goal. Like anything else in life, you have to go for the next goal. But I also had the attitude that if the book I was working on didn't sell, then I would just write another one. And I wasn't going to stop until I had one published."

One thing you'll never read, he says, is a nonfiction book bearing his byline. "I don't even read nonfiction," he says. "I don't even like to research my own books. I make up the stuff. What I usually do is call a friend who's in the business or something like that."

Developing great characters is one of Harlan's trademarks. Take "Win" for example. Windsor Horne Lockwood is a wealthy, handsome, amoral and appallingly lethal investment banker. A pleasant, attractive, golf-loving psychopath whose only loyalties are to himself and to Myron, Win is capable of astonishing feats of martial arts and comes equipped with a staggering amount of good old-fashioned firepower. He's one of Myron's two best friends; the other being a stunningly beautiful bisexual woman named Esperanza. Throw in the huge (well over the 300-pound mark) female exwrestler named "Big Cindi," and you begin to wonder where Harlan comes up with his characters.

"Well," he admits, "Win is based on somebody I know, except that the person is not a psychopath. My college roommate, who has a name equally obnoxious and was a member of all the clubs and looks like Win and acts like Win, is also—like Win—not at all what he appears to be. He's certainly not a psychopath by any means, but a lot of people do realize it's him [Harlan's inspiration for Win], and he sometimes tends to get better tee times."

That character aside, Harlan says, "I rarely base my characters on people I know. Friends always think I do, though. They always think that the cool sophisticated guy who gets all the girls is based on them. I try to start with some sort of a core. Other writers will know everything about their characters before they start. I have to kind of feel my way around—and then sometimes have to rewrite. I didn't intend for Win, for example, to be quite as damaged as he was. He just was. This guy was formed, and he was more violent than I had anticipated. And that sometimes means going back and rewriting—even if it was going well in the beginning."

Harlan's advice for aspiring mystery writers has very little to do with writing groups or continuing education courses on the novel. He encourages new writers to read the people who have made it to the top of the genre. "But," he says, "the first piece of advice is just to write. Writing is one of the few activities where quantity inevitably makes quality. Don't get discouraged. One yes will make all of the no's disappear. That's an important thing to remember.

"Also you have to be a good self-editor. I find that criticism paralyzes me. If I give somebody something to read and they say, 'You spelled this word wrong,' then I immediately think the whole thing stinks, and I have to throw it all away. So I don't need it. The only person who reads my early drafts is my wife, and her job is to tell me that it's brilliant beyond words."

Speaking of first drafts, Harlan encourages writers to lighten up on themselves in the early stages. "It's important to write and not worry so much at the beginning. You just worry about writing. Later on you can stop and look and worry if it's not good or whatever.

"Writers are so insecure. I'll be writing a new book and I'll end up saying, 'This is crap. I was so great before. What happened? I lost it.'

Then on the next page I'll say, 'This is brilliant!' And that happens within five minutes of one another. We're very insecure. I don't like being ruled by that, but that's the way it is."

Harlan is a writer who enjoys his fans. So much so that he even publishes his e-mail address (Bolitar@aol.com) in each of his novels, something that some authors might consider an act of insanity. "I would say that 99.9 percent of the e-mails I have gotten have been great. I try to answer every single one of them. I mean, I get to talk to you for 450 pages, you should have the right to talk to me for three or four sentences. Mostly, I enjoy the feedback. I enjoy what people get or don't get out of the books. It's really been great. I had one guy write to me saying that he'd had prostate surgery, and some friends had given him the books and it helped him through it.

"I never buy books from people who say they write for themselves. Writing is about communications. It's about other people. If a tree falls in the woods and no one hears it, did it make a sound? As a writer, if I write and no one reads it, I don't exist as a writer. I don't live. And every time somebody reads it, it's sort of like that Arabic expression that says when one person dies, a whole universe dies. When one new person reads one of my books, a whole new universe of Myron and Esperanza and Win is created. That's still a thrill for me."

CHAPTER EIGHT

Go for the Money, But Do It Right

Legend has it that a distant ancestor of mine once sold his neighbor a dead horse. Propped it up against a rail fence and sold it from across the yard.

I mention this only because I'm about to ask you to get into a "show me the money" kind of mood, and it's only fair to disclose that I may have something of a genetic "leg up" when it comes to asking for money. Also, I was a carny for a while, so there you go. Gimme a buck. Right now. Hand it over.

Learning how to negotiate for dollars is one of the most important skills a freelancer can develop.

There are several ways of going about this task. When my dad hired farm hands, they almost never talked about money up front. By some unspoken cowboy agreement, the hired hands and my dad would wait until the field was cultivated or the fertilizer sacks unloaded or the cattle rounded up before they would even discuss the subject of compensation.

"Well, what do I owe you?" my dad would query, with his hand on his wallet.

"Oh, heck, I don't know. Whudda you think?" the hired man would say, rubbing the toes of his boots in the dust.

After a few moments of this, my dad would suggest a figure, and the hired hand would insist that the amount was far too much for the little bit of work that had been required of him. My dad would insist, and the guy would reluctantly take the money.

I think those guys would have taken any amount offered just to avoid looking greedy to a neighbor. Of course, if they thought my dad had ripped them off, they probably would have been politely busy the next time he was hiring. By the same token, if the hired hand had demanded an unreasonably high wage, my dad probably would have paid him without comment, but it would have been the last time the guy set foot on our place.

Then there was the service station owner near Lake Tahoe, California, who fixed a tire for me. When I asked him how much the bill was, he just said, "Give me whatever you think it was worth." I gave him a five-dollar bill and asked him how he could survive financially with such a laid-back pricing policy.

He told me that in all the years he had done it that way, no one had ever given him less than a fair price. Some of them paid way more than he would have dared to ask.

I don't recommend that you adopt either of these approaches when negotiating with editors, creative directors or any of your other clients. You'll soon be working for bylines and contributor's copies.

Of course, even if you take a fairly hard line, there's a good chance you could leave some money on the table when negotiating for your writing services.

What you need is a plan for upping the ante. Here are some techniques I've used successfully in the past. Feel free to apply them to your own efforts.

1. Make sure your work is worth what you're going to ask. Nothing will undermine your efforts like shoddy work. Take an objective view of the quality of your work. I don't mean just whether you put words together well. Look also at the degree of aggravation (or lack thereof) that your work brings to the buyer. Are you on time? Do you check your facts? Do you interact well with your client's clients? Does your work produce money or some other benefit without which your client's business or life would be diminished? Be painfully honest with yourself. I once hired a freelance writer—a former *Newsweek* reporter, no less—to write an investigative story on a local medical scandal. She turned in a great story, well researched and written—except for that little error of fact that caused my publisher to be sued for $1.9 million. The plaintiff had a very weak case and eventually settled out of court for a reported $1,000. This did not erase from my publisher's mind the fact that I'd commissioned the piece, edited the piece and even made it the cover story. He was professional about it, but I bet he still remembers it. I know I certainly do.

2. Negotiate from a power position. The best time to suggest a higher freelance payment is when you least need it. Say you just landed a huge book contract or you just signed on to write a column for a lot of money or your spouse just got a great high-paying job. You'll be able to think clearly, speak without fear of losing your income and comport yourself like the successful writer you are.

3. Tie your request to a significant event or accomplishment. Perhaps your work just won an award for the magazine or ad agency or whomever. Maybe something you did brought in new business for your client. Or maybe you've just completed your first year as a columnist for the local paper. Now is the time to allow your client to express his or her gratitude in a tangible way. Don't push too hard, though. It's important for an employer to feel that you have the best interests of the company at heart. Try to give him the impression that you really are committed to his or her success. The famous self-help guru Dale Carnegie used to say that people have a basic need to feel important. They can do that either by saying no and crushing your hopes, or they can show their importance by saying yes and helping you. It's up to you to help them decide which way they choose. I highly recommend Carnegie's book *How to Win Friends and Influence People*.

4. Never threaten what you can't or won't do. I used to work for a trucking company in Arizona. My partner was a retired air force noncom who threatened to quit about once a week. Sometimes he actually did grab his toolbox and stalk off the lot. But he always came back—and the boss knew he would. The drama was amusing to the rest of us but not very effective for him. Think very clearly before you threaten to withhold your services if your pay request is not met. Don't bluff. Be prepared for your client to cut you loose.

5. Always be pleasant, not confrontational. I've been on both sides of the hiring equation, and I can tell you this: Nobody likes to deal with a disgruntled, confrontational loony. Always be professional. If you do decide to move on, be sure you give proper notice. Who knows? You may want to come back sometime with another project or another offer. Don't torch those bridges.

This can be difficult to do. There's something downright delicious about righteous indignation. There's a certain self-destructive satisfaction in howling with rage over injustice, stupidity and other of your client's character flaws. But don't do it. You have to decide in these situations if you want to be right or if you want to get your way. Again, read Carnegie's book. It was the first and, for my money, the best of the whole self-help genre.

6. Always look for the next gig. Personally, I think this is the most important part of negotiating. At least half of your time as a freelance writer should be spent marketing—looking for work. If you have ten assignments going at once, there's a good chance that you can convince your client that the best way to get his or her projects to the top of the "In" box is to make the payment more attractive. It's also important to understand that even the happiest, most satisfied, best-paying client can sometimes go south on you for no apparent reason. I had a great relationship with a trade publisher in New York City a few years ago. I wrote just about every kind of direct mail, circulation promotion project you could imagine for them. They were happy with the results and my fee structure. They took me to lunch. They laughed at my jokes. And then one day, they quit calling me. I've talked to them since then and they were still friendly. I think I'd just done everything I could for them, and they wanted to try out some other writer. Not much you can do about that, except wait for a few years and then try to be the new guy again.

Along with these techniques for squeezing more money out of your writing, I should also say that sometimes you'll get an offer that just looks too good to mess up with negotiation. When I first started copywriting, I was doing small-time stuff for local ad agencies and supplementing my income with the occasional magazine article and PR story. I was paying $100 per month for an office over a popular yuppy saloon and wondering sometimes how I was going to get enough money to keep the doors open. Then one afternoon a guy named Bill called me from a local recording studio. He had a job for me, he said, if I was interested; something about a slide show script on earthquake preparedness. It was a state government job. The budget, he apologized, was only $2,000. "Is that $2,000 for the copy alone," I asked, trying to keep the nervousness out of my voice. "Yeah," he said. "I know it isn't much, but I'd appreciate it if you could help me out."

I calmly agreed, hung up the phone and did an awkward little dance around my compact office. Years later, when I owned an advertising agency in the same town, I used Bill's services frequently. I confessed one evening over a cup of coffee that I'd been floored by the price he'd paid me. "I knew that," he said. "I just thought you could use a break." He had no idea how right he was. That job not only paid the rent for quite a while, it also got me thinking in terms of more money and bigger jobs. Nowadays, I'd probably try to get him to go for an additional $500, but at the time I felt like I'd won the lottery.

I hope you'll experience that same rush of pure joy when you make the deal for your next fee. Good luck, be brave and remember that the increased pay you negotiate is like free money. What a concept!

Raw Material for His Travel Writing Article Factory

LYNN SELDON, JR.

Utter the words *travel writer*, and most people will conjure up a vision of supreme romance.

Here's mine: I'm flying into Aruba in a small seaplane piloted by an expatriot American with a four-day beard and no respect for authority figures. I'm met at the airport by a jolly man in a straw hat who calls me "Mon" and delivers me to a breezy hotel veranda where I sip a drink with an umbrella in it and talk to an obviously wealthy couple dressed in white. The woman, stunningly beautiful and at least four decades younger than her aging millionaire husband, is flirting with me shamelessly.

Later I will sell the story to a high-paying travel magazine . . . and then use the whole Aruba trip as the lead story in a fascinating, critically acclaimed, best-selling travel book . . . or perhaps a hot megabucks screenplay. Naturally, I will write off every cent I spend as tax deductible.

Describe that scenario to travel writer Lynn Seldon, Jr., and you'll probably get a very blunt answer. "With travel, there's no free lunch," he says. "Nothing is free with travel writing." (See the sidebar on travel writing ethics below.)

Point out to him that travel writers often don't have to pay cash for their trips, and he will reveal a side of the business that is far from your romantic vision. "In that sense, some of the trips are free," he says, "but they still take up time, and my time isn't free. I don't take trips just for the free nature of them. I take them because I want to sell stories."

"Am I Going to Have a Good Time?"
The Ethics of Travel Writing

A couple of decades ago, I found myself in a restaurant in Hermosillo, Mexico, with my friend Rosie and a couple of middle-aged, underworld-type big shots from what was probably some sort of local chamber of commerce.

Rosie was pitching them hard to buy advertising from the Arizona-based magazine for which we both worked. At one point in the conversation, one of our dinner companions fixed a baleful eye on me and said, "What are you doing down here?"

I guess he wanted to know what part I was playing in Rosie's pitch. I just smiled at him and said, "I'm writing some travel articles about Hermosillo and Kino Bay."

"Are they going to be nice articles?" he inquired.

"Gosh," I answered, "I don't know. Am I going to have a good time?"

With that, he grinned at Rosie and asked, "Why do we need you?"

I may still have a scar on my shin where Rosie kicked me under the table. The fact is, though, our friend was right. Travel editorial is probably a whole lot more valuable than travel advertising—and a lot cheaper if you see it from the point of view of the person promoting the destination. This can cause some ethical problems for the travel writer.

As travel writers, we are sometimes in the same position as an elected official facing lobbyists: We have to develop our own code of ethics. That can be difficult. It's expensive to travel, stay in fine hotels and eat in fine restaurants. Magazines often do not offer to cover the cost, nor do they often pay enough per article to make a single-story trip worthwhile. However, if we accept the free trip, the complimentary room and the on-the-house gourmet meals, we may feel our objectivity eroding.

Some writers solve the problem by paying for themselves but only going on trips when they have a dozen story commitments from various editors. That makes some sense, but what if we're not willing to hurl ourselves full time into the business of travel writing? What if we only want to take that one trip to Togo or that one cruise around the Virgin Islands and then head back to our main business of sportswriting or advertising copywriting or whatever?

My solution, though it may be a little controversial, is to take the free trip, enjoy the room, eat the meals—and then write the story exactly as if you were there on your own bankroll.

Simply forget that your destination host may feel he is owed something for his largess. That's not your problem. Do your job. Just because some hotel or resort is giving you the red carpet, don't be afraid to go beyond the program laid out before you by some friendly PR person. If your luxury hotel is sitting on a hill overlooking a squalid slum (and many of them are), don't be afraid to let your readers know. Your obligation is to your readers, to giving them an accurate picture of the travel experience offered by a particular destination. You are *not* a cheerleader, and you are not beholden to your host to do anything other than what any guest would do: Evaluate your experience and tell your friends (in this case, your readers) what it was like.

There are, of course, conflicting opinions regarding travel-writing ethics. I asked Robert N. Jenkins, the travel editor of the *St. Petersburg Times* and the national vice president of the Society of American Travel Writers, to give me his take on freelance stories that result from free junkets. "My employer," Bob told me, "has a policy against taking press trips, comps, press rates, etc., and from buying stories that originate from such discounted travel. We prefer to avoid even the appearance of a conflict of interest that such huge discounts present. We do not, however, refuse to buy *any* copy from a freelancer who has taken such trips, just no copy from *those* travels."

Furthermore, Bob would seem to take exception to my "take the trip and report as if you'd paid for it yourself" approach. "How can we present such a story to our readers as objective and fully typical when the readers cannot receive the same discounted experience? I have heard the disingenuous argument that freelancers who take comps and press trips are 'bartering' their creative services for the discounted travel; I don't buy that for a minute. The freelancers would not be *at* that particular destination, *on* that cruise without the offered discounts. How many of them would honestly recount a dreadful travel experience without worrying that it diminishes their currency among the travel providers?"

Well, I can say that I, for one, would quite happily take the trip and write a bad review of the destination or the cruise or whatever, if such a bad review were deserved. I wouldn't hesitate. But that's just me, and I don't make my whole living out of the travel writing game. In fact, I do very little of it. Even so, I stand by my own ethical standard on this issue.

In the words of travel writer Lynn Seldon, Jr., "It's the writer who controls what gets written."

Lynn told me that he usually stays away from publications that refuse stories generated on paid-for trips. "There's probably less than 25 percent of the magazines I know of that object to the paid-for junkets—and they usually pay the worst."

The Society of American Travel Writers has an ethics section on its Web site (www.satw.org). Principle I discourages plagiarism, encourages the use of reliable sources or first-hand knowledge and prohibits any conduct that embarrasses the society. Principle II forbids members from, among other things, selling rights they don't own or claiming co-authorship of articles upon which they have done no work. Principle III prohibits members from misrepresenting assignments in order to secure participation in a press trip and states that "a member shall personally pay for all services required by that member that are personal, or over and above the services voluntarily provided by the host."

I don't have a problem with any of these rules, nor with Principle IV, which says that "no member shall accept payment or courtesies in exchange for an agreement to produce favorable material about a travel destination, service or supplier that is contrary to his or her own professional appraisal."

These rules (and the handful of other admonitions you'll find at the Web site) make sense to me. I find it unreasonable for editors to demand that a writer pay for a $2,500 trip herself, especially if the publication offers to pay none of the expenses and coughs up a $150 freelance fee. The fact is that most of these travel destinations are going to get a favorable review even by the most objective, demanding travel writer. Being fun to visit is what these places are all about. It's what they do. I also don't think that travel providers will blackball writers for being objective, even if some particular story doesn't appear as a total valentine. The PR professionals I know don't work that way. They lay the material out, give it their best shot, hope for the best, and they get on with their lives and their jobs. They are far too busy for vendettas against good writers.

My advice then is to check out the SATW code of ethics and make it your own when it comes to travel writing. Enjoy your travels, write your stories as accurately as possible and try to sell to magazines and newspapers that have enlightened policies. And remember, there's a reason why travel writers are among the most envied of freelancers.

By the way, I did have a very good time in Hermosillo and Kino Bay.

For Lynn, travel writing is a business, one he runs with remarkable efficiency. He started back in the early 1980s selling articles and photography to the military newspaper *Stars and Stripes*. It was, he says, a sort of creative outlet while he was traveling overseas. When he mustered out of the military, he decided to make travel writing his profession and went about it with a typical businesslike attitude. "I bought a copy of *Writer's Market*," he recalls, "and followed it to the letter. I've pretty much been doing that ever since. I buy every edition. I read through it to find new leads and contacts. I change my databases [with the information in *Writer's Market*]. It's still my number one resource."

His attention to the business side of writing has rewarded him with an income that has increased steadily ever since he started. "Last year," he says, "was my best year ever revenue-wise." His number of regular clients has also increased over the years. "On the average," he estimates, "I complete one hundred assignments a year. I would say 50 to 75 percent of them are repeat business."

That means he is averaging a couple of articles a week, which means he has to pick his excursions carefully. "If I don't feel that I can sell a trip five times over a year," he says, "then I won't take the trip." That two-per-week total, by the way, does not include photography or reprint sales, both of which he actively pursues.

Like a lot of successful freelance writers, Lynn knows the information he gathers while traveling is the raw material for his article factory. Sometimes he gets a remarkable amount of use from one set of notes. His highest number of resales on a single batch of information came from a West Virginia white-water rafting expedition. "It's probably been picked up, including newspapers, as much as twenty-five times," he says. "I can't give you a very accurate number because I've reworked it so many times over the years. I think the lowest I ever got for it was $100. The original sale, I think, was $700."

Maintaining a vast inventory of past articles while continuing to research and produce new pieces for his clients requires an impressive organizational effort. "Basically," he explains, "I have used the same software from the start, Microsoft Works. Within the database portion of the software, I keep records of whom I submit articles to, what I sent, when I sent, that kind of thing. I just did a postcard mailing that went out to more than ten thousand contacts. It was my highest total ever. Next time I'll send fifteen thousand."

These postcards and Lynn's other marketing efforts are directed to word buyers in a variety of categories. "I have an editor category," he says. "I have a magazine photo editor category. I have a book photo editor category. And I have a public relations contact category. Those are my four main ones. That's what adds up to ten thousand. So the public relations people help me learn about new places and story ideas that I then pitch to the people in the editors category. The photos I usually sell individually; they're usually looking for certain things."

Not every freelancer takes these kinds of marketing steps, even though it makes perfectly good business sense, as Lynn's successes tend to prove. "I think that the key," says Lynn, "is that they don't want to invest in their business. It's an unwillingness to spend the money to make the money. My postcard mailings pay for themselves within weeks, no matter what the cost. Including postage, it generally comes in around $3,000."

He uses his list of contacts both before and after his trips turn into articles. "I had a special section in USA Today," he recalls. "It was a work-for-hire situation where I wrote the whole thing. I sent out an e-mail to the public relations community, basically telling them that this was in USA Today and that it was going to be in other major newspapers. Just telling them that this is the type of writing I do and that if they had an appropriate client they should let me know. The response was incredible. Out of the six hundred e-mails I sent, I had more than one hundred people respond to me somehow.

"I need to figure out how to make it even larger. My next goal is to do a similar e-mailing to editors asking them to visit my Web site. I have a lot of articles there that may interest them for reprint possibilities."

Keeping up with his marketing efforts while still producing a steady flow of articles has forced Lynn to develop a pretty strict system. "I try to keep it at fifty-fifty," he says. "The mornings are my writing time and the afternoons are for marketing. I'm pretty good at keeping it that way. Generally, in the mornings I don't answer the phone. Rules are made to be broken, of course, but I try to follow that as much as possible. I've gotten into the bad habit of checking e-mail all the time. I'm trying to get away from that, not mess with it and then respond to all of it in the afternoon."

Over the years, Lynn has learned to recognize the kind of trip that will yield the most stories and earn him the most money. "For me," he says, "it's a resort destination. Let's say a Caribbean island. Someplace that has lots to do, lots to see. And not just one thing like golf or diving or hiking. I want all of those to be available at the same destination. And I don't want to be pigeonholed in one hotel or resort. I want to be able to cover other things. I may stay in one place, but then I'll rent a car and I'll go and do a lot of other things."

He has to, because there's no free lunch in the travel writing business.

CHAPTER NINE

The Dookie Factor

Sometimes the answers to the really big questions are hidden in your daily routines.

Homer Cheeseman, the legendary Arizona handyman with whom I used to work, once accidentally explained to me the secret of a successful life. It was amazingly simple.

We had been sent out by the service manager to liberate an egregiously plugged mobile-home toilet. Further complicating things was a short circuit in the home's electrical system, which provided a mild shock when you touched the aluminum siding or grabbed the doorknob. The people who owned the house had maybe washed their dishes once or twice in the several months they had owned the trailer. Moreover, they had attempted to overcome gravity by hooking their sewer pipe to a connection that was not only uphill, but was also shared by another trailer that was also uphill from them. So, when the neighbors flushed their toilets or drained their sink, the water and whatever it carried came rushing down the pipe and lodged somewhere in the long black pipe under our client's house. It was not a pretty sight.

We spent a good hour or so trying to remedy what was largely an unsolvable problem. Finally, Homer found the short circuit and made it safe to touch the house. Then we held our noses and bailed out the potty. When we left we told the folks they were going to have to either raise their house or lower their sewer connection. They said they'd take care of it right away. We never heard from them again.

On the way back to the office, I was complaining bitterly about the job and the smell and life as a trailer repairman in general. Homer, a philosopher who grew up and learned his trade in New York City, told me that he thought it was a good idea to learn how to do something that nobody else wanted to do. That way, he explained, you could charge a lot of money for it—plus people would be grateful.

The concept was further refined for me by a North Carolina plumber when I asked him how he could in good conscience charge so much for what he did.

"It's the Dookie Factor," he explained, as he tucked most of my cash into a bulging wallet. "If you don't want to clean the dookie outa your own pipes, then I guess you just have to pay. And the worse the dookie, the more you pay." The worst kind of dookie, he explained, was the kind he'd just pushed out of my kitchen sink.

How can we apply the Dookie Factor to the field of freelance writing?

It may be easier than you think. A lot of folks out there are terribly afraid of writing. They lack the experience. They lack the skills. They lack the confidence and courage to lay out their thoughts on paper for everybody to see and judge. Many of them will avoid admitting their shortcomings by saying they just don't have the time.

Saving these timid souls from the writing tasks that frighten and intimidate them can be quite lucrative, especially if you can maintain a certain healthy arrogance when it comes to the matter of compensation. A motivational speaker once called me to help him write a book based on his oral presentations. He outlined the project, gave me an idea of his time frame and asked me what I'd charge. My answer was followed by a full thirty seconds of stunned silence. I asked him if he was having a little sticker shock, and he stammered that he couldn't afford to pay my price. We negotiated and arrived at a price he could afford to pay and I could afford to accept for the amount of work he had in mind. He became one of my most enjoyable and easy-to-work-with clients, mostly because he is a genuinely decent guy with a great sense of humor—but also, I think, because he respected me for asking a fair price for my services. I continue to do work for him, and he continues to be a no-problems client.

If you're going to ask people for large amounts of money to do their writing for them, you're going to have to cop an attitude not only in terms of compensation, but also when it comes to the actual writing.

If you don't think you're a great writer then it's going to be difficult to convince anyone else you are. Make this a "humble but self-assured" kind of thing. Think of the surgeon about to put a baboon's heart into a sick human's chest. Think of the airline pilot who tells you the skies may turn "a little choppy." Let your confidence show, but make sure your customer understands that what you are about to do for them is not easy; in fact, it's extraordinarily difficult for most mortals. When people, businesspeople especially, hire someone to do a job, they want to know that they have hired the best person available. Creating that impression about yourself is one of your most important jobs.

Another important step is defining what services you can offer. This may require you to take a personal inventory, which can be a little intimidating, but it can also provide you with a pleasant surprise. There's a good chance you may have skills and experiences and talents that you never realized. We'll talk more about this later, but for right now here are a few genres of writing you may want to consider: speech writing (particularly good since it involves the twin bugaboos of writing and public speaking), guest columns in local papers, brochure writing, radio spots, press releases, Web site copywriting, annual reports, direct mail solicitations, ad copy. The list goes on. Anytime you find someone who is painfully trying to write something that they absolutely have to have, you've found a customer. I spent an afternoon a few years ago talking to a woman who writes love letters and mushy poetry for a fee.

I have a client in New England who pays me very well to write e-mail messages to his subscribers. The individual messages aren't very long, but the research and the editing process can be time-consuming and difficult. I got the job because the client couldn't find anyone else to give him exactly what he wanted.

A songwriter I know in Northern California once collected a nice handful of green rectangles for writing a birthday song called, if I remember it correctly, "Sweet Little Grandma Gal." There is practically no limit to this market.

The next task is finding customers. A lot of potential customers are readily recognizable; some no farther than your yellow pages. Doctors, lawyers, chiropractors, CPA firms, old-age homes, retail companies, research firms, massage therapists, car dealers—just about anybody with a service or product to sell.

Pick up the phone and call. Tell them you're a freelance writer specializing in business and professional communications. Ask for an appointment to discuss ways you can help them accomplish their goals. Always make it clear that your primary objective is to help them. Sometimes you can do this by offering a free critique of their current written material. Just remember to make it a general critique. Don't give away your store.

You may also want to buy a list of businesses from the chamber of commerce or from a professional list broker and simply send out a letter to introduce yourself and explain your services.

One freelancer I know works for a temp service specializing in clerical work. Every time she is assigned to a new job she analyzes the writing level at the client's company and offers her help. This approach works well for her, she says, plus she gets paid while she's there. A word of caution is appropriate here. When you are conducting your analysis of the company's writing skills you may want to keep your findings to yourself, at least initially. The writing you criticize could very well be the product of the person to whom you will be pitching your services. Be very careful how you express your analysis. The same mindset that makes people reluctant to write can also make them a trifle sensitive to criticism.

Another important thing to remember is that you won't sign up everybody you pitch. Just keep pitching and stay confident. They hate to write and are no good at it. You love to write and are great at it. Sooner or later that equation will produce dollars for you.

Once you start landing clients, put out press releases announcing that these "area firms" have retained your services. It's best to check with the local newspapers and electronic media to find out who should get the press releases and what form they should follow. I do this locally, even though most of my clients are from out of state. The reaction is remarkable. I might have a press release in the paper just three or four times a year, but people in town are always coming up to me and commenting on the "article" they saw about me. In some ways it's just an ego gratification. But, who knows, I might someday want to pitch some local business, and those long-term impressions may help land an important local client.

Once you get your new client, be sure you charge enough. It's important to both of you. It's a lot easier to do good work for a client who is paying top dollar. In a way, then, you owe it to your client to charge as much as the market will bear.

Asking a fair price is one of the most difficult and important skills you can acquire. Earlier in this book we explored ways to find the going rate: call up creative services agencies and ask their price, get to know your fellow copywriters, join the local writers/PR/advertising clubs, etc. Finding out what to charge is largely a matter of plugging into the professional scene.

Fighting the temptation to lower your prices to get work, however, is something you'll have to do on your own. Be as brave as you can be. Resist this urge as vigorously as you can. Nothing erodes your position as quickly and profoundly as undercharging. How would you feel about a heart surgeon who offered you a huge discount for the privilege of splitting your sternum? Or a plumber who charged you $2.75 an hour? Besides, if your price is truly too high, it's always easier to negotiate down than it is to negotiate up. And if your client cannot possibly pay a top rate for top work, then you're better off looking for a better client.

Keep in mind that you have a very valuable skill. You write well. You owe it to yourself to make the most of that extraordinary skill. Remember, the worse the dookie, the more they have to pay.

The King of the $100 Story

JAMES RAIA

I call James Raia "The King of the $100 Story." He calls himself "highly unemployable." Actually, we're both correct.

James is a freelance sportswriter who specializes in endurance events and NBA basketball. That's not to imply that he would refuse assignments outside his specialty. In fact, he's pretty much open to any form of writing that includes a paycheck at the end of the project. I've hired James for a variety of projects and have always been happy with the results.

Like a lot of freelance writers, myself included, James started freelancing when he became jobless. He had been a sportswriter on the *Sacramento Bee* for about eight years when he got a notice that a combination of union difficulties and other unpleasantness was forcing a "consolidation" of positions at the paper.

Self-employment suddenly seemed like a good idea to him. "I'd done a little bit of freelancing," he recalls, "and it dawned on me that there were things that I liked to do—sporting events, particularly endurance events—that a lot of people didn't like to cover.

"To complete [the set of unlikely] coincidences, the Sacramento Kings had just become a franchise here after moving from Kansas City, and at the same time there was a major bicycle race being held in Colorado for the first time. So I got an assignment to cover the Kings for the now-defunct UPI [United Press International], and I went to Colorado and covered the Coors International Bicycle Classic and the World Cycling Championships for thirty-one days straight."

James will tell you the pay wasn't great, what with UPI being in the throes of death, but those assignments did give him a niche as an NBA and bicycling writer. That was a long time ago, and he still covers the Kings and most major bike races. A couple of years ago I had breakfast with James in the Grove Park Inn (a huge luxury hotel in Asheville,

North Carolina) before the start of the Tour Dupont. After that race he was off to some other more exotic locale. It's a great life, and James makes the most of it. I regularly get e-mail from James while he's traveling in Germany or Italy or some other bicycling race venue. He's expanded his specialty to include golf now, so he also gets invitations to some of the more prestigious golf tournaments around the world. I don't know anyone in the writing business who is more devoted to the life of a freelance writer than James, or anyone who enjoys it more.

"[Since] the summer of '87," he says, "I've been freelancing full-time. It's just the best thing. I love it. I think I'm highly unemployable. I don't know what else I could do. There is rarely a day when I don't look forward to coming to work, and it just takes me in so many directions that it's constant stimulation. I travel all over the world. I'm not living beyond my means, but I am living a lifestyle that I couldn't afford if I weren't a freelance writer."

An accomplished long-distance runner himself, James has been able to provide a point of view that's often missed in traditional sports coverage. "I do a lot of marathons and ultra-marathons. The people I write about have jobs, families and other responsibilities, and yet they somehow find time to do this. They're not doing it for the money. They're in it for an entirely different reason. I love those kinds of interviews, because these people don't get a lot of exposure. They're not the same tired, clichéd athletes. You go to talk to somebody about what it's like to run a hundred-mile race. You give them a chance to talk, and you get a lot of good stuff. As a person who does that kind of thing myself, at a sort of marginal, middle-of-the-pack level, I have an appreciation for what they've done."

When I last spoke to James, he was gearing up to cover his tenth Iron Man Triathlon in Hawaii. Getting a handful of well-paying freelance assignments for this event is a matter of knowing whom to call, he says. "What I do is call up people I might string for three or four times a year, like the *Dallas Morning News*. They're not going to spend the money to send somebody to Hawaii, but I can cover their local athletes just as if I were a staff writer. I'll do three or four stories for them. Then I'll call up the *San Diego Union* or the *Baltimore Sun* and say all of the same things. I'll have seven assignments, and I'll make $1,000—and I'm going to be in paradise for five days."

If James is handy at getting several assignments out of one trip, he's equally good at squeezing a lot of usable information out of one interview. Take his solitary interview with skiing legend Jean-Claude Killy, for example.

"He had developed a very high-end line of ski wear," James remembers, "and a line of sunglasses. He had debuted them at a ski show in Las Vegas. I knew the PR guy there, a real professional, and he asked me if I wanted to interview Jean-Claude Killy. I knew a little bit about his history, but not as much as maybe some full-time skiers knew. It didn't matter, though, because when I got there nobody else had showed up, and I got this one-on-one interview. He was a delightful guy, charming, and he gave good answers. He'd run the New York marathon once, so when I told him that I had done some running, we had some common ground there. I ended up writing a story for Reuters that went out on their international news service. I also wrote a story for a Japanese skiing magazine. They translated the story into Japanese characters. The only thing in English was my name. Everything else was in characters. When I got the check, they had converted from yen to dollars. I also wrote a story for *Singapore Airlines Magazine*. I think I ended up doing four or five stories. The hotel was expensive, but they had a media rate, and I had an inexpensive flight. I also got to do some new-product stories at the ski show, so somehow it all worked together.

James still writes regularly for that Singapore-based in-flight magazine. "It's not a high-paying market," he says. "It's about thirty-five cents a word, something like that. But it's a beautiful magazine, and most times they're just buying either airline in-flight rights or second publication rights. It's not a bad gig. I spin it around, change the lead. It takes an hour, and maybe I'll make three or four hundred dollars. I've done the same thing with Tiger Woods stories. Usually they want profiles. Sometimes health and fitness stories. They've changed editors a few times, so I might not do anything at all for them for a year and then I'll do two or three stories in a row. Then maybe not anything again for a year."

Like any good marketer, James has great respect for the shelf life of his products. "I have about thirty or forty columns I've written that are very service oriented. How to buy a pair of running shoes. How to prevent sunstroke. How to stay hydrated. New products. That sort of thing. They're all very basic, timeless stories. I save them on my laptop in a folder. Just the other day a guy called and was looking for something like that. He has a special section and was looking for maybe ten stories. So I printed out ten of them and sent them to him. He might pay $25 to $50 [each] or maybe $100 at the outside. If it takes me two hours to get everything all said and done, and I make $300 or $400, then I'm making well over $100 an hour. All I've really done is package the stuff and send it off. Sometimes it doesn't even require a rewrite. Just make sure it's in the proper envelope, put a stamp on it and send it off."

Even though his stock-in-trade seems to be small stories that he can sell repeatedly, James still makes fairly frequent big-ticket sales, as well. The biggest, he says, was for an annual golf magazine put out by a company in Chicago. They asked him to write miniprofiles of about three hundred words on the top thirty golfers on the PGA tour. "I ended up getting six or seven thousand dollars for that assignment, and I turned it around in about two weeks. That's pretty good pay. Plus, I didn't have to interview anybody. I saved quotes from golf tournaments, and there are a lot of Internet sites full of what you call public domain quotes. I wrote four profiles a day."

I once asked James what kind of advice he would give to freelancers just starting out. Here's what "The King of the $100 Story" told me: "I would say that 60 percent of it or more is putting your nose to the grindstone, to use an awful cliché. Be a businessperson first and a journalist second. When you're starting out, never say no. If someone offers you a nickel say 'Yes!' and take it. Cultivate contacts. The term *hustler* has a bad connotation, but I think that it's a wonderful word. If you want to succeed, it's up to you. If you want to fail, it's up to you. I don't want any middle-management person looking over my shoulder."

CHAPTER TEN

Pitching, Schmoozing and Maintenance Lunching

A decade or more ago, I received a unique Christmas card from a California public relations agency.

The card featured a traditional Santa riding in a traditional sleigh pulled by traditional reindeer. The caption read: "What good is Public Relations?" Inside I found a leering, disheveled, disreputable-looking Santa. The inside caption read: "Without PR, Santa Claus would be an unshaven, overweight burglar who hangs out with little people and thinks reindeer can fly." The card was a big hit in town. I even heard a morning drive-time disc jockey talking about it on the air. He seemed to think it was a bit over the top. *Crude* was the word he used, if I remember right.

Well, sure, it was crude. But I'd have to say that the card did contain at least a grain of truth. Presenting one's image or one's actions in an intelligent fashion can make a lot of difference.

I learned early on about the value of public relations. When I was a kid I had a Daisy BB gun, the Red Ryder model. For the first few weeks I owned it, nothing was safe on the farm. Everything was a target. My reign of terror ended one sunny afternoon when I put a round through a garage window, leaving a neat little hole in a 12″ × 12″ pane of glass. Thinking quickly, I immediately ran inside and told my dad that I had smashed some windows in the garage. He, of course, flipped and ran outside to inspect the crime scene. When he saw the actual damage, he was so relieved that he actually patted me on the shoulder and told me not to worry about it. He did, as I recall, mention that if I wanted to keep the BB gun I'd have to learn to line up my shots a good bit better.

I've never forgotten the incident and the value of presenting information in the most effective, beneficial way. The fact is, just about any business can profit from an effective public relations effort. That's something for freelancers to think about on a couple of different levels.

For one thing, PR services are a nice addition to your freelance product line. Nothing warms the client heart and loosens the client purse strings like seeing his or her business featured in the local press or on the television screen. It's actually not that difficult to get some media attention for your client. The main thing to remember is that you're not going to get an article every time you pitch something. Not every press release is going to see publication. Not every story idea that you and your client cook up is going to appeal to the assignment editor upon whom you bestow it. Think of it as a cumulative effort. Some of your stuff will stick, some of it won't. You need to make your client understand that simple fact. You also need to let the client know that even the press releases and story pitches that don't come to fruition are still beneficial to his or her business. The more well-written, legitimate press releases an editor gets from your client, the more that editor will begin to think of your client as an expert source. If you're lucky and persistent, the assignment editors and reporters will start coming to your client even without the benefit of a press release or a phone call from you.

Conducted correctly then, PR can be a very tasty profit center for the freelancer and a very valuable service for your client. A caveat: Make sure you charge your clients enough for your services to make them take you seriously. And make sure your clients are aware of all the work you've done to get them where they are media-wise. If you don't do that, clients may start believing their own publicity and could begin to imagine that they would have gotten all that ink even without you.

If PR is so good for your clients, isn't it just as handy for your own business? Of course it is, and it's not all that difficult for you to put into practice on your own behalf. A good self-promotion campaign can start with nothing more than some press releases about yourself and your business.

Not long ago, I did a circulation promotion project for *Atlanta Magazine*. As soon as I had the contract signed and in my hand, I sent a press release to the local business editor and to a couple of trade journals that serve the publishing industry.

The local paper ran the release almost word for word and included a photograph. One of the trade magazines put an abbreviated version in its industry notices. The other trade magazine pretty much blew me off. Not a bad result, really. Ask any PR agent if they consistently get their stuff published two out of three times.

About a week later, I landed a marketing contract with a psycho-
therapy group that was planning an expansion into another market. The
local paper ran a release on that job as well. For a month afterward,
people all over town commented on how well I must be doing. I've been
offered a handful of local marketing jobs since then, almost certainly
because of the publicity I developed for myself earlier.

Here's an example of a press release I sent out on my own letterhead
when I signed the contract for this book:

For Immediate Release   Contact: John Clausen
July 27, 1999   Phone: (828) 555-5555

Local Writer Signs Book Contract

Hendersonville, NC—Freelance writer and Hendersonville
resident John Clausen has signed a contract with Writer's Digest Books to author a book on freelance writing. The 85,000-
word book, titled *Too Lazy to Work, Too Nervous to Steal: How
to Make Money and Have a Great Life as a Freelance Writer*, is
scheduled to be in bookstores in the spring of 2001. The book
is based on Clausen's twenty-year career as a freelance writer
and journalist.

"It's definitely a how-to book," said Clausen, "and it definitely has to do with making money. But I also try to make
people understand how much fun they can have as a freelance
writer. You know, the really remarkable thing about it is . . .
you really don't have to have all that much talent. You just
have to understand the marketing, know your way around a
page of copy and develop a certain level of confidence. It's not
that hard to do, and it really is a great way to live. I know a
lot of marginally talented writers who earn a perfectly good
living simply because they had the guts to give it a try. That's
what the book is all about—making money, having some fun
while you're doing it, and living an interesting life."

Clausen also publishes *Writing for Money*, an online journal
for freelance writers at www.writingformoney.com, and provides marketing consultation for clients in Hendersonville and
Asheville.

The local paper was very generous in its coverage. The item, whittled down a little bit, ran on the front page of the business section—right where it would do me the most good as a marketing consultant. After it came out, people stopped me on the street and demanded autographed copies, even though I hadn't finished writing the book yet. No doubt some of them will open their checkbooks at the local bookstore—at least I hope they do.

I am constantly amazed at freelancers who do not send in press releases on their accomplishments. That article you sold to the national crafting magazine might be a small thing to you, but it could be big news to the local media. Let them know about it. Use my press release sample as a template. Make sure the release still makes sense if an editor cuts off everything but the first paragraph. Once you have the essence of the information in the lead paragraph, don't be afraid to load the press release with a quote from yourself and as much self-serving information as you can pack into it. Don't make it over two pages long. One page would be even better, as long as you can get everything you want into it. You might want to add (as I did not in this case) that you are available for speaking engagements and writing seminars.

Please understand that there is little chance your press release will survive in its entirety. It's likely that the editor will chop it up and take what he or she wants from it. And don't expect them to agree with you about what's important about the story. The press release I sent out about this book generated a nice story, but the emphasis was largely on the fact that I said that it didn't take much talent to be a freelance writer. But that was OK with me. They spelled my name and the name of the book right. That's about all I could ask.

I also try to write a piece for the local paper about once every quarter, even though the pay is laughably low. It's the same principle—keeping my name out there as a writer and a part of the local media. Writing for the local paper is also a good way to unearth story ideas that may have a potential life beyond your hometown. I once wrote a piece called "Best Sellers" for *Sacramento Magazine*. Basically, I chose a dozen or so overachieving salespeople (one of them was my exwife) from a variety of businesses and interviewed them about the secrets of their success. I wrote up the interviews, tossed on a snappy lead paragraph or two and shipped it off. The magazine ran it complete with artsy photos of the interviewees. I think it was a very nice piece, and it produced a fairly decent payday for a city magazine article. When I moved to Hendersonville, North Carolina, I did a similar piece for the local paper. I even used some of the same lead. I'll wager that any one of you could sell the same thing to the various papers and magazines in your areas. In fact, feel free to pitch the story. I'll bet you get some takers.

Let's move on now to the art of the schmooze.

When I was working in Northern California a few years ago, I called up an assignment editor at one of the local radio stations (the one that launched Rush Limbaugh and Morton Downey, Jr., no less). I invited her to lunch at one of the city's trendier sushi bars.

She immediately asked me what I was selling.

When I told her I didn't have a thing in mind, she said, "Oh, so this is just a maintenance lunch." I admit that her rather cynical point of view was right on the money. I really didn't have a story to sell her, but I was pretty sure I would have one in the not-too-distant future. A few scraps of raw tuna and some seaweed seemed like a small enough investment. And besides, I love watching the little train that brings you the sushi at that particular restaurant. Plus, she was pretty good company. A classic win-win situation for me.

The ability to execute a successful maintenance lunch is a skill worth cultivating. Not everybody knows how to pull one off. When you're on "maintenance lunches" with potential assignment editors or some other word buyers, it is important to avoid seeming overeager to sell them something on the spot. If they bring it up, fine. Go for it.

But if they don't offer assignments or invite a pitch, clam up and wait a week or so. Then send a query or make the call. Experienced editors/word buyers will know what you're up to. They will, however, appreciate the fact that you didn't try to jam the story down their neck along with their club sandwich. I've been on both sides of the press release/PR equation and I can tell you this: Reporters and editors hate (and I mean really hate) to be seen as the unwitting dupes of PR people. So give them a little respect, make sure your story is worth pitching and be persistent, whether it's for a client or for your own accomplishment.

While you're whipping up self-promoting press releases and arranging schmooze lunches, don't forget the ever-popular (and tax-deductible, in many cases) "client gift."

I've given my clients crystal balls, signed and numbered prints of paintings, Christmas cards, pens and pencils, screaming brass monkeys, wine, books, sausages, smoked salmon, Swiss Army pocket knives, liquor (including one jar of genuine North Carolina moonshine) and several other forms of tribute. (The numbered prints and the Swiss Army knives brought the best response, by the way.)

Many of my larger clients spend several thousand dollars on my services. I find that a small, tangible token of my appreciation goes a long way. Before we end this discussion, let me reemphasize one extremely important thing to remember when you're doing any sort of self-promotion: Try to avoid *looking* as if you're promoting yourself. The press releases must have legitimate news pegs. The maintenance lunches have to be nothing more than peers getting together for a bite to eat. The gifts have to be things that the recipients can really appreciate.

The objective is to make yourself appear as you are—a charming, media-hip, helpful friend who also just happens to be a professional freelance writer.

An Industrial-Strength Copywriter

BOB BLY

Bob Bly is probably the best business-to-business, high-tech, industrial, direct marketing copywriter in the country.

His client list reads like a corporate Who's Who list: IBM, ITT, McGraw-Hill, AT&T, General Electric, Hyperion Software, George-Town Publishing and many more tasty big-business accounts. He's won awards from the Direct Marketing Association and the Information Industry Association, as well as two Southstar Awards, an American Corporate Identity Award of Excellence and the Standard of Excellence Award from the Web Marketing Association. He's written some forty-five books on copywriting, marketing and related topics. His Web site (www.bly.com) sports a nearly interminable list of testimonials, including one from the late great guru of advertising, David Ogilvy, who positively gushed over Bob's book, *The Copywriter's Handbook* (Henry Holt and Co.).

A truly inspired industrial-strength copywriter, Bob is also a master at hanging onto clients—no small feat in the quick-shifting world of advertising.

His explanation for his success and longevity in the business is characteristically to the point. "I'll give you the simple answer," he says. "To me, you hang on by concentrating on the work before you. I remember interviewing Bert Manning, who was then CEO of J. Walter Thompson [advertising agency]. I asked him, 'What made you successful?' He said, 'I was always interested in the task in front of me. I concentrated on the work.'

"So, to maintain clients you do the best job with the job before you. I know some freelancers who are so enamored of self-marketing that they like that better than the work. Or maybe they're always looking forward to the next job. They really don't like what they're doing, so they do it but they don't do it well, and they lose a client. The other secret [to hanging onto clients] is something I call 'fit.' That means only doing business with clients who you are compatible with, who are a good fit for your business. I had a guy call me, a Web site designer, looking for a copywriter. I asked my assistant to call him back, and he said to her, 'Why are you calling me?' She said, 'Well, Bob's not available right now. He wanted me to set up a time to talk to you.' He told her, 'That's going to be a problem. I really need him when I need him.' When she told me about that I asked her to tell him very politely that we weren't interested. He was a client who wanted his copywriter at beck-and-call availability. I don't do that. So, for me to take him because I wanted the business or I wanted the money would have been a strained relationship that would eventually dissolve. I like to work with a client who gives me an assignment, is accessible when I need him and other-wise leaves me alone—gives me three or four weeks and the only thing he cares about is that when the copy comes back it's as good as it can be."

Bob, a very pleasant man who nonetheless prefers to work away from other people, employs what he calls a virtual staff. "The people who work for me," he explains, "are not strictly employees. They are vendors. They're freelancers. I have a full-time secretary and a half-time agent who reps me to corporate clients and seminars. I also have an accountant. I have a bookkeeper, which most freelancers don't have. And I have a couple of literary agents."

All of these support people work either from their homes or from offices of their own. They maintain their own equipment and office supplies and they have other clients. "It's interesting how that came about," Bob says. "I had an assistant leave, and I said to somebody, 'Now I have to hire somebody new.' She said, 'Why don't you just get a freelancer. Look in the local penny-saver paper. Call some of these word processing shops.' So I called them and said that I was interested in buying forty hours a week of their time, a month at a time, and that I would pay the month in advance. They were all thrilled to get it, because apparently that's a very touch-and-go business."

Using a third-party representative to hunt up new business is not the usual freelance copywriter marketing procedure. Most of us spend half our time looking for new business and the other half desperately trying to finish the projects we've sold. Bob has a different idea and it seems to work well for him.

"I don't do anything [in marketing] at this point," he says. "I have more than enough business. More than I can handle and much more offered to me. I turn down a lot of work.

"I have no direct mail; I don't do any PR or mailings. I don't have a newsletter. I don't send out mailings or promote myself. I don't call people. In terms of leads—those people who contact me—if we don't close them right away or for whatever reason they don't hire us, if they're good prospects they get a call. But it's not from me. So there's activity going on, but I am usually unaware of it."

It may seem possible that clients would be turned off by not getting to deal with the top guy. Not so, says Bob. "I think it's actually better," he explains. "A lot of people do cold calls, and I'm not completely against this. But if you, Joe Blow the writer, are so busy and successful, how come you're sitting at the phone calling me up asking if I have any business for you? It's better with a third-party person. I can't measure that or prove it, but I know it's true.

"When you are demanding a higher fee, it's even harder when you're cold calling. How can you call someone, hope to get his attention, and then say, 'I need a billion dollars'? I'd rather have them come to me than have to go to them. Sid Rosenbloom, a very old-time direct response copywriter told me, 'I only get paid to write and think. Everything else I can outsource.'

"But, would I advise all this to a novice freelancer? Probably not. At the beginning you probably want to be more flexible and accommodating. I've been doing this a long time. I have a huge waiting list, I have more freedom to do what I want. If it changed, if suddenly someone in my family got sick and I had to spend every penny on a life-saving operation, and we were all of a sudden poor, then I would probably act differently."

CHAPTER ELEVEN

The Care and Feeding of a Model Press Release

A couple of years ago, I sold a short article to the local newspaper on a local woman who designs and creates preserved floral arrangements.

There were a few aspects of her life that gave the piece a little extra buzz, but not a whole lot. She was born and raised in Sweden where, at a fairly early age, she became a high-fashion model. After she moved to the United States, she got into the travel business and enjoyed a good living and had some interesting adventures. Dinner with Scandinavian royalty and trips to exotic destinations—that sort of thing. The floral arrangement work grew from a hobby to a full-time business after she got divorced.

She led an interesting life and is a pleasant person to talk to, but there really was no "gee whiz" factor to the story. Oprah Winfrey has one of her creations, but other than that she is pretty much just a talented woman making a living selling her art to local folks with enough money and taste to indulge themselves in what could be called a rather esoteric art form.

The story ran with some nice color photography on the front page of the local Sunday lifestyle section. I made $30 for my efforts (when the check finally arrived). The following Monday, people started showing up at the woman's shop, and business began to thrive. They kept coming in and mentioning the article right up until she moved her store to Sarasota, Florida, to escape the annual snowstorm that we get here in the mountains. (Don't ask me why a Swede couldn't take a little harsh weather.)

My point in all of this is that the stories we write as freelance journalists can have a profound effect on people, specifically on their commercial success. The florist told me that a dozen or so of her friends in the antique and flower business stopped by and demanded to know why she had gotten her story in the paper and they hadn't. She told them in her charming Swedish accent that it was because they didn't know John the writer, which made them turn their attention to me.

Some of them were even a little bit hostile about it. The stories that we write about the people and businesses around us are extremely valuable to them. There is no question about that.

The problem is how to exploit for ourselves some of that value— without venturing into some ethical minefield.

Obviously, editors are going to get a bit peevish if they find you're getting paid by the subjects of your stories as well as by their publications. You can easily put a major kink in your freelance career by indulging in this sort of double-dipping. Back before I really understood the ethical considerations, I did myself some considerable damage with the press in the town where I was working as a freelancer. I'd turned in several freelance stories to one of the local daily newspapers. The editor was very pleased with them and ran them on the front page of the Sunday magazine section. In fact, he told me that one of them, an adventure-style story about the paintball wars that were just then becoming popular, was the best thing he'd ever printed in the magazine. I was happy to hear that, but the fact is I only made about $75 for the piece, which took a good bit of research time. There was no way I could keep writing for them at that paltry rate of compensation.

About that time, a public relations firm asked me to do some writing for them. They paid more and the work was considerably easier. I did a bunch of stuff for them, including an article or two that I passed off on the Sunday magazine editor as pure freelance material. I got paid from the paper and from the client. It was an exceedingly stupid—not to mention unethical—thing to do. I guess I could try to square it up by saying that the paper should have paid more so that such temptation wouldn't occur. I tried telling myself that later on when the editor found out and screamed at me over the phone. But the fact remained that I'd done a bone-headed, dishonest thing, and I deserved the tirade that followed, which, by the way, was considerable in volume and duration. I doubt I could sell anything to that editor today.

The only winner in the whole affair was the public relations firm's client who benefited from the story and was relatively isolated from the hubbub. All in all, it was a painful situation, one I only bring up now to help you avoid falling into the same trap I did. That said, I would hasten to add that there is a way to help people in business get valuable coverage without endangering your own good reputation.

It's called the "model press release."

Here's how it works. You find a business owner who would benefit from the kind of exposure we're talking about. Just about any business qualifies. Look the business over carefully and try to figure out a few angles that might make viable newspaper or TV stories. Next, you call up that business owner and offer your services as a public relations consultant. Set up a meeting to discuss how you can help his or her business get the exposure you feel it deserves. Tell the business owner that you already have some ideas, but you'd like to explore more specifically the business's potential for media coverage. During the meeting, explain your ideas and how you feel the business would benefit. One of those ideas should be a "model release." The owner is almost certain to ask you to explain what you mean.

At this point, explain that the piece you will produce won't be an article in the usual sense. It will be more like a superdeluxe press release, one that will make it obvious to the editor who receives it that there is merit in pursuing the story. It will look like a regular story and will be written and researched like a regular story, with the main difference being that the client gets to approve the copy.

Once you've explained the concept of a model release and are certain that the owner knows exactly what you are proposing, you're ready to proceed. Interview the owner just as if you were about to do a regular article. Don't make it a single-source story. Instead, do a good job of covering the topic from as many sources as you can find. The key to success here is making it a good piece of journalistic writing. Once the story is complete, you let the business owner look it over and make sure it's completely accurate. The owner is bound to make at least a few changes. The urge to edit somebody else's writing is one of the strongest in the human experience. Brace yourself for the possibility of some truly laughable suggestions. Your job at this juncture is to make your argument and then let the client have his or her way. I usually say something like, "OK, you're the client and you get to win. You get to have your way. But you hired me to do a professional job for you, and I feel obligated to give you my honest opinion. I wrote it that way for a reason." Then I give the owner the reason and conclude, "Like I said, you get to have it the way you want it, but I wanted to make sure you understand why I've written it the way I did." Sometimes they will actually come up with a perfectly good reason why the piece has to be the way the client suggested. The client knows the business better than you, and there may be things at play you don't know about.

For a lot of freelancers, letting the subject see and, in effect, edit the piece can be difficult. Get over it. Make your point politely and then move on. Keep it professional. Don't take the client's editing personally.

After all, we're not doing journalism here. We're not writing that Great American Novel. We're doing public relations, and you need to have a clear understanding of the difference. Letting the client (or subject) see the copy will help you get comfortable with the role of a consultant.

Nevertheless, your writing will have to be top-notch, because the editor will be looking at it with the same jaundiced eye he or she uses on press releases. When you turn the piece in, make it crystal clear that you are not selling freelance journalism. The best way to do that is to tell the editor, "This is the way my client and I see this story. If we can add anything to it or if you need anything further from us, contact me through my client. Here's her phone number and other contact information. Thanks for taking a look."

Both you and the client need to understand that there's a better than average chance that the piece will never run. If the editor sees it as overly self-serving and fails to detect a news peg, it will just be ignored. Or the editor may look your work over and decide that the story is worth assigning to one of his or her writers.

If the story runs, grab the champagne and celebrate. If the editor assigns it to a staff writer or reporter and that person spells your client's name right, grab the champagne and celebrate. You've done your job well. Your client has his or her story in the paper (or on the radio or TV), and you have earned a tidy sum of money—probably far more than the $30 I got for the floral arrangement piece—and you've done nothing underhanded or unethical. In fact, you've helped everyone concerned, including yourself.

Let me repeat myself to make a point. The key is to make sure that both your client and editor know that this story is nothing more than a "model" of how you think the story should be told. The editor has to understand that you are doing the work on behalf of your client, and the client has to understand that there are no guarantees that the "approved" story will get in the paper the way you originally wrote it.

The idea is simply to get exposure.

To increase your chances of getting the piece placed, you should include a list of sources (even ones you didn't use yourself), material for sidebar stories and all the information a writer would need to get in touch with your client. Clippings on a similar subject from *The Wall*

Street Journal or some other impressive publication can help your chances as well.

Now let's move on to the matter of compensation. What you charge for this service is, of course, up to you. Keep in mind how much an advertisement the size of your story would cost. Or figure it out by the amount of time it takes you to do the piece and make the arrangements with the publication. I think that you should charge no less than $55 per hour, even if you're completely new at this line of work. Go ahead and cop a little attitude about this if you need to.

You may want to charge the client only if a story runs, but if you choose that option make sure you charge plenty. I really don't recommend this. It's pretty easy for unscrupulous clients to stiff you after they've enjoyed the benefits of the article and realize that you have no recourse short of burning down their house. If you're doing it for a flat fee, make sure you get at least a 50 percent deposit before starting work. You may want to do it for a modest up-front guarantee with a fat bonus if the piece gets published.

Because not all of your model releases are going to see publication, you should explore several possible story angles at the same time. Call it a "shotgun" approach. The more stories you try to float and the more publications and other media that see them, the more likely you are to do some good for your client.

Here's one important thing to remember when you're dealing with your client: Let him or her know that once the story is suggested, the editors and writers will pursue it according to their own abilities and ambitions.

If there is anything, *and I mean anything*, in the story that is potentially damaging to your client, drop the whole project and move on to something less dangerous.

Remember that you're wearing the consultant's hat. People will pay you good money for your expertise and experience. Give it your best shot—and don't forget the attitude.

"I Can't See Myself Doing Anything Else."

JAN LATIMER

Jan Latimer bought my first freelance story.

I don't remember what it was about now, but I do remember her telling me that I was a pain in the rear to edit. Maybe it was the way I hung around watching over her shoulder saying things like, "Hey, how come you changed that? If I'd have wanted it that way, I'd have written it that way." I guess I wasn't completely obnoxious, though, because she eventually hired me to work as a staff writer at *Tucson* magazine and later at *Reno Magazine*, as well as at *Sacramento Magazine*. I have to say she was one of the best editors I ever worked with. She was very calm under fire, even when a minor, innocent mistake I made brought a $1.9 million lawsuit (unsuccessful, thank God) down upon us. She was, and is, possessed of a finely honed sense of humor and a remarkable tolerance for the quirks one sometimes finds in good freelance writers.

She was also adept at recognizing a potentially good story when she saw one. That's probably why she was so successful when she switched from magazine editing to public relations.

Jan is refreshingly honest about herself. I asked her what made her get into journalism in the first place. This was her answer: "Do you want a true answer? I'd done some journalism in high school with this friend of mine named Susie. She was a year younger than me. I think I did news and she did sports or something like that. So, anyway, we both ended up going to the University of Arizona in Tucson. I was an English major. She came up to me and said, 'You gotta take journalism. It's really fun and the classes are longer, but there's no big midterm or final because you do most of your work in class.' So I did it for those two very good reasons: Because it was going to be fun and it probably wasn't going to be as hard as the rest of the classes."

Actually, Jan started out to be a teacher. "When I got to student teaching in my senior year," she recalls, "I hated it. I liked teaching, but I didn't like the other teachers in the teachers' lounge. I was afraid I would turn out like them. They just seemed miserable, and half of them were divorced. I didn't want that to be my future, so I got a little more serious. My dad had already told me that I was off the payroll the minute I graduated, so I had to do something. I remembered something about a magazine in Tucson, a city magazine that somebody had started. So I went over and asked for a job. The guy I talked to told me there were no openings but that I should stay in touch. So I did. I didn't tell anybody in the journalism department about the magazine, though, because I didn't want any of them to get the idea. I knew I wasn't the best student, and if the competition got worse I probably wouldn't get picked. Then one day they called me up, and they had an opening. I did a freelance story, and they asked me to apply for the job."

She worked there for two years, during which time she hired both me and a fine writer named Leo Banks (see the profile "No Pants Before Noon!" on page 151). After that she moved back to her native California and worked for a business publications company based in Newport Beach. "It was a lot of fun," she says, "because I was learning about all the businesses in the area, plus I was living on the beach. It was a great lifestyle."

Money and perks eventually lured her away from Southern California to a company that owned magazines and radio stations in Sacramento and in Reno, Nevada. It was a good job, she says, but it was still working for somebody else. "My hands were always tied working for other people. I didn't want to do that anymore, so I quit and started my own company. Public relations seemed like a good option. I'd worked with a few really professional publicists, and I'd seen what they could do for their clients just by working hard and coming up with good ideas. I'd seen some very good firms when I was working down in L.A. Sometimes they would call me back then to plug a story. Always legitimate business stuff. They'd basically just organize it and then get out of the way, just put their client with the writer and let the story happen. I thought, well, maybe Sacramento is ready for that. So I slowly started getting clients. One of the first was the local dairy, Crystal Cream and Butter Company. That ended up being more promotions than press, though."

Her list of clients eventually grew to include a top CPA firm, a leading-edge biomedical company and a prominent local bank. It was an event for the bank that seriously tested Jan's skills as a publicist.

"Everything was going great," she says. "They were just quality people to work for. It was exciting. They'd fly me up to their corporate headquarters in Portland [Oregon] before making any big decisions, so I was in meetings with the chief financial officer and the head of the product division and the chairman of the board. They'd get every opinion. Usually as a PR person, you are just given the news and told to do something with it. This was the best thing. I was involved, giving pros and cons and deciding how decisions they made in the boardroom would affect them on the ground in Sacramento and elsewhere. That was wonderful.

"They came into the Sacramento marketplace and their performance was great. At the time there was an old office building being renovated downtown. It was on the same block as the old original city library, a beautiful old marble building. The architectural plan was to kind of build a high rise above it. Sort of incorporate the old library into the new building. This was during a time when the economy wasn't very good, and the library couldn't afford to stay open very many hours. My clients rented the top two floors of the renovated building. I convinced the president of the company to give the city enough money to open the library on Sundays for a year. The year after that they would donate just a fourth of that amount and get three other corporate sponsors to donate. We had a five-year plan, so that eventually the library would start picking up some of those costs. By the end of the five-year period, the library would have developed their own financing. It was a wonderful thing and some really great PR. We had banners lining the streets downtown. We had a ton of press. Everybody in town was talking about how great my client was.

"So we had a big event, a promotion on the first Sunday that the library was open. People are taking tours. We had all these activities going on. All the media came, all the TV cameras. We had clowns and storytellers and everything else you could imagine. Then, like fifteen minutes before closing time, a homeless guy with a gun got into the library on the third floor and held a bunch of people hostage and killed two people.

"By then I'd already gone home. I turned on the TV and Channel 13 was showing the police shooting the homeless guy from the top of the parking garage. They showed the bullet hitting him and him falling. The camera followed him down. He flopped three times before hitting the ground and bouncing.

"It was a total panic. He'd just come in and started shooting. People were hidden in the library. I wasn't sure if some of my staff had gotten out. A lot of people were just hovering outside the library on little ledges. They had to close the library for a month, give everybody psychological counseling and cover bullet holes. A lot of people didn't want to use the downtown library after that. I guess they considered the whole incident proof that the downtown area wasn't safe."

It was no doubt a difficult public relations position to be in, but Jan and her client rose to the occasion. "The first thing I did," she says, "was call up the TV station and ask them if they could maybe quit showing the flopping scene. For some reason they went along with us on that. They showed the attack. They showed the SWAT team trying to negotiate. And then the president of the company came on and said how sorry the company was that this horrible thing had happened. Somebody asked him if they intended to keep on opening on Sundays, and he answered that this really wasn't the time to figure that out. He promised to work with the city and the library system to determine the best thing to do. I don't remember exactly what he said, but he wasn't trying to sweep it under the carpet. He realized that we needed to tell people the truth. There weren't any deceptive official corporate statements. The bank was just wonderful about it."

Thanks to Jan's efforts and the enlightened attitude of the bank's management, the disaster did not tarnish the bank's image or permanently affect the library. It also helped make Jan's reputation as one of the best crisis-management PR pros in the area.

But it takes more than a single incident to make a career in PR. According to Jan, the best way to achieve success in the business is to turn yourself into a resource for the press. "I feel that because I'm friends with a lot of reporters I can call and suggest story ideas to them. Sometimes they say it's a great idea, sometimes they tell me that it's completely stupid. But I never insult their intelligence or try to force-feed them some bogus, self-serving story on a client.

"If you're going to be effective for your clients and for yourself," Jan says, "you have to be pretty self-sufficient. Come up with ideas and figure out how to get things done, because your clients are in business, and businesspeople don't want to hear excuses. They really judge you on your results. That's the best part of being in this business. You don't have to play office politics to get ahead. It's all up to you. If you work hard, pay attention to the details and have a little luck, you can make good things happen. I can't see myself doing anything else."

CHAPTER TWELVE

Lessons Learned From a Master Teacher

I probably never would have met Ralph Chavez if it hadn't been for a broken sewer pipe under an old trailer house in Tucson.

I was working for a mobile home dealership, delivering trailers (the salespeople called them *coaches*) all over Arizona. I also picked up repossessed units and filled in on service work when necessary. The money was lousy, and the work was sometimes quite hard, what with three-figure summer temperatures, thorny plant life and stinging bugs of all descriptions. But, hey, it was a job, and it funded my modest lifestyle at the time.

I wasn't exactly the senior guy on the crew, so if something particularly nasty showed up on the service schedule there was a good chance I would find that work order in my box. That's how it was that I found myself at Mrs. Jones's (I don't remember her real name) aging home in a dusty, two-bit trailer park somewhere on Tucson's south side. Mrs. Jones told me that she had noticed an unpleasant smell coming from underneath her house. She also said the flowerbed alongside the trailer's skirting was sort of mushy. The smell, she reported, had been noticeable for about a week and was getting somewhat worse every day. These were not good signs.

I put on a heavy pair of coveralls and a pair of thick, rubber-coated gloves and crawled through the skirting door. I was soon creeping through what my flashlight revealed to be a pool of raw sewage. After a few truly unpleasant moments, I reached the trailer's main sewage outlet. Sure enough, the pipe was lying on the saturated ground beneath the outlet. Apparently the metal band that was supposed to secure it to the outlet had failed. I was just lining up the assembly when I heard a loud "whoosh" from above. Mrs. Jones, apparently not making the connection between the toilet and the broken sewer pipe, had chosen that moment to flush. I got my face out of the way, but took a pretty much direct hit on the chest. I'm normally a very peaceable guy, but I think that I could have murdered at that moment.

That evening I looked up the number of the local community college. Education, I had always heard, could lift a person out of poverty and dead-end jobs. I was ready to check it out.

That's when I met Ralph Chavez.

Ralph is a short, compact man with (at that time) dark hair, a chiseled Aztec profile and an aura of crackling energy. He calls it his *vamonos recio* attitude, which, loosely translated means, "Hurry the hell up, let's get something done right now."

If I know anything at all about journalism, writing and ethics, it is because of Ralph and his boot-camp approach to journalism class. I stuck to my light schedule for one semester. That's all the time it took for Ralph to indoctrinate me with his work ethic. In the next two years, Pima County Community College became my home away from home. The last semester I was there I took something like twenty-four credit hours and edited the school newspaper. I'd arrive at 7 A.M., and I'd be there until at least 10 P.M. And I wasn't alone. Several other Chavez junkies were right there beside me, churning out copy, laying out pages and plotting against the forces of evil. Ralph was in and out all day, teaching classes, advising us on newspapering and generally lashing us on to bigger and better things.

When one of our reporters broke a story about sex-related discrimination (which eventually drew Gloria Steinem to Tucson and inspired a handful of class-action suits), Ralph was right there with us. We were all over the administration asking questions, jotting notes and generally irritating the people in charge of the school, operating in what could only be called a hostile environment. It was great training for a beginning journalist. There are few things as satisfying as asking a sidestepping official a pointed question.

I was in Ralph's office one day shortly after the paper had come out with yet another piece on the controversy. The phone rang. Ralph picked it up and listened for a while with the muscles in his jaws slowly flexing. Then he very calmly told the caller that he considered it his job to teach his students the fundamentals of journalism and to let the chips fall where they may. He wouldn't tell me who the caller was, but I was sure right then that my newspaper colleagues and I had pretty much worked Ralph out of a job.

Later that year, the whole staff loaded up into a school van and headed off to the Rocky Mountain Collegiate Press Association conference in Colorado Springs. In true *vamonos recio* fashion, we came home with trophies and the contract to host the convention the next year. When I came back from the awards dinner with a first prize in newswriting, I think Ralph was more proud of it than I was—but just barely. I still have the trophy on my mantel twenty-five years later.

I learned a lot of things from Ralph. I found out, for example, that there is no such thing as "good writing." There is only good rewriting. That philosophy helps me a lot, especially when I'm writing something longer than a one-page press release. A lot of writers have trouble writing long pieces because they edit themselves as they go along. If you were to survive the Ralph Chavez school of journalism (or "churnalism" as he sometimes liked to call it) you learned to churn the stuff out, fix it up in the second draft and then get on with the next thing. *Vamonos recio!*

We also learned bare-bones writing. The first day of class, Ralph strode to the front of the room and wrote a lengthy description of a particular kind of soap, including the chemical formula that allowed the product to displace water at a certain ratio and various other lofty descriptions of benefits and features. It covered the whole blackboard. When he was done he said, "Shorten this up as much as you can," and left the room. He came back about fifteen minutes later to find us toiling away at the project. Ignoring our protests, he erased the whole board and wrote in large letters, "It floats." It was probably the most valuable lesson I've ever had, especially when it comes to the kind of commercial copywriting that I often do now.

More than anything else, Ralph was a champion for his students. He was squarely in his element at any kind of awards ceremony. He loved telling parents and the community at large what a great bunch of students we were. And he meant it, too. Nothing pleased him more than seeing his students win awards or get some kind of recognition for the hard work we'd done. That doesn't mean, however, that he was easy on us. He was as strict a teacher as I've ever had. In fact, a fellow student once got the ultimate high mark on an article he wrote for one of Ralph's classes. He received a zero. That's right, a big fat goose egg at the top of the page indicating that he had made no mistakes, committed no errors of fact or style. Paul probably still has that article. It was the only zero I remember seeing during the entire time we were all in Ralph's clutches.

The classes were tough, but Ralph was always a gentleman as he was breaking your back with work. He told me once that he felt a duty to show students what the real world of journalism was like. It was far better for them to discover any weaknesses in class rather than on the job later on. The truth is, a lot of students did wash out. But the ones who stayed on got a first-rate journalism education.

His ability to weed out his classes notwithstanding, Ralph was also a great one for recruiting talented folks who might otherwise have overlooked a career in journalism. Carmen Duarte, a classmate of mine who went on to a distinguished reporting career at the *Arizona Daily Star*, told me that she never would have thought about writing for a living if it hadn't been for Ralph. "He came to Pueblo High School and talked to us about scholarships. I didn't know what I wanted to do with my life. I was just planning to work in clerical because I've always been good at typing; I was thinking about joining the military so that I could travel and see the world. I really didn't know what I wanted to do. I hadn't applied to any colleges. He came to class and talked to us and said scholarships were available. So I talked it over with my mom and decided to go for it."

Getting the scholarship meant that Carmen would be able to attend class, but it didn't mean that life was a bed of roses for her once she decided to take Ralph's help. In the heat of a Tucson summer, just commuting to the college to fill out the paperwork was an ordeal, she says.

Carmen wasn't the only one to benefit from Ralph's attention. He believed that the newsroom should reflect the community, racially as well as economically. "He took us all under his wing," Carmen remembers. "There were some professors who made comments to him, saying that he was recruiting more minorities than Anglos, that he wasn't giving a fair chance to the Anglo students. He let us know what was going on. I think he wanted us to be strong and learn to fight for ourselves. I remember when he told me [about the professors' comments] I was very hurt. It must have been my Catholic upbringing—everybody had to love everybody. Anyway, I went into the bathroom and just cried and cried. But knowing about all that toughened me up. And Ralph was always there to pick up the pieces, but also to let us know that we had to stand up for ourselves."

As an Anglo student who spent two years working under Ralph's direction, I can say with absolutely no doubt that I got the same breaks and the same treatment as any other student in his classes.

The thing about Ralph, and mentors in general, is that he never really got anything for all the good he did. He got paid for his efforts whether we learned anything or not. He could have put the clutch in and coasted through his classes using age-yellowed notes from past classes (believe me, I've seen it happen). But that wasn't his style.

So what does all of this mean to freelancers? It means simply that the world is a better place and journalism is a better profession because of people like Ralph Chavez. And it means that all of us in the business should use Ralph as a model for helping other writers of all types. And it means that, for me, meeting Ralph was well worth that long crawl under Mrs. Jones's trailer.

CHAPTER THIRTEEN

The Klan Comes to Hooterville

It was one of my most memorable phone calls.

I'd been gone from the farm for about six months, knocking around in Idaho, dividing my time between playing cowboy, installing mobile home awnings and keeping the Coors brewery staff working late into the night.

I'd called my dad back on the farm in North Dakota just to catch up on crops and the local gossip. About halfway through the conversation, Pop told me he had some mail I might be interested in. He and my mom had a strict policy against opening other people's mail, but I could tell he was dying to know what was in this particular letter.

There was no return address, he said, just a big, bold, three-word sentence that read, "Defend the Bastards."

Who knows what goes through a parent's mind at a time like that? But, true to his ethics, he had waited until I OK'd him to open it. It turned out that the envelope contained a fund-raising letter from the American Civil Liberties Union. In the years since then, I've written a score of similar pitches for a staggering variety of good causes and not-so-good causes. But I will always remember that one.

The text described another letter, one that had arrived at the ACLU offices from a Holocaust survivor now living in the United States. He had seen a news account of the ACLU's efforts to defend the First Amendment rights of some neo-Nazis in some now long-forgotten controversy.

He told them in no uncertain terms how he despised everything the Nazis stood for and hoped that no one in the country would be swayed by what they said. But he also said that he loved this country for its Constitution and its unique notion of free speech. He expressed his patriotism by enclosing a small donation and telling the ACLU folks to use it to "defend the bastards."

I suppose that wise old gentleman is gone by now, but I wish he could have been with me when the KKK staged a rally in the little mountain town where I live.

The Klan had been denied a permit to march through the city because they hadn't filed their request in time. Because of this, they had to make do with a rally on the old courthouse steps. The leaders of the group said they would be sure to get their application in promptly next time. Most of the people I know around here are not looking forward to seeing hoods marching through our streets.

Nevertheless, the marchers do have a right to free speech.

That single premise—that Americans can express their thoughts and feelings without fear of official reprisals—is what makes us what we are. It's what makes our borders crowded with people wanting to get in.

But freedom of speech only works if it works for all of us.

A lot of my friends completely missed the philosophical boat when the Klan showed up. One of them, a police officer, planned to hover around the courthouse to make sure they didn't step a toe into the street. "They leave the courthouse and they are mine," was how this peace officer put it.

Others wanted the city to put a stop to the rally. Temperatures were running pretty high for a while, but I'm proud to say that several groups came up with alternative activities for the morning of the rally. The hood heads ended up playing to a nearly empty street, an apt metaphor if ever there was one.

All in all, the whole controversy was a good experience for the community. I got to wave my ACLU card around and weigh in on the side of the Constitution. My coffeehouse pals got a chance to express their righteous indignation. The Klansmen got to see just how few people around here consider them significant. And we all got a chance to see, once again, that the grand old system—flawed though it may be in some ways—really does work.

This is important stuff for everybody. But to freelance writers it's even more important. We are, more than anyone in the country, dependent on free speech. I can't imagine how sadly different the country would be if it weren't infested with folks like you and me running around jotting notes, snapping pictures and jamming microphones in the faces of outraged captains of industry and government. And I don't even want to think about what my life would be like if I were prohibited from writing about what I observe and what I think. No matter how shrill or annoying our freely spoken ideas may seem at times, I say that we all owe the Founding Fathers a major debt.

So here's what I want you to do when whatever extreme group that may deeply offend you shows up in your town. I want you to wave that First Amendment under everyone's nose. I want you to be a complete jerk about it if you have to. Stand up for the God-given right of human beings to say what they think.

In other words, I'm asking you to "defend the bastards."

———••◄———

When the above comments ran in a column in *Writing for Money*, I received a letter from a Kansas subscriber named Jim. He objected, he said, to my support of the ACLU and the First Amendment rights of the KKK.

There are limits to free speech, he explained to me, and in his opinion, the KKK had clearly stepped over the line by inciting people to violence. He offered some Supreme Court opinions and said, "The ACLU and local law enforcement agencies that protect rallying KKK groups are violating the laws of the land and giving credence to what they (KKK members) have to preach." He feared that simply ignoring ranting such as that offered by the KKK and other similarly minded groups would endanger society and could even "swamp a culture."

He certainly has a right to that opinion, but I'm happily inclined to disagree.

I am absolutely sure that no long- or short-range good can come of denying people the right to express their opinions. That one thing is what makes this country what it is, what it has been and what it can become. As you may have gathered, I take the First Amendment very personally. I don't care, for example, if a speaker suggests to the world that I should probably be horsewhipped—as long as the speaker doesn't act on his own suggestion. The opinion and the action are two different things under the law.

After I received Jim's message, I expected that the Kansas *Writing for Money* subscriber and I would continue the First Amendment/ACLU discussion via e-mail for some time to come. I like a good debate with a civilized opponent. Jim presented an interesting point of view, wrote well and was extremely polite. I even invited the rest of the readers to join in, throwing the forum open to any subject at all that tightened their jaws or lifted their spirits. I was braced for a deluge of discourse. Of course, that never happened. I wrote back to him once and never heard from him again. We'd both stated our cases, I guess, and that was that. No need to flog a dead horse. And this, I suppose, is the great danger. We actually take free speech for granted. In a world where bombs flatten dissent and free speakers disappear in the middle of the night, we sit here in this wonderfully free, wretchedly flawed country and dare to forget about the First Amendment. I hope this chokes you up the way it does me.

As a sort of addendum to the message, Kansas Jim mentioned that he had "noticed a great concretizing and narrowing of mind in the younger generation, those in their twenties." These kids seemed to him to be very intolerant, and he wondered if I could tell him why they were like they were.

Here again, I had to disagree.

I have several friends in the twenty-something category. There are entire herds of them at a local coffeeshop I visit in the morning, and I can't say I've ever sensed any serious narrowing of minds. Quite the opposite is true, in fact. They generously tolerate my presence as a token geezer. In turn, I generously tolerate body piercing and music groups I've never heard of before. I even overheard one of them describe me to his pal as a "cool old guy." That was gratifying in a way, as well as a little hard to take.

The truth is, I really like these people—despite my envy of their unclogged arteries and their spectacular muscle tone. Idealism runs deep in their crowd. One of them just left her job at a domestic violence shelter to work at another shelter, this one for battered, neglected and abused children. Another one of them is juggling her time between two jobs as she prepares to join the Peace Corps.

Almost all of them have tremendous respect for writing. A few have even been published—poetry, mostly, or other small, intimate pieces of work. Many of them, even that really strange young man with the steel ring through his septum, share a great sense of humor. Almost all of them want to do something worthwhile in the world. So far, they are largely unsullied by the events of their lives. Give them a few decades, and maybe they'll see things differently. But maybe not. Maybe they will keep their youthful optimism. Some of us kept a few albums from the sixties, didn't we?

A One-Way Ticket to Bogotá

JACQUELINE SHARKEY

Jacqueline Sharkey hates to be bored.

She was working on a journalism degree at Northwestern back in 1966 when it became obvious to her that she needed to make a change.

"I hated school," she remembers. "I was in my freshman year, I was bored and depressed. I didn't want to go home, so I just decided to run away. I'd always wanted to go to South America; it had been an area that had interested me since I was a little kid. I had enough money to buy a one-way ticket to Bogotá, Colombia—with fifty dollars left over.

"I called my parents one night and said, 'Well, I'm leaving tomorrow for Colombia. I hate school, so I dropped out and—bye.'

"I think they didn't know what to think. I think they were so stunned that they didn't know how to react. But I give them a lot of credit. They didn't try to talk any sense into me. They didn't urge me to be sensible. They didn't tell me not to do it."

So, Ms. Sharkey, with little or no knowledge of the Spanish language, an appallingly small handful of greenbacks and the bewildered blessing of her parents, got on the plane and headed south.

"I knew somebody in the Peace Corps down there, so I had a place to stay. I made some money teaching English and did freelance on the side. Most of what I was writing was either news analysis pieces about U.S. economic policy or U.S. foreign aid. Or sometimes feature stories. I lived in Bogotá for a year and taught myself Spanish.

"When you're totally immersed in a language every day, you have to learn it. It's absolutely the best and fastest way to really learn a language," she says.

Before long she picked up a regular gig as a Copley News Service stringer and also started sending articles home to the *Tucson Daily Citizen*. "It paid very little," she recalls. "The *Citizen* paid maybe fifteen or twenty-five dollars, something like that. When you live abroad you have to have either a huge cache of money or you can teach English.

"The people taking my class were all businesspeople, people in-volved in the country's political and economic life, and they often gave me great story ideas. Or they knew government officials I could talk to. My students ended up opening a lot of doors for me."

In those days, Bogotá had not yet become the dangerous, drug-infested place it is now. "In fact," she says, "there were no drugs at all in Colombia at that time. Bogotá was a small and beautiful city, the cultural center of North and South America. It was known as the Ath-ens of the Andes. Then the drugs started in the early seventies. The last time I was in Colombia was in 1979, and I swore I would never go back. It was like being on a different planet. But in the sixties it was a wonderful place to live and work. It was a small city, very cosmopolitan.

"It was also a country in which the United States had a tremendous interest. It was close to Panama, and it had been a democracy that had experienced some problems. The U.S. was pouring a lot of foreign aid into the country, so in terms of being somewhere where the U.S. media would have some interest, it was a great place to be."

At that point a lot of freelancers would have been quite satisfied with life as a foreign correspondent in a charming, exotic city. Not Sharkey. She began to feel bored again and decided to travel around a bit more—see the sights, so to speak.

"I wanted to see the rest of it, so I went about thirteen thousand miles through South America, Central America and Mexico over the next twelve months. I financed it all through my freelancing. I would simply travel until I found an interesting place I wanted to be or some interesting person I wanted to interview. I'd stay there long enough to write the story, then I'd ship it off by airmail with the instructions to send my check to some embassy two countries away. I did that whole year on about $450.

"Things were cheaper back then. We're talking about twenty-three years ago. I hitchhiked everywhere. I was sleeping in churches, sleeping in jails. I'd go to the police station and ask if I could sleep in an empty cell. On the road, if no one stopped to pick me up I'd throw my poncho on the ground and just roll up in it. It was a very inexpensive way to travel. Most people thought I was nuts. People picked me up. They fed me. People would take me home even. Today that would be a very foolish way to do things. It's too dangerous now. The world is a different place from what it was then."

She did manage to find a few kindred souls along the way, like the itinerant deer hunter from New Zealand who showed up walking a pig on a leash at an apartment where she was staying. "I asked him where he got the pig, and he said that someone had given it to him. I asked him what he was going to do with it, and he told me that, of course, eventually he was going to eat it when he ran out of money."

After she spent a year filled with hardship travel, borrowed typewriters and high adventure, Sharkey's brother joined her.

"My brother said he was going to come with a couple hundred dollars. Instead, he shows up with $12 and an alarm clock, which I promptly grabbed and sold. We ended up basically hitchhiking to get to Central America . . . from there we got a ride on a mail plane that was pretty cheap and then hitchhiked some more. That stupid alarm clock. I was furious. I don't know how we ever survived.

"I was just eighteen and sleeping on the side of the road, not knowing where I was going to be the next day or the next week or where my next meal was coming from sometimes. It was very exciting and romantic. It changed the whole course of my life."

She's been back to Central America since, again as a freelancer writing about the contras in the eighties. It was, of course, a whole new ball game for her.

"I couldn't put up with the stuff I could put up with at eighteen. I mean, I would do it because it was my job. I would slog through four feet of mud in the rain forest with the contras to get a story. But I didn't enjoy it. It wasn't romantic. It wasn't an adventure. It was a pain in the butt."

Her Spanish and her objectivity stood her in good stead among the contras. "Nobody in Central America was going to tell you the truth if you had an interpreter," she says, "because [the interpreter] probably worked for the government. I never asked anybody's permission to go anywhere. I made it clear that I was going to talk to everybody on all sides of every issue. And I did. I had a reputation after a while as being somebody who was fair. And that if you talked to me, your side would be represented fairly. That opened all kinds of doors for me—accuracy and fairness."

Today, Sharkey is a very popular University of Arizona (Tucson) journalism professor who confesses that she still misses her days on the road in South America. "I miss the excitement, definitely. And the freedom that I had when I was younger. I tell my students that they should follow their hearts while they're young, because they won't always have that freedom."

CHAPTER FOURTEEN

The Importance of Being Flamboyant

Telling people what I do for a living is one of my great pleasures.

I'll be sitting at a party talking to BMW-driving attorneys and wealthy, scalpel-wielding doctors and hard-charging entrepreneurs when somebody will turn and ask me what I do.

"I'm a freelance writer," I answer. That confession always inspires a small rush of interest among those assembled, after which someone will ask what it is, exactly, that I write. I have a lot of stock answers to that—junk mail, magazine articles, ad copy or whatever I'm working on at the time. For a while, when I was writing for Time-Life Books, it was easy to make a definitive answer. Everyone knew Time-Life Books. I'd just have to make it clear that I didn't write the ones about do-it-yourself home maintenance or cowboys in the Old West.

The strange fact is that no matter what I tell them I'm writing, people always seem extraordinarily interested. High-powered professionals with bulging stock portfolios, gold watches and triple-A credit ratings hunker right down and want to know everything about my writing life. Most of them have an aunt or a sister or a pal who writes—or would like to. I've been asked how much time I spend writing, where I get my ideas, how I find work and even how much money I make, a question most of them would consider quite crass if I were to direct it at them. There's something about the fact that I swap words for money that resonates in almost everybody I meet.

Can anyone tell me why this is so?

Personally, I think it has little or nothing to do with the process of writing, a task that the vast majority of people don't enjoy at all. By the way, I have a couple of theories why people don't like writing. For one thing, it's very much like public speaking. You're slinging your talent out in front of a bunch of potentially hostile judges. Also, unless you're quite talented, writing can require a lot of work. But most of all, society as a whole has made writing into a chore. Cops on TV grumble about paperwork. College students dread essay exams. Misbehaving grade-schoolers are forced to write essays as punishment, or at least they were when I was one of them. A buddy of mine once had to write a five hundred-word essay to pay for some insignificant sin he committed during school hours. In an inspired bit of rebellion he wrote "I- I- I- I- . . ." for the first 499 words and then ended the essay with the word "stutter." The teacher was not impressed. The whole episode, which I felt should have earned him an A for his imagination, ended with him spending a bunch of recesses sanding old desks and doing other slave labor for the teacher. He never liked writing much after that.

So, I doubt that it's the joy of writing that attracts people to a writer, and I seriously doubt it's the money, although, planned carefully, a writing career can pay well. Of course, just about any career, planned carefully, can make a comfortable living.

So, if not money or the pleasure of writing, then what's the big deal? Personally, I think what's at work here is the image of the flamboyant writer, the eccentric scribe who lives life according to a unique set of priorities and terms.

I once worked as an editor at a magazine in Tucson. One of the writers we used frequently was a guy I'll call Joe.

Joe wasn't a particularly skilled writer. In fact, the other editors and I used to pass his stories around hoping that someone else would have to edit them. Nevertheless, he did get his stuff in on time, and he did have some great ideas, and he did make a living strictly from writing books, articles and anything else someone would pay him to put on paper.

Most of all, though, Joe was eccentric.

I remember seeing him marching past the headshops and saloons on Fourth Avenue in Tucson, wearing a fancy hat, Bermuda shorts, black socks and white high-top sneakers. He was speaking into a small tape recorder.

That kind of behavior on the part of, say, a family lawyer could be somewhat damaging career-wise. It did not, however, do a bit of harm to Joe's credentials. In fact, we sort of enjoyed knowing him because of it. It certainly never kept us from giving him an assignment. It didn't stop other editors, either. Today, he is one of the most successful free-lancers in the business, with numerous books to his credit and what must be a huge stack of clippings.

Another one of my old pals from Tucson was what Billy Joel once referred to as a "real estate novelist." A series of truly heart-wrenching personal misfortunes had made it impossible for my friend to bear the mental rigors of peddling ranch homes, even though the job paid very well. To escape, he simply took off one morning and hitchhiked around the country. This became his way of life. He just sort of wandered from one interesting place to another. When he got bored, he'd just stick out his thumb and move on. Seems like he always made it back to Tucson, though, sort of a homing instinct. I saw him once walking down by the university wearing a Jesus-like robe and sandals. A few days later, he stopped by my house to crash on my couch. Then he borrowed a few bucks and a Swiss Army knife and headed north.

I saw him years later. He was still traveling on a whim and a short budget. If anyone inquired after his profession, he told them he was a novelist "gathering material." Everyone seemed to be OK with that and, who knows, maybe he actually did write a book at some stage. I'm certain that he had enough adventures to fill a volume or two. The point is that by assuming the identity of a writer, he was almost instantly forgiven for appearing to be a few fries short of a Happy Meal.

Please do not infer from all this that I advocate insane behavior as a business tactic for freelance writers. On the contrary, I urge you to be as professional as you can possibly be, while still preserving the romance of the writer's life.

You see, it's important for society to have a few mavericks, a few folks marching to the beat of Thoreau's different drum. We need people who are daring enough to live life on their own terms, maybe because they might just be daring enough to seek the truth and share it with the rest of us.

So the next time some Armani-wearing aristocrat asks you what you "do," hold your head high, look the poor devil in the eye and modestly admit that you're a freelance writer. Note the respect (dare we say envy?) that you receive.

Most of all, though, learn to enjoy your profession. Sure, freelancing may have its ups and downs, it may have scary moments and frustrations, and it doesn't pay as much as open-heart surgery.

But if you are a freelancer, you are doing something extraordinary with your life. People pay you to express your thoughts and observations. You're making a living by your intelligence and creativity. You deserve to be envied.

"No Pants Before Noon!"

LEO BANKS

Several years ago I called up Leo Banks with a writing assignment. He'd been traveling with a baseball team in the Mexican leagues, and I wanted a short piece on his experiences during the season.

I figured he'd duck out of it when he heard I was only paying $100 for the piece. But Leo and I have been friends going all the way back to college, so I figured I could get to him on that level.

"Sure, when do you want it?" he asked after hearing the price. I told him not to kill himself over it. Just put it together in his spare time and get back to me when it was done. Roughly forty-five minutes later, the piece came crawling out of my fax machine.

When I stopped to do the math, I understood why Leo was eager to accept the assignment. Written off the top of his head, no further research necessary—and at a rate of about $130 per hour. That's exactly the kind of situation he looks for.

"I work pretty fast," Leo says. "I'm the primary income in my family, so I've got to do it to make a living. I draw a distinction between that situation and people who have a wife or a husband with a good job. They don't have to do it to pay the bills. That's a very different ball game."

Leo is in the freelance business, he says, because "I was a failure as a novelist." He quit his job at the *Arizona Daily Star* in Tucson after seven years as a general assignment reporter. "I had this idea of writing novels, which I have done over the ensuing fifteen years. I've written four or five now. I haven't sold a single one, so freelancing was essentially something I got into just to pay the bills."

The shorter the story, he explains, the more money you make. "The question to ask yourself when you're freelancing isn't 'How much?'— it's 'How long?' If you got an assignment at the national level and did nothing but front-of-the-book shorts that run 250 or 350 words, if you could just do those exclusively and get a buck a word, you could make a living at it. But when you start getting into 1,500- to 1,700-word stories, the amount of effort is huge, and you don't get paid for your time—you get paid for completing it. When you're the primary income and you've got to make $40,000 a year, you can't sit there and look out the window."

As you might imagine, a writer with Leo's businesslike attitude loves multiple sales. One of his best sales was an article involving a woman and a bookstore called Singing Wind. The bookstore was (and may still be) located in a ranch house near the town of Benson, Arizona. "It's a bookstore in a working ranch, and it's run by a woman alone. The bookshelves are all though her house.

"I heard about her at a party one night. I told myself, 'That sounds like a story. I can hump that.' I did it for the *Tucson Weekly*. It was a long story. Maybe three thousand words. I think I got about $850. It was not a profitable venture."

Of course Leo did not let the story die there. He sold a shortened version to the *Los Angeles Times*, another shortened version to the *Boston Globe*. Then he repackaged the story and sold it to a business magazine in Phoenix and an airline in-flight magazine before making his last (so far) sale to the leisure and arts section of *The Wall Street Journal*. By the time he was through with that tiny bookstore on a small ranch in a relatively unknown Arizona cow town, he had wrung several thousand dollars out of it. The story now reposes in Leo's twenty-year "inventory" of stories, which he numbers in the "hundreds and hundreds."

This veteran of the freelance business will tell you that there are a handful of things you need the most if you are to succeed in the business.

"Number one is story ideas. You have to know where you find them. You have to have a regular supply. You have to have a billion of them sitting around. You also have to know the market, what magazine buys what, what newspaper is looking for what. Basically, you have to know what an editor will buy. I was talking to a guy who wanted to freelance, and he'd been around a long time as a newspaper reporter. He says, 'Yeah, I got a great story on making tequila.' There's this little town in Mexico where they grow the agave plant. That's where they make tequila, he tells me. He says he's going to sell it to this certain airline magazine. I didn't have the heart to tell him—well, I almost didn't have the heart to tell him—that the airline didn't fly there. In-flights only buy stories on their route system. It's a matter of market knowledge."

Leo calls the third freelance career ingredient the "butt in the chair." By that he means you have to get to it. "You just gotta do the work, and you gotta stay in the chair and do it. And a lot of people as freelancers have a problem with that."

The fourth thing is an ability to take rejection.

"I've had mail queries returned to Neil Bags, Leo Gangs, Leo Barks, which is at least a complete sentence. One time I was in Mexico covering the Latin American Baseball World Series for *USA Today*. I phoned in the story. They run about four hundred words at the most there at *USA Today*. When the story came out the next day the byline was Leo Woods. Which is OK, I've gone under aliases before, so this is no problem. But whom are they going to make the check out to? Sure enough, it was Leo Woods. It took quite awhile to get that situation rectified."

About the least important ingredient in the freelance soup is writing ability, according to Leo. And just below that is creativity.

One of the most important things about freelancing, he says, is to become an instant expert. "I remember one time when the phone rings, and it's an editor at an airline magazine calling me. 'Leo, do you ski?' he asks. Well, I know the son of a bitch isn't calling to ask me if I ski, you know? Not just for conversational purposes. Well, I always advocate telling editors the truth, but once in a while it just isn't possible. So he says, 'Do you ski?' And I say, 'Are you kidding? I'm from New England.' I'd never been on skis in my life. The only time I went skiing I never got out of the lodge for reasons I don't want to get into.

"The editor says, 'We got a story we need in a hurry. It's "How to Pack for a Ski Trip"; do you think you could do that?' No problem—Twelve hundred words, $400. That's all. It's very simple, but you have to do it. You just call a ski shop or find somebody else to be your expert and do the piece."

Sometimes it's easy to outsmart yourself in negotiations with an editor. "I had a call one time from some [young editor] in L.A. who was starting up a UFO magazine. . . . I'd done a story for the *Los Angeles Times* on a patch of southern Arizona desert where there'd been all kinds of bizarre occurrences. The editor at this new magazine wanted to reprint the story for $100. I was in a sour mood so I said, 'You know I got $500 for that originally. How about $500 for the reprint?' We dickered around back and forth. I wouldn't budge, and he probably wasn't authorized to go over $100. So he hung up. I have to admit it felt kind of good to tell him to buzz, but of course, ever since then I haven't stopped thinking about the hundred dollars I lost."

Lost hundred-dollar sales notwithstanding, Leo is happy being a freelancer. It's a matter of freedom, he says, being able to live life as he wishes. "Do you know what the freelancer's motto is?" he asks. "No pants before noon."

"I mean, you're by yourself. Your hair could be standing straight up. You could be wearing your drawers. I've interviewed several famous people in my underwear. I haven't been to a meeting in years. It's a huge advantage. The other thing is you save on clothing. You don't have to wear suits, although you have something on hand in case you need it. The overall benefit, though, as far as I'm concerned, is just the sense of being independent. Being able to do your own stuff."

Although Leo obviously relishes his self-employment, he isn't afraid to admit that at least one of his regular jobs helped put him where he is today.

"The best thing I ever did was work for a newspaper. You do all kinds of stories. You meet all kinds of people. You learn how to write. You learn what not to worry about when you're doing a story, so you can get it done quicker. I just never could do what I do if I hadn't worked for a newspaper. It was at times a tortuous experience, but mostly it was good."

It's been a good career for Leo, who has yet to see his fiftieth birthday. Especially good when you consider that he started out as a "failed" novelist, something he plans to change someday in the not-too-distant future. "I was confident I could do it as a novelist. I still am, by the way. And I still do it, which is either a triumph of hope over experience—or you're talking to a real idiot."

CHAPTER FIFTEEN

Pondering Predictability

Sometimes even a bad piece of writing contains a nugget of wisdom.

There is, for example, a great scene in an otherwise fairly frothy Tom Selleck movie. *Her Alibi* was the name of the flick, if my memory serves me. Selleck plays a blocked mystery writer who meets this beautiful, mysterious woman (complete with foreign accent). They fall in love but have some problems, starting with her suspected attempts to kill him. You can probably fill in the rest on your own. It was entertaining in its own way, but believe me, nobody in the cast or crew needed to buy tuxedos for Oscar night after this one was released.

However, like I said, there was at least one scene worth remembering.

A peevish Selleck complains bitterly after some other writer (who happened not to be blocked) describes Selleck's writing as "predictable." His agent tells him that, yes, he *is* predictable and that his predictability is what makes his readers love him.

Now there's something for a writer to ponder.

As writers, we spend a lot of time trying to root out predictability in its many forms. I knew a reporter in Kansas who could hardly sleep at night if she happened to use the same word twice in one paragraph. Whole careers have been built on the foundation of unpredictability. Many famous writers, actors and performers have done remarkably well simply by surprising their audiences.

François Truffaut, the famous French filmmaker, exhibits a great knack for putting unpredictable scenes into his delightful movies. In *Small Change*, for example, we watch a tiny boy named Petite Gregory crawl toward an open window four or five stories above the street. He falls out the window, but lands in a shrub without so much as a scratch.

Truffaut's movies have a lot of that sort of humor. In fact, I'd dare say he's somewhat predictable that way.

There is a certain comfort level in knowing that François was not going to make us watch Petite Gregory bash his brains out on the sidewalk. That comfort factor extends itself to a lot of other entertainment, as well. When I used to travel from San Francisco to New York City on a semiregular basis, I would take along three Dick Francis novels: one and a half for the trip out and one and a half for the return.

Francis, a regular occupant of the international bestseller lists, writes mystery novels that have to do with horse racing. In his youth, Francis was the Queen's steeplechase jockey. His books, full to the brim with great details about racing, are some of the most predictable on the market. The plot: Usually a charming, sympathetic male character in the horse racing world gets entangled with bad guys, falls in love, gets the stuffing beaten out of him, escapes the clutches of the bad guys and saves the day. Very predictable—and very, very entertaining. He's just the thing for a long, boring airplane ride.

I don't want this to sound like a complete rejection of surprise and unconventional plotting. Ivan Doig, author of *This House of Sky*, *English Creek* and a handful of other truly magnificent books, takes his readers on an emotional roller coaster ride that is anything but predictable. His novel *Dancing at the Rascal Fair* is the best book I've read.

Another great, unpredictable work of dramatic fiction was the 1973 movie *Charley Varrick*, which starred Walter Matthau as a bank-robbing crop duster. Charley and his band of thieves rip off a small-town bank, which just happens to be laundering mafia money. Skulking (and a bit predictable) bad guy Joe Don Baker pursues them, leaving a wide path of destruction and bushels of machismo-laden quotes. ("Now I'm going to hurt you very badly," he tells one of the gang after he's already thrown the poor lad through a couple of mobile home walls.) The ending, however, caught me completely by surprise. Great movie, great unpredictable ending.

So where does this leave us regarding the question of predictability in writing?

Maybe predictability is like sarcasm or irony. If you are going to use it in writing, you'd better do it well—and intentionally. Creative fiction writers stray from accepted genre predictability at their own peril. I once had a mystery novel rejected by an agent because I had trod on the conventions of mystery writing. I thought I was breaking new ground, pushing the creative envelope. She looked at it and knew that I was wasting her time with a project that wouldn't sell.

Many other forms of writing require creative use of predictability. When you're writing junk mail (some of us call it "direct response") copy, for example, you learn to use certain terms that have been proven to generate response. The word *free* is one of them. You can be pretty sure it's going to show up in my junk mail copy. Likewise with the phrases *Owe nothing* and *Send no money*. These are predictable but powerful words that reach the reader on an emotional level. Another convention of the junk-mail-writing world is the four-page letter. I'm betting you have received dozens, maybe hundreds, of direct mail pitches, each of which contained the famous four-page letter. I'm also betting that you haven't ever read one of these epistles all of the way from "Dear Friend" to "Here's how to order." Very few people do. They read the Johnson box (that little box at the top of the letter that tells you, "We have reserved a FREE gift in your name . . .") and the P.S. On rare occasions a letter will pull its readers all the way through, but mostly the four-page letter is there to give emotional weight to the package and because if it weren't there, people would miss it. All of which is yet another form of predictability doing its job.

In commercial writing it's important to arrange your priorities. Results trump creativity every time. Most of my direct mail clients would mail letters written in crayon on toilet paper if they were convinced it would lift response by half a percent. I once had a direct mail client ask me why I always used the same brochure format. Why, he wanted to know, didn't I try something different. I could do that, I explained. I could make up something entirely new and different and visually uplifting—but I couldn't guarantee that it would do as well as the brochure format I'd been using. A format, I pointed out, that had been a part of winning packages for years. He got the point. Nobody wants to risk $100,000 worth of postage on a new, untested idea. People absolutely crave predictability. They beg for it.

This does not, however, argue for the use of tired old ad copy. For example, the phrase *and much, much more* turns up in a lot of amateur advertising copy. It really means nothing to the reader. It adds nothing to the process by which a sale is made. In fact, it may be so predictable (and uninspiring) that the reader just glosses over it without much thought.

Perhaps we should call this an argument for deliberate writing. If a writing situation calls for predictability then, by all means, be predictable. Just make sure you're doing it on your own terms and for a good reason. But I bet you knew I'd say that.

Defying Death for Fun and Profit

ROBERT YOUNG PELTON

Some freelancers are completely content to write brochure copy for the local chamber of commerce. Some find fulfillment in dreaming up billboard copy or powerful junk mail teasers. Magazine articles, how-to books or any other project can bring in money, independence and satisfaction. No doubt about it, freelancing is an adventure, no matter how you pursue it.

Some of us, however, require a bit more adrenalin in our lives. Robert Young Pelton is a great example of how freelance writing and extreme adventure can come together—sometimes quite literally—with explosive results.

Take that time he was sitting in a bar in Uganda. "They were fighting a war with three different groups," he recalls. "Bill Clinton had been in town the week before, and his wife had made a speech about how she was personally going to combat terrorism and all that sort of stuff. And then she left, of course, with her limousines. The rebels . . . went looking for an American to kill, and I just happened to be sitting and having a beer in this place. So anyway, this guy with a backpack dropped his pack and asked for a glass of water. I wasn't really paying attention to him. Then, for some reason, I got up from the table to see where my traveling partner was. . . . After I got up, the bomb [in the backpack] went off and blew the shit out of these people. Then another bomb went off up the street. We spent the night basically trying to save people's lives . . . commandeering pickup trucks to take them to the hospital.

"The guy I was with was a mercenary, a former Green Beret. He really did a good job patching people up. There were twelve people injured, and I think he saved quite a few people's lives. The only unfortunate thing was when we got to the hospital they were just sitting there on their gurneys bleeding to death. They don't do that much for you in

Africa when you're injured. Some of the people were just blown to bits. There were pieces just big enough to put on blankets or whatever."

Robert is, among many other things, the author of the acclaimed guidebook *The World's Most Dangerous Places*. He's the kind of guy who responds to grim State Department warnings by hurrying to visit the countries he's been warned away from. As a result, he has been in just about every hairy situation an adventure travel writer can experience. Oddly enough, he started his writing career as an advertising copywriter at age seventeen. "I started in the mail room," he recalls, "and got promoted to copywriter. I also used to take time off and travel to adventurous places, but I never combined the two."

Over the years, Robert acquired a reputation as a top strategic planner. He developed products and wrote advertising. It was, he says, extremely lucrative. "I hate to tell you this," he says, "but in 1993, I was a business consultant for Marvel; they paid me $500,000 a year. And I just dumped all that to do this.

"I was forty-four years old, and if I'm going to do what I'm going to do I might as well get to it. It kind of forces you to figure out how you're going to survive."

It's tempting to think that one of the most dangerous things Robert has ever done was to go home and face his family and tell them that they no longer were going to be enjoying a $500K income. Not so, he says. "The thing is, I always knew what I wanted to do. And part of what made me worth a lot of money in the business community was that I'd spent so much time in war zones. There's very little difference between writing a marketing plan and writing a battle plan. It's the same terminology and the same end result. Then I realized that I was going . . . from the boardroom to the rebel camp, and I thought, you know, this [the adventuring] is real and the other one is bullshit. So at some point I had to get real." His wife and two daughters have always been supportive, he says.

So, with the approval of his family, a minimum of equipment and a couple hundred gallons of testosterone, Robert headed wherever he felt the most unwelcome. When I spoke to him last he was just back from Chechnya, where he was one of the last people to leave as the Russian tanks sealed off the capital city of Grozny.

"I had to cross three kilometers of the Russian front lines," he said. "I don't know if you've ever seen thirty tanks lined up about a hundred yards away and crawling with soldiers. God knows how many soldiers . . .

and then they're setting off illumination flares. We were so close, too close. I think they didn't open fire on us because they couldn't actually believe that we'd [dare to] cross the front lines that way."

Robert and some of the rebels from the city were driving what he describes as "a crappy Russian car." One of his companions kept a thumb over the choke light to avoid providing the Russian soldiers with an easier target. "We got on this road that was being hit with SCUD missiles," he said. "I don't know if you've ever been hit with a SCUD missile attack, but it was an interesting thing. The mountains were on fire. It was a narrow chasm that had been blown to bits and the road was just kind of notched out above the river—one of the most amazing sights I've seen, all these mountains on fire with these missiles hitting them."

At one point Robert counted, in a sixty-second period, eighteen strikes by missiles slightly smaller than SCUDs. "It's just a sight you'll never see in your life," he said. "Maybe back in Stalingrad or some place like that. But I wanted to take somebody in to see what was going on, because all of the journalists had buggered off. So I took in a photographer and [also] a writer, a gal who had never been in a war zone before. She was twenty-six years old. The photographer was a Turkish friend of mine.

"We got out of Grozny one hour before the Russians circled the city. They woke us up and said, 'The Russians are coming, you have to get out.' As we were leaving the city our car ran out of gas, so we had to go back. We could see the Russians coming at us."

At that point, most of us would have seriously considered a career change or spent a few minutes contemplating the joys of being an accountant. But not Robert. "Well, I choose to do this," he says. "I'm not sent by anyone. Yes, it can get pretty miserable. But the people, when they see you, they are so thrilled that somebody's come to see what's going on there. That has become sort of my cause, that nobody else will go in for whatever reason. I will go in. I was in Algeria without a bodyguard. I was in Afghanistan with the Talaban when they first started.

"By going in there I can at least tell people what's going on. The important thing to me is that somebody's got to see this. The secret is really being one-on-one with these people. Not having an agenda. Not having to file stories every day and conform to some editorial [political correctness] policy."

Robert has learned how to make his living doing exactly what he wants. He writes books, he's written and starred in a Discovery Channel series, and he writes for magazines. Along the way, he has put together a downright scary Rolodex of people from all over the planet. "Yeah," he admits, "I've got lots of weird friends. People I met under fire in other countries and people who are just trying to fight a war. They don't have a lot of resources or friends. I don't try to get involved in the wars, but I think they respect the fact that I'm risking my life to understand why they're fighting a war. If you look at how many people are actually covering wars you'll see that it's very, very few."

Not all of his adventures are dripping in gore. Sometimes things get downright funny, absurd even.

"I always sit down and plan these things very carefully," Robert says of his journeys, "and they always end up completely different from how I planned them. I was in Eastern Turkey once. As you know, they're having a war between the Kurds and the Turks. Anyway, the governor heard that there was a travel writer in town. I guess nobody told him that the name of the book was *The World's Most Dangerous Places*. So he had these people come and snag me off the street and invite me to dinner. I accepted. He lives in a compound, and that night, while we're eating, we come under attack by the Kurdish rebels. By the way, I was the only guy at the dinner table who didn't have a gun in his belt.

"I didn't want to be rude, but I'm thinking 'Should we go somewhere, should we do something, should we stop?' All the while he's sitting there telling me all about the potential for tourism in the region. He didn't even notice the fact that we were being rocketed and shot at. He was going on about hiking and camping and the beautiful scenery they have. I thought it was the most surreal experience I've ever had in my life."

CHAPTER SIXTEEN

Only the Lonely Know How We Feel

Writing, at its best, is a lonely life. — ERNEST HEMINGWAY

I used to have an old yellow cat who hated me.

Goldie would accept food from me if I would put her dish outside and then carefully back away from it. One false move and she was gone.

Goldie had earned her distrust of humans on the streets of downtown Sacramento, where she and I first became acquainted. Still, you would think that she, like other rescued animals, would have developed an obsessive affection for someone who took her in and spent big bucks on designer cat food and even the occasional catnip toy. Nothing could have been further from the truth. She showed absolutely no gratitude toward anyone for saving her from life on the streets. No gratuitous purring. No possibility of scratching behind her ears. No sitting on my lap watching TV. OK, once when I was flopped on the couch she actually climbed up on my stomach and appeared almost friendly. Then a car backfired outside, and she nearly eviscerated me in her escape. She spent the next half-hour crouched underneath the furniture growling and giving me the old evil eye.

Despite all of this, she remained a part of my household for several years after her rescue and stayed with us through two subsequent moves.

She finally attached herself to a strange but kind man who lived next door. I left her with him when I moved out of state. On the day I moved, I saw her on the guy's front porch, sitting on his lap, purring away like a well-tuned Evinrude. I bet he was scratching her ears before I was a block away.

One might wonder why I put up with that old cat, as well as with the bedraggled legion of animals that followed her (a one-eyed, malevolent weenie dog; two psychopathic black cats; a shockingly flatulent, nearly blind English bulldog; a hyperactive junkyard mutt who has been shot, but not killed, at least three times by my neighbors). Life without them would have been much easier and certainly cheaper.

I've become convinced that all of this tolerance of mutant livestock has something to do with the loneliness of writing. Maybe writers just need animals.

I know a writer in Northern California who keeps a cat named Sweetie Pie on his desk whenever he's plying his trade. He also has a Jack Russell terrier who regularly tries to assassinate his fellow pets. I know another scribe who keeps horses and German shepherds. And one who owns one of those miniature Vietnamese pigs. Look around any writer's home and you're likely to find some strange representative of the animal kingdom. Papa Hemingway himself was reported to keep company with several six-toed cats, the descendants of which still inhabit his old Key West neighborhood.

When you think about it, writing almost has to be a lonely profession. Even in the noisiest, most crowded newsroom, the writer is still there, alone, with a blank page and a handful of notes. For the freelancer, the loneliness is even more profound.

So, of course, a nonverbal companion—even one with a bad attitude or a serious emissions problem—might take the edge off the feeling of isolation that we've all felt at one time or another in our freelance careers.

We're never going to completely remove the element of solitude from the writing profession (and it's probably a good thing that we can't). That doesn't mean, however, that there aren't some steps we can take to mitigate the loneliness. Here are a few suggestions:

1. Join a writers group. Just about any city has at least one writers group. If there isn't one where you live, perhaps you should start one. Just make sure you don't have any unreasonable expectations about what you will be getting out of the group. As Hemingway said, "Organizations for writers palliate the writer's loneliness, but I doubt if they improve his writing." I was once foolish enough to bring a short story I'd written to a meeting of local writers. I'm not an accomplished fiction writer, but I did think the piece had some merit, and so did the assembled writers, except one who said she found it "anticlimactical." I ignored her comment and focused on the obviously more intelligent members of the group who had the good sense to praise my writing lavishly. If you do decide to become a member of a group, I recommend that you not take criticism too personally. Just use the meetings as an occasion to hang out with people whose interests are somewhat similar to your own. Eat some brownies, drink a little punch and just have a good time.

2. Do something besides writing. Consider taking a part-time job that is unrelated to writing and involves a lot of interaction with the public. Bartending comes to mind, as does selling shoes, selling Christmas trees, waiting tables, working for a funeral home, being a tour guide, etc. One of the most talented writers I've known is a truck driver in Northern California. A former magazine staff writer, he says that working at something besides writing has given him a better perspective on life and has improved his writing enormously.

3. Try team sports. Running up and down a hardwood floor with four comrades, all aiming to drop a ball through a hoop more times than the opponents—now there's a fine diversion. No threat to Mr. Jordan's legacy, I usually go for more sedate sports, mainly because I tend to go blind from throwing up or have a minicoronary about the second or third trip up the court. Nevertheless, team sports can be a remarkably efficient way to remove loneliness. Try softball or volleyball or street hockey if basketball doesn't suit you. Joining some colleagues for doubles tennis works pretty well too, especially if you're all on about the same level vis-à-vis skills and competitive urges.

4. Scare yourself and a friend or two. There are lots of ways to accomplish this. Hiking the Grand Canyon with an old friend worked for me several years ago. After making a primitive camp and climbing up what was essentially a seven-mile ladder, my friend and I felt an extraordinary sense of teamwork. Hunting or fishing trips might have the same effect for some people. Or perhaps a group hike on a difficult trail. If nature stuff doesn't do it for you, try something more urban. I've ridden with the county sheriff's patrol on night shift. We didn't get involved in any car chases or gun battles, but there were a few tense moments, not the least of which was early in the shift when the cop I was riding with patted the short-barreled shotgun racked up between us and said, "I don't really think anything will happen, but if it does and I'm down, this is yours. Do you know how to use one?" Now I'm pretty sure he was pulling my chain, a favorite cop thing to do, but it did give me pause. I could just see myself hunkered down behind his lifeless corpse pumping buckets of lead at the bad guys.

5. Do some charity work. Working in a soup kitchen or a homeless shelter will make you appreciate what you have and make you feel good about yourself in the bargain. Some other suggestions: swing a hammer for Habitat for Humanity, visit retirement homes or hospitals or work in domestic violence shelters. Make sure, for our purposes here, that you work in a teamwork situation. The point is to help you combat the loneliness you may feel as a freelance writer and do some good for your fellow humans.

I guess the lesson here is that even if we ply a lonely trade, we don't have to be lonely people. The choice is ours. As François Mauriac once wrote, "A writer is essentially a man who does not resign himself to loneliness."

CHAPTER SEVENTEEN

Blame It All on Michael Wiley

It was Michael Wiley's fault. That's my story and I'm sticking to it.

There I was with a perfectly good job as a managing editor for a multititle regional magazine publisher. I had my own office with ergonomic furniture, ample tack surfaces and perfectly acceptable office equipment. I had an extraordinarily efficient assistant and a whole battalion of interesting and talented colleagues. I even had a parking spot. I'll admit that the salary reeked and the benefit package wasn't much, but at least I had a job in the journalism business, right? Something to go with that bachelor's degree for which my parents had paid so dearly.

Life was simple. Life was good.

Then Wiley, my old drinking buddy and former landlord from Kansas, blew into town calling everyone he met "darlin' " and raving about his new calling as a carney. Yeah, a carney—a corndog-loving, beer-swilling, young-girl-chasing, live-in-a-travel-trailer outdoor amusement professional. His news did not come as a shock to me.

I'd first met Wiley when I was working as a reporter in the small college town of Lawrence, Kansas. Most of the reporting staff from the paper hung out at a place called the Catfish Bar & Grill. I guess the best description of the place would be "grizzled." Although it was right on the edge of the University of Kansas campus, I don't remember a lot of coeds spending much time there. Mostly they'd walk in, look at the assembled hard drinkers, mutter "eeuuwww" under their breath and do an about-face. We were not a pretty sight. Interesting, for sure. Maybe even colorful. But not pretty. It may have been some kind of hallucination on my part, but I could swear that Ron Kube, the famed left-wing attorney who took over William Kunstler's practice, used to bartend there. Nice guy—and a pretty good poker player, as well.

Michael Wiley was also a regular patron of the Catfish. Did I mention that Wiley holds a doctorate in sociology and was a tenure-track professor at the university? I got to know him pretty well through the media of draft beer and cheap wine. He always seemed a friendly, clever fellow with a fine, twisted sense of humor. Time eventually revealed him also as a devotee of conspicuous consumption on many levels. But always a good friend. At one point, when I needed a new place to live, he rented me a room and kitchen privileges in his house. Another one of the newspaper crew already rented a room from him, so it was quite a sociable household. One of my female acquaintances referred to the house (with only a little sneer) as "Boys' Town."

After a few months on the paper, I packed up my old truck and headed West to work for the aforementioned multititle regional magazine publisher. I did, however, manage to keep in touch with Wiley. His father lived in Sacramento, where I eventually ended up, and one day Wiley called me to say he was stopping in town and wanted to talk to me.

We met for dinner at a Chinese restaurant. He proceeded to tell me, between mouthfuls of fried rice and chicken lo mein, that he had changed his life. He'd sold his house and his tree farm, resigned from his university teaching job, dumped his Mexican restaurant and invested the entire proceeds in a handful of carnival games, some rolling stock and a .357 Magnum pistol. One of the carnival contraptions, a "high-striker"—the thing you whack with a hammer and ring the bell, would be *perfect* for me to run.

At least that's what he told me. The good professor also raved about the Serious Money that was easily available in the outdoor amusement industry and, of course, the fine adventure of it all. So, he asked me, did I want to come out and play?

I said I'd do it if I could get a magazine interested in an article on the whole experience. We shook on it. I wrote one query to *Rolling Stone* and figured I'd narrowly avoided a serious dip on the professional dignity scale.

About two weeks later, I got a response to my *Rolling Stone* query. After gently questioning my sanity, one of their associate editors gave me a tentative go-ahead. Not really an assignment, but at least a promise to look at the manuscript if I managed to survive the research. The next thing I knew, I was standing in front of the publisher's desk asking if it would be OK if I didn't show up at work for five or six months.

He was disturbingly quick to agree.

I packed a few clothes and a little traveling equipment, sublet my apartment and headed the old station wagon east. In North Dakota I traded my car for my dad's old Ford Econoline van, which came complete with a tiny fridge, a fold-down bed arrangement and a pop-up roof. It was the very epitome of carnival chic—and it got pretty good gas mileage, too. From there I drove to southern Wisconsin and joined the show.

I have to tell you that I was a little nervous as I drove onto the carnival lot. Carnival folks do not have the best reputation with town marks, which is what I was at the moment. (A "mark" is anyone who isn't a carny.) When I finally found Wiley, he welcomed me with his usual enthusiasm and put me to work immediately. Interestingly, none of the carneys offered to shoot, stab, beat or otherwise molest me. In fact, it was as if I were invisible to them. Nobody talked to me, and if I made so bold as to chat one of them up, he or she would give me a single-syllable reply and find something to do elsewhere. It was like that for the first few towns we played. Then on the jump to Peoria, I spotted an elderly specimen named Wrangy Bob on the side of the road with a boiled-over radiator and a lot of uphill left to travel. I stopped and dug out my trusty water can for him. Left it with him in case he needed it again. That single act of kindness, small as it was, changed the way the rest of the folks on the show treated me. I think it wasn't so much that I'd stopped to help. It was more about the fact I'd trusted Bob with some of my personal property. Carneys are very "us and them" when it comes to dealing with the world in general. Unless you can convince them you're on their side, you'll always be a "mark," which is one of the most derogatory things a carney can call you. The term carries with it a whole mixture of scorn, loathing and disgust.

So now I was a carney, a green one, but a carney nonetheless. I worked the highstriker, the checkerboard darts and a couple of other hanky-pank games. I took money from drunks, children, honeymooners, city councilmen, beer truck drivers, oil-field workers, farmers, cowboys, pretty young girls, college football players, senior citizens and one gentleman wearing a fuzzy, plum-colored fedora and sporting an attractive maiden on each arm. He, by the way, was unable to ring the highstriker bell and left my joint considerably deflated in the eyes of his companions. I was also on the lot when Mud, a 350-pound ride jock, received a 150-stitch knife wound from one of his colleagues. I regularly watched girls on the midway in the company of a very funny English lesbian, and on more than one occasion I had lunch with some truly strange folks from the sideshow.

I won't inflict the whole substance-abusing, customer-cheating, head-banging experience on you. Suffice it to say that I had a great time, no formal charges were ever filed and the scars have all but disappeared. All together, I spent about six months on the road, after which I was definitely more carney than mark. When the show closed in Mobile, Alabama, I was sad to see everybody go. In fact, it reminded me a lot of the way men my father's age talk about World War II. That may be a little over the top, I suppose, but think about it. We were a bunch of people thrown together by a very warlike enterprise. Soldiers moved across a country taking real estate from hostile forces; we moved across a country taking money from people who were often at least a little hostile. Just like the soldiers, our shared experiences made us form closer bonds. We helped each other out. We even fought each other's battles. And then, when the season ended, we grabbed our gear and headed our separate ways—just like the GIs returning from overseas. Like I said, that's a little overdramatic perhaps, but I did feel a loss as I watched Lurch and Cherokee and Big Bird and all the others leave the lot.

To overcome the feeling, I traveled up to Washington, DC, to drink heavily with my old college roommate for a week or so and then headed to New York City to deliver the goods to the editor who had been so farsighted as to give me the go-ahead. Once there, I picked up a part-time job typing letters and invoices for a restoration architect in a field office near the Fulton Fish Market.

It took me about a week to write the piece the way I wanted it. Then I showed up, manuscript in hand, at the swanky Manhattan offices of *Rolling Stone*. Unfortunately, the editor who had given me the nod had long since quit and gone into hiding. It took a few days to run him down. He was living with his artist girlfriend in a Soho loft.

We met for a few glasses of stout at the Lion's Head Tavern in Greenwich Village. He sympathized with my plight and suggested that I take the piece to a friend of his who edited *The New York Daily News Sunday Magazine*.

After looking over my manuscript and declaring it a swell piece of writing, the *Daily News* guy told me it was a bit too raw for the Queens housewives who constituted the larger part of his audience. He suggested I try *Penthouse* magazine.

OK. I figured *Penthouse* probably had several cubic yards of unsolicited manuscripts moldering away in their editorial offices. I didn't want my stuff to end up in that pile. So, dressed in a navy watch cap, jeans and an old sweatshirt, I marched right up to the *Penthouse* headquarters (which is a heck of a walk from Greenwich Village, by the way). I took the elevator to the editorial offices and confronted a receptionist with a thick New Jersey accent. I was a messenger boy, I told her, and my very job depended on my placing this package directly in the hands of an editor by the name of Peter Block. After a few moments of alternately beefing and demanding, I let her persuade me to leave the package at her desk. She promised to give it to Mr. Block the minute she saw him. I hadn't seriously thought that she would let me into the inner sanctum of the magazine, but I figured if I made a big enough fuss she might remember to give it to the man.

Apparently she did. By the time I got back to my temporary job downtown, Mr. Block's assistant had already left a message. When I called back, Block himself answered the phone and offered me $3,000 for the piece. I calmly replied that, sure, I could let it go for that much. Those funds, combined with an income tax refund and a couple of other writing assignments, allowed me to stay in Manhattan for an entire year. I should also mention that they invited me up to have my photo taken for the table of contents section. Who would have ever thought it? My photo in *Penthouse* magazine. Actually, the piece never ran. Some problem with lawyers and releases. I never did find out what the glitch was, but I can tell you that it made my dad very happy. He'd never been nuts about having his son's work (and photo) in that type of magazine. He was, however, pretty enthused about the money. He got the best of both worlds.

I later divided the amount of money I'd made on the story by the number of hours I had spent researching it and discovered that I would have been way better off on paper if I had simply gone to work in a convenience store. Of course, when you work at the Stop'n'Shop you don't get to have lunch with Zabora the Gorilla Girl on a regular basis.

Anyway, like I said, it was all Michael Wiley's fault.

CHAPTER EIGHTEEN

Editors May Forgive, but They Never Forget

Back a couple of decades when I was working as an editor in Northern California I received an unsolicited manuscript from a writer who described herself as a "national and international freelance writer." The logo on her letterhead took up at least three inches of the page and listed phone numbers, fax numbers, a telex number (I still don't know how to use one of those) and an address with an impressively small street number.

The article she was offering was completely inappropriate for the publication I was editing, plus it wasn't written well at all. I put the whole package in my outbox and went back to the job at hand, putting out a magazine.

A week or two later, my publisher, a man with a relentless sense of humor, appeared in my doorway with a twisted little grin on his face. He was holding an envelope gingerly between his fingers. "What am I gonna do with you, Clausen?" he asked. "Take a look at what landed on my desk this morning." Then he tossed the envelope on my desk and walked out shaking his head and chuckling wickedly.

The envelope was from the "national and international freelance writer." Apparently, I hadn't responded quickly enough to suit her so she had sent an invoice demanding payment for the article. The frosting on the cake was the "late charge" she had added to the bill to compensate herself for my tardiness. As you might imagine I was not favorably disposed toward buying this article, or toward hiring her to do anything in the future. No doubt she thought she was taking bold measures to further her career. All she really did was seriously aggravate an editor, who, by the way, remembers the incident, as well as her name (and middle initial), some twenty years later. Editors may forgive, but they almost never forget.

Another writer—this one from Mexico—sent me an ill-advised note. First he told me that he had deduced from my photo that I drank too much and suffered from a degenerate lifestyle that showed up clearly in my "bulging" eyes (which, by the way, are an adorable hazel and do not bulge in the least). Then he berated the publication as nearly useless. And finally, he offered to write an article for me if the pay was right. Trust me here—this is not the way to get an editor to say yes. Sure, this guy had a right to think what he may about me and my telltale eyes, but those observations certainly had no place in a pitch letter to an editor. There is, after all, a certain element of salesmanship that is vital to the successful query. Can you imagine your own reaction if you went into the local Chevy dealership and were confronted with a salesman who spoke to you as this writer addressed me?

I very seldom get into arguments with writers, probably because I identify with writers more than I do with editors. I like writers a lot. I can't think of a more caring, spiritually seeking, genuinely friendly bunch of folks. Sure, there can be some massive egos involved in our profession. We have to be a bit self-absorbed just to want to do what we do. But I've taught writers in workshops, extension classes and as an editor, and I've never been more welcomed and appreciated than I have been by people who write. Writers are great—that's why it's so painful for me to see a fellow scribe sabotage himself or herself with an ill-chosen approach to an editor.

The mistakes don't have to be as egregious as the two I described earlier. Sometimes it's just a matter of timing or even format. I handed over a screenplay once to an acquaintance who used to read for one of the big studios in Hollywood. This was a work I had spent several months on, one I figured was as good as it could be. I heard from him the next week. "Don't send it to anybody," he told me. "You'll only embarrass yourself." This was, as you might imagine, a bit hard to accept. When I asked him what prompted his low opinion, he told me that I didn't have the thing in a proper format. Anybody in the business who read the first two pages would know I hadn't ever written a screenplay before and, thus, would toss it on the heap of other amateur attempts. Plus, he said, the story sucked. That last bit hurt my feelings, but what really burned me up was the fact that I had followed a format in a book by an allegedly professional screenwriter who was supposed to know what he was talking about. I still have the screenplay, by the way. It's sort of a totem, a reminder to myself that a little diligent research at the front end of a project can save a lot of wasted time and effort.

Over the years, I've seen a lot of mistakes in query letters and story pitches. One query I received promised me a story that was so astounding, so well-written, so utterly compelling that it would no doubt cause the circulation of the magazine to soar and elevate me to a whole new level of respect among my peers. This magnificent article, complete with first North American serial rights, was mine at my standard rate of pay and could be delivered on any deadline I cared to impose upon its author. Wonderful. Stupendous. Unfortunately, the author of the query never told me what the piece was about, so I was forced to continue my lackluster career unaided by its brilliance.

Another writer, an amazingly enthusiastic poet, queried me in rhyming verse about selling me her poetry. She was undeterred by the notion that the magazine had never purchased poetry, or by the fact that we had no plans to begin doing so. That's not to say that I would have categorically rejected a good poem—assuming, of course, that she had provided me with one (which I believe she did not) and that I could recognize good poetry when I saw it (which I probably could not).

I've seen writers bury their chances in an amazing variety of ways. One wrote me a query in crayon. Another chose a medium that looked suspiciously bloodlike. Yet another, a veteran freelancer, got so angry over a missing byline on a piece she'd written (even though the byline did appear in the table of contents) that she stormed into my office and lathered me with invective and a fair amount of airborne saliva. One of the staff writers at the magazine was convinced the irate visitor was a scorned woman demonstrating the fury that hell hath not. Interestingly enough, I continued to use that writer's services—but only after explaining to her that her next such outburst would seriously damage our ability to work together. I did that because she was an excellent writer who normally gave me great work and no trouble. If she'd been a first-time freelancer I would have given her the gate permanently. By the way, she later apologized and told me that she had double-parked at my office and gotten a rather expensive ticket while she was screaming at me.

These have all been relatively dramatic mistakes by writers. Be warned that you can mess up in all sorts of small ways. Misspelling an editor's name is a classic. So is getting the address wrong, or mistaking the editor's title—or the title of the magazine. Sending queries on subjects the magazine doesn't cover is a common but potent misstep.

Experimenting in mass marketing once, I sent a simultaneous query to about two dozen women's magazines. It was a perfectly good story about the art of arguing with your spouse. "Fighting Fair" was the title, and I figured it for a sure sale to at least half of the magazines. I did end up selling it a few times, but I got more than one angry letter suggesting that I study the magazine before bothering them again. Any market research you do will help your success rate. Sometimes it takes a lot of time and effort, but it almost always pays off.

Sometimes you can actually sabotage yourself by *accepting* an assignment. This is more prevalent in commercial copywriting than it is in the magazine business. I once brought my advertising portfolio to show the creative director/managing partner of a relatively large agency in Sacramento. It was a case of instant dislike. The man, who claimed to be a former professional soldier, started the interview by saying he wished he'd stayed in the military so that he could be "down south killing Spanish-speaking people." I found this highly offensive, partly because my mentor in the writing business was a Mexican-American man for whom I have undying affection and partly because anyone with more than a room-temperature IQ could tell the guy across the table was an idiot. It would have been a big mistake for me to accept any work from this source. Even though I needed the dough, I couldn't stomach the thought of bringing written words for him to approve. He apparently didn't like me much either because I never heard from him again. It was a narrow escape.

I'd like to think that I've always been the hero in these confrontations between writers and editors. I'd like to tell you that I've always been the consummate professional, that I've never violated a deadline or angered an editor. That, of course, would be a vile lie.

Here's an example: A few summers ago, I was sitting in my office fuming over the audacity of a local contractor. The scalawag had promised to come by and fix a handful of small problems—plumbing, a little carpentry. Small stuff for which he wouldn't make a lot of money, but hey, he'd made the commitment and taken an up-front deposit on the job. I was waiting at the appointed hour and he wasn't there. Boy, the nerve of some people, huh?

I had a little time to kill while I was waiting for this obviously unprofessional scamp, so I thought I'd check my e-mail. The first message I found was from an editor in New England. Where, she wanted to know, was the piece I'd promised to deliver on that very date? It was a deadline about which she had reminded me no fewer than three times.

I had completely forgotten about the job. I'd gotten totally wrapped up in some circulation promotion job (OK, junk mail) I was writing for a national magazine. You see, the small article paid less than a tenth of what the junk-mail job paid, and I guess we'd have to say I had "back burnered" it.

To make matters even worse, it wasn't the first time I'd been a tad late for this editor. She was steamed—to the point of idly (I hope) threatening my life. I snapped around and got the piece done by the next morning, but not before doing some serious damage to my relationship with this person, who it turns out, had another writer go completely south on her that same day.

This is not how I like to think of myself in the profession.

I've been on the editor's side of the desk many times. I've dealt with slow writers, blocked writers and arrogant writers and experienced just about every form of writer-related unpleasantness an editor can have on the job. Remember the irate freelancer screaming (complete with flying spittle) at me over my own desk right in my own office, for something that was not even remotely my fault?

I know what this sort of thing does to the folks who make our assignments and OK our invoices. Blowing deadlines is about the best way there is to get out of the freelance business. Editors don't forget. They may forgive you (especially if you happen to be a very talented writer and they need your stuff), but they will remember for a long, long time what you put them through.

And it's not just the rookies on the way up who need to mind their level of professionalism. A friend of mine who used to work at *Rolling Stone* once described to me the remarkable fact-checking effort that the magazine was forced to mount just to protect itself against libel and errors of fact. Interestingly, it wasn't the new writers who made this necessary. It was the grizzled veterans who were more likely to slap something together carelessly.

Another editor for a national publication told me about a cartoonist who had promised to write a piece on the ins and outs of being a professional cartoonist. This guy had major credentials. His stuff appears in top magazines. He obviously could have gathered enough material right off the top of his head to put together this piece.

On the day of the deadline, he called the editor and said he'd been "swamped" and could probably get the piece done by the end of the week. This was simply not good enough. He lost the assignment and any chance of doing work for that editor anytime in this century.

He could have salvaged his relationship with a phone call about a week before the deadline. In the words of the editor: "He had to know he was swamped sometime before the deadline day. All he had to do was call and give me a little time to arrange for something else."

The good news was that the editor found somebody who could put together a replacement article in a matter of three hours. It was a good piece, the editor told me, and arrived in pristine condition requiring almost no editing. Can you guess who's getting the next plum assignment from that editor? (By the way, the heroic "pinch" writer also got paid double the standard rate!)

Perhaps it's a part of human nature to relax our standards and drift into carelessness. The fact is, however, that the path of least resistance is also the path of least compensation.

My point in all of this is that as freelancers we should keep in mind that the relationship between word sellers and word buyers can be a delicate one. Try to be businesslike without losing the human touch. Be professional without being a hard case. Respect the other person's dignity and intelligence, always do your market research before making your pitch, and always make it as easy as possible on your buyer. Don't be afraid to turn down an assignment that doesn't seem right. Always give good value for the money you receive.

The preceding opinions and observations are strictly from my experience. I've heard similar stories over the last twenty years. The following are some comments and suggestions from professional word buyers around the country.

Denise Dersin: Time-Life Books

Denise Dersin is a veteran project editor with Time-Life Books. Before coming to work with the company in the early nineties, she was a freelance writer and researcher for a variety of publishing companies. During her tenure as an editor, Denise has worked with a wide variety of writers and has developed what could almost be called a sixth sense for finding good writers.

"It's always important to see something else that a person has written," she says. "It really gives you a good sense of what they're capable of doing. It's really more of a feeling that you get from a person, how eager they might be to do the work in the way that you might want them to do it."

Apparently, some writers have a tendency to stray from the fairly strict Time-Life Books format. "And then," Denise says, "they argue with you about it after the fact. Certainly if I give someone a sample of what we're doing, it's up to them to figure out how to fit their assignment into the mold. Being a freelancer involves a lot of intuitiveness. You need to figure out what someone is asking you to do—even if they don't exactly say it. You have to listen to their instructions very carefully and try to figure out what it is they're looking for from you. The sample is the best way to figure that out."

The "sample" she mentions is usually a copy of an already-published Time-Life Books edition. "I tell them how this new one might be different from or similar to the sample. In the past when I've just been getting little pieces from people—a picture or a single chapter or whatnot—I'll give them the best example that I have of that kind of piece and tell them 'This is what I'm looking for.' That might mean in terms of how many quotes I want sprinkled throughout the text or how I want the text to go together with pictures—or how different I want it to be."

In her career, Denise has seen a lot of writers come and go. One of the big things that makes freelancers fail is inattention to details. "We have to have all of the pieces," Denise explains. "What I mean by that is that we need to have the bibliography, we need to have the work annotated. We need to have it checked after it's gone through the editing process. If it's an international product, we need to have quote cards done, because when people are translating they need to know where the stuff comes from. These things all need to be done, and every piece is as important as the other.

"Certainly, if we have someone with an absolute gift with words, we might let some stuff slide—but hardly ever. Someone might feel that once they've gone through what they consider to be the really hard part, which is digesting the information and regurgitating it to you, they are less likely to want to follow up on those details. But those are the things that make me not want to use somebody again—if they don't come through with the things I need."

Denise says she's never had anyone completely blow an assignment, but she did have a writer who rebelled at the editing of his manuscript. He refused to assist her in the task of post-editing fact checking. This was, she says, pretty much like resigning from any future work.

The occasional bad experience notwithstanding, Denise says she has generally enjoyed working with freelancers. "I've had so many good people. They're so anxious to have everything done perfectly that I think they wind up making a nickel an hour. I don't really want people to do that. I want it to be as worthwhile for them as it is for me. I like them to find a balance as far as the time they spend. Overall, it's been a real joy to work with freelancers—just extraordinary."

Greg Sanders: Journalistic, Inc.

Greg Sanders is an editor with Journalistic, Inc., a North Carolina trade magazine company that publishes *The College Guide for America's Brightest Students*, *Sign Builder Illustrated*, *QSR* (which stands for Quick Service Restaurant), *Backlist* and a contract publication for Kentucky Fried Chicken's franchising division. Journalistic, Inc., buys freelance material for just about all its magazines, which means that Greg gets to see a lot of query letters, both good and bad.

"When I open a query letter," Greg says, "there are two things that I'm hoping to see. One, of course, is a good idea for my magazine, with the idea well presented. [The second is something to inspire] the feeling that the writer will be able to deliver on it.

"We used to publish a magazine called *Young Scholar* [now sold to another publishing company]. I got a lot of queries that [looked as if] the person had read my one-line mission statement for the magazine and then came up with a very shallow, very common idea that I'd seen a million times. We prefer [for any of their publications] something a bit more thoughtful. Something that peels back the layers and goes in a bit deeper. I'd say that in the hundreds and hundreds of queries that we received over the course of the several years we published *Young Scholar*, there were maybe twenty or thirty that we actually ended up commissioning a story from, because the majority of it was crap. I mean, it didn't fit our audience or it was a bad idea, or the writer didn't seem like the kind of person who could handle his own idea—that sort of thing. It just floors me when I think back on how few of those queries were any good. I don't know why they couldn't be better. That's sad. For me, it goes back to the idea that a lot of people see writing as some sort of romantic or glamorous thing to do, but also as something that doesn't take any talent or training."

If you doubt the value of researching a magazine's style of writing, consider the following. "Actually," Greg says, "here at Journalistic, we were looking for an editor, and we ended up hiring a guy almost solely on the fact . . . that he had proven himself very adept at mimicking a set style of a magazine. That's what we wanted. Maybe some people find mimicking a style distasteful, but for better or worse, in magazines that's a big part of success."

Despite the fact that disappointment can be an editor's lot in life, Greg still finds working with freelancers to be a rewarding experience. "When a story turns out the way you want it to," he says, "or even better than you wanted it to be—it's all the disappointment that makes those moments really stand out."

Marie McTague: Harcourt Learning Direct

Marie McTague is a project manager for Harcourt Learning Direct, a publishing company specializing in business, medical, legal, educational and other professional books. In the course of a year, she works with as many as seventy-five freelance authors.

Finding new writers, she says, has gotten easier with the increasing presence of the Internet. "It used to be really difficult," she says. "We'd do a lot of cold calling. We tend to make the rounds of community colleges and undergrad programs. Adjunct faculty members tend to make very good authors. They're mostly not employed full time, and they're very interested in their fields."

To Marie—and a lot of other editors and project managers—first impressions are very important. "I'd say the first thing is the cover letter," she explains. "Even if it's just an e-mail note, you can't believe the stuff that people write to me. They'll write stuff like, 'Send me more information,' and then they'll sign their names. They don't even attach a resume or anything. I don't mind sending somebody information if they attach their resume and I can see that there is some [hope] that they might be good for the project."

A working knowledge of modern technology is pretty much required if you wish to do business with Marie. "A lot of times people make it really obvious that they have no idea how to use e-mail," she explains. "I don't think that's always a problem, but if you are trying to get work, you really should make a big effort to learn the basics of e-mail, just attaching files and [knowing enough not to] type with all caps. That kind of thing. The first thing I look for in the cover letter is just a short summary of what you've done that . . . makes you qualified for the project."

That doesn't mean she wants you to repeat the resume you've attached. Say something about the number of years you've spent in the field or how you've been volunteering in a related organization or the time you've spent teaching.

"A lot of times," Marie says, "people aren't great writers but they have a really good background. We can get around some of the mechanical problems if they can just find a way to express their thoughts and their knowledge."

I asked Marie to give me an example of a truly bad query letter.

"I don't get too many really bad ones," she said. "But one time this woman sent me her husband's obituary. She sent it to me in the mail. This whole long, sad story about how her husband had died and now she was raising her children and she needed work. I mean, it was really horrifying to read, but it just struck me as being so inappropriate—and she wasn't qualified anyway. It was just the strangest thing that has ever happened to me. I felt bad, not calling the person.

"I think there's a really large pool of good candidates, a lot of qualified people out there. They just have to figure out how to present themselves in a positive light. Because if I read a cover letter and it doesn't tell me immediately why I should hire you, then it's probably going to end up in the garbage at some point."

Don Nicholas: The Blue Dolphin Group

Don Nicholas is the CEO of the Blue Dolphin Group, Inc., a publishing and consulting firm in the Boston area. He is one of the most well-known circulation promotion consultants in the magazine publishing industry. I know this because several years ago Don helped me get started in the direct mail copywriting business. I've worked as a freelancer for him frequently over the last decade, as have several other copywriters, freelance journalists and graphic designers.

Don's a very blunt fellow. Ask him what you need to break into freelance writing, and he'll tell you it's something he calls "the personal inventory."

"Figure out what you know," he says. "If you're a lawyer, you better start out writing about law. If you're a botanist, you better start off writing about plants. Take whatever you have that's a strength. Figure out what core expertise you have, something you're good at. If you're a great cook, if you're a great parent—whatever it is. I very seldom run into anybody at a cocktail party—a housewife or a student or whomever—who doesn't have a couple of things, or at least one thing, that they're passionate about. Whether it's snowboarding or French cooking or whatever."

Progressing from a fledgling freelancer to a well-paid professional is a matter of image, he says.

"Go out and find a market that's looking for people who have your expertise," Don will tell you, "and they'll probably be willing to overlook the fact that you don't have a lot of clips. Then you flip that around. Once you've got the clips, people will believe that you can write about other topics, even if you can't."

This does not mean that you should mislead your prospective clients or editors. "Taking jobs you're qualified for is the way you get paid more," he says. "Taking jobs you're not qualified for is the way you get paid less. What skill do you have that you can sell? Who is out there buying that skill? You make phone calls. You do some research and find out who's paying."

Negotiating skills play a big part. "There tends to be a budget for these things," Don says, "whether you're talking about a magazine article or a column or a textbook. They may have some flexibility, but the bottom line is that [the word buyer] has a number to play with. You may get 10 percent more. You may get 10 percent less—but largely, you're going to get what they have in the budget. The trick is targeting the guys who have more money to spend on the things you're qualified to write, and then figuring out who's got what in their budget."

Of all the many traits a freelancer must develop, Don rates persistence as number one. I asked him if having a "thick skin" wasn't also up there on the list. "I think it's more than a thick skin," he told me. "It's more like having a permeable skin, because you're going to have to develop some pretty strong listening skills. You really want to learn from the experience.

"The better your clients, the better you're going to be as a writer. The more feedback, the more time they're going to give you, the more you'll learn. That's the kind of conversation you want to have with a client right up front. You say, 'Look, I know the field really well, and I'm a pretty good writer, but I'm going to want to spend as much time with you as I can so that I can understand what you want. I need to get into your head and see what your vision is so that I can make you happy.'

"It's amazing how much time somebody will spend with you to help you learn to write better for them—so that you can improve and eventually charge them more. It's one of the great conundrums."

CHAPTER NINETEEN

Indiana Jones and the Examined Life

Looking back on the night, I'd have to admit that the quart of Old Overholt 90-proof bourbon whiskey was not a particularly good idea.

It was during my last year in journalism school. A favorite professor told me about two old desert rats living in a cave up above his place in the mountains near Tucson. The cave, he said, was actually an old mine shaft, although I don't recall what sort of minerals had been extracted from the mine. These were, he assured me, a couple of genuine characters—something right out of the Old West.

Always looking for a potential freelance sale, I asked the professor (we'll call him Mr. Green) if he might see fit to introduce me to the cave dwellers.

Mr. Green agreed immediately, offered to lend me a good horse and volunteered to guide me to their camp. I borrowed about $1,000 worth of camera equipment, pocketed my tape recorder and a notebook and showed up at the Green rancho just as the sun was setting.

We mounted up on a couple of small, surefooted (so Mr. Green claimed) mountain horses and headed up a deeply rutted logging road. The camera equipment shared the saddlebags with the jug of Old Overholt.

Just before dark, we reached the narrow cliff that served as a porch to the cave. After introductions to Nevada Jack and Shorty, we broke out the bourbon and poured generously. It soon became apparent that I was in the company of enthusiastic, if somewhat inept, drinkers.

I won't trouble you with the whole story, which involved grown men wrestling in a campfire, gunshots from a bone-handled .38 revolver and a headlong, pitch-black plunge on horseback down that rutted logging road. I'm pretty sure that it was as close as I've ever come to the Great Permanent Hurt.

It's also one of my fondest memories of my college days.

At the time, of course, I was far more concerned with survival than with the romance of it all. Since then, though, I have come to see the whole debacle as one of the defining moments in my life, one of the things that nudged me into being a freelance writer as opposed to an employed, responsible, hanging-on-until-retirement journalist.

Adventure is good for a freelance career.

Please understand that I don't necessarily mean you have to parachute off El Capitan (although I'm told that's a real rush) or swim the English Channel. Perhaps a better term would be "a sense of adventure."

Adventure comes in many forms. The birth of my son Pete was the beginning of an ongoing, ever-changing adventure for me. Freelancing in New York City for a year was an adventure. Spending six months as a hanky-pank agent on a traveling rag-bag carnival was an adventure. Taking over *Writing for Money* and putting it on the Internet was another adventure.

My point about freelancing is that there are very few other professions so well suited to the concept of "life as adventure."

Think about it. As a freelancer, you are living the real-life equivalent of an Indiana Jones movie. The big round rock trying to squash you is the mortgage payment. The pigmies shooting poison darts at you are rejection slips. That huge, snake-filled pit over which you are dangling is a bad case of writer's block. The evil Nazis are looming deadlines. What a romantic figure you are. What fun you are having!

Seriously. You are living by your wits, leaping over pitfalls and emerging with the Holy Grail, which, in your case, is a check that actually showed up in the mailbox when it was supposed to.

Contrast your life with that of the poor sap who drags himself to the office every day, puts in his time until 5 P.M. and then heads for his two-bedroom subdivision ranch house, complete with station wagon and lawn mower. Probably he lies awake at night pondering his future retirement, at which point he will be able to do what he wants to do— which is what you are able to do right now!

You have no ceiling on the amount of money you can make. You have nobody "managing" your work. Nobody tells you what to do and when to do it. You are free to create, free to try anything. You're even free to fail. You get to take chances and, occasionally, you get to win big. Trust me on this. A lot of people would like to have a life like yours, if they could only muster the courage to give up their "security."

Personally, I think that security is overrated, which is OK with me, because it's also virtually impossible to achieve. You and I are walking around in a bag of bones, blood and viscera, a truly flawed vessel that could malfunction at any time in response to a staggering number of physical hazards. Other than an indestructible, unassailable soul, we have nothing that lasts. Nothing. So, really, in the final analysis you have just as much security in life as the billionaire in his mansion. Perhaps you even have more, because your lifestyle and resources may not make you a target of envious, money-obsessed, violently disposed folks.

I'm not knocking financial well-being. I like money. There's nothing wrong with that. But, as a friend of mine likes to say, "Money only achieves monumental importance when you don't have enough."

Another friend of mine, an intellectual gentleman who has accumulated almost no money at all in his nearly eighty years, lives a life of quiet adventure every day. His slowly deteriorating home houses a collection of approximately seven thousand very good books, mostly philosophy and religion. A grand piano, covered with sheet music, dominates his living room. I've spent hours at his house discussing some esoteric bit of writing or listening to him read his poems. The last time I spoke with him he was starting work on a new novel and studying classic literature in the original Greek.

Sometimes he's frightened. Sometimes he's supremely confident. But he's always thinking. He's always great company. And he's almost always broke. Now that's what I call a real adventurer.

CHAPTER TWENTY

Journalistic Widgets vs. Deathless Prose

My old pal Danny is a truck driver.

That's what he does for a living. But on a deeper, almost cellular, level Danny is a writer. Something like eighteen years ago he sold me his first magazine piece, an opus on the crawdad harvest extracted annually from the Sacramento river.

Since then I've been regularly amazed at the man's talent. We'll go a year or two without contacting each other, and then he'll call me up in the middle of the night to get my take on the opening paragraph of a short story or the lead to a magazine article he's putting together. I'll pick up the phone, and he'll start reading to me before I even get a chance to say "hello."

The man is brilliant.

No question about it. Words seem to perform more willingly for him than for other writers. And if words love Danny, he more than returns their affection. I've never seen anyone who enjoyed a well-turned phrase more than he does. Tell him a great joke, and he'll repeat the punch line to himself, savoring it in the way you might savor a great wine.

Danny is easily capable of writing something significant, something that would make him a celebrity and take him out from behind the dash of the eighteen-wheeler he pilots around Northern California. Something important.

The only thing that might stand in his way is a powerful perfectionism. One evening several years ago, Danny sat down for an all-night writing session that was supposed to produce an article I needed in the morning. When I left the office that night he had a scant three paragraphs on the screen in front of him. The next morning the office was littered with spent espresso cups, the ashtray was overflowing, and he had only two paragraphs on the screen.

In other words, he'd spent the whole night to come up with a net loss of one paragraph.

I tried my best to instill in Danny my own rather commercial approach to writing for a living. "Make a damned outline," I'd tell him. "We're making journalistic widgets here, not deathless prose." One does not make a fortune in the writing business, I'd explain, if one does not produce pages and pages of writing, some of which may not be total genius. Perfectionism is the enemy of "good enough"—and "good enough" is often the money-conscious freelancer's most valuable stock in trade.

He'd agree with that shamelessly mercenary philosophy and then go back to his desk and edit his lead for the twenty-third time. I'd shake my head and mutter to myself that he was never going to make it in the harsh world of commercial writing.

And I was right.

Today, after years of trying to make a living as a freelance writer, Danny is jamming gears and hauling freight. The funny thing is that he isn't any less of a writer for having taken honest work. In fact, in the absence of any money pressure, his writing has gotten far easier and more productive—and even more skilled.

So what's the lesson in all of this? Should we all get day jobs and work on writing in the wee hours of the morning? Should we all treat writing like a factory that produces necklaces of words? Should we turn our attention to commerce or to art?

As far as I'm concerned, the lesson is that you should follow your talent without trying to mold your writing to fit the ideals expressed by your colleagues and mentors. And be prepared to change your life to accommodate that talent. If you have art in you, the world deserves to experience it. If you have a knack for making money with writing, you deserve to bank it.

CHAPTER TWENTY-ONE

Writing for More Than Money

I spent a recent Wednesday evening playing Scrabble with Thomas Gray.

About halfway through the game, just after he had landed the word *vex* on a triple word score, Thomas grinned at me and said, "I kinda like this game."

I was gratified to hear that, partly because Thomas is a good guy and I like to see my friends enjoying themselves, but mostly because when I met him, Thomas was considered functionally illiterate.

He showed up at the Blue Ridge Literacy Council looking for a tutor. A kind lady who lives where Thomas worked as a gardener noticed that he had trouble writing and suggested he try the Literacy Council. He laboriously filled out some paperwork and took an evaluation test to see where he was, educationally speaking. Then he waited to see if they could find him a tutor. I happened to be on deck at the time waiting for a student. I'd done a little tutoring before.

My first student was Abraham, a nice fifteen-year-old kid from Mexico whose family had moved to North Carolina looking for work. He spent his days working for a textile company and going to school. After school, he was supposed to come and meet with me. That didn't work out well. His English skills were almost nonexistent, and his motivation was pretty low. I can't say that I blame him. All day he listened to people talking in a language he didn't understand and then had to listen to me in the evening. His uncle used to go fetch him for me just about every session. The only time I noticed a marked increase in his motivation was when he acquired a girlfriend who spoke no Spanish. I'm not sure how they got together, but I suppose some things just transcend language barriers. I lost track of Abraham after a couple of months and sort of drifted away from the tutoring work. When I finally decided to give it another try I told the supervisor that I wanted a student about my own age, one who spoke English but needed help with reading and writing. I asked her to make sure the person they chose for me was motivated and ready to learn. That's when I met Thomas.

Thomas is unusually driven. He wants his high school equivalency degree, and he plans to someday own a machine shop. To achieve those goals, he is willing to do what needs to be done, no matter how difficult.

But more impressive than his attendance record is the progress the man has made in a relatively short period. He reads and spells on a much higher level, as witnessed by his Scrabble triumph. He wrote a little essay for a Literacy Council contest. It is a measure of his growing confidence that he was a little peeved when he didn't win the contest. As I write this, Thomas is getting set to take his fourth (of five) exams for the GED program. His scores on the first three have gotten progressively better. This one is on math, and I'm almost willing to bet that he knows more about math right now than I did when we started working together. (Of course, my math skills are right up there with my pole-vaulting skills.)

Nevertheless, I'm sure that Thomas will pass the math test with flying colors and will then plunge himself into studying for the fifth and final exam. I'd like to take credit for his successes, but the fact is, Thomas is just unbelievably persevering. He works hard at learning.

The remarkably baffling rules and regulations of the English language are often difficult for him to apprehend. The definitions and usage that you and I take for granted are a nearly impenetrable code for someone who early on slipped through the cracks of public education. Just finding out how to study is a major accomplishment for him. Applying himself the way he does to this kind of a learning task, using his decidedly limited resources while working more than full time, is, well— nothing short of awe-inspiring.

I can only imagine the courage and determination it takes to face the task of learning to read and write at age forty-eight. I do know that it sometimes takes repeated sessions before Thomas can comprehend some of the work. And sometimes a hard-won piece of knowledge will drift away between sessions. But whenever Thomas does gather in a bit of information or finally understand a thorny point of grammar, he locks it away as securely as he can and incorporates it into his life.

It strikes me that writers have both the privilege and the obligation to use their skills to help out around the planet. We are a sort of priesthood, if you want my opinion, and that carries with it a responsibility.

I try to fulfill my own responsibility by tutoring at the Literacy

Council, as well as with high school and college students. This also helps me satisfy a lifelong teaching ambition—without the horrifying 60 percent cut in pay that taking a teaching job would entail. One of the guys I helped through a first-semester writing class announced the other day that he'd gotten an A from a tough history professor—plus a compliment on his writing skills from the instructor. I couldn't have enjoyed the news more if it had been my own A.

There are, of course, lots of other philanthropic ways to use your skills. You may, for example, want to spend some time reading the newspaper aloud or writing letters for retirement home residents. Keep in mind that some of these folks are a little confused. Some of them can be downright weird and even annoyingly rude. I had one old gent grab my wrist and demand to know when "the next damn train" was pulling out. I told him "ten minutes," and he let me go. Older folks need some spice in their lives, and you're equipped (and, in a larger sense, obligated by your own good fortune) to provide it.

While you're there, keep an eye peeled for some tasty "old-days" stories. There's a very good chance you'll find something marketable. Nobody said you couldn't make a buck while giving somebody a chance to dust off their memories. Just don't let story hunting become the primary focus.

Maybe you could use your copywriting skills to help promote a good cause: helping a local food co-op attract more members, for example, or pumping up the response to a charity drive. It is not written in stone that salesmanship has to be used solely in the service of avarice. Find a worthy but struggling business and give it some free writing or marketing services, just to help it get moving.

Or how about writing a play for the local school or teaching journal writing at the local domestic violence shelter? Once you start looking, there will be no shortage of places to apply your talents. Keep in mind that your finely honed skills as a reporter, interviewer and organizer/ marketer of information are formidable. Your contributions can be extremely valuable to people less comfortable with the process of communication, and your spiritual life will be enriched.

That's not a bad payoff for a few hours of your time.

CHAPTER TWENTY-TWO

Sometimes a Good Deed Goes Unpunished

Somebody once told me that no good deed ever goes unpunished.

I've never liked the idea of that, but I have to admit that I have seen it happen. Take my old pal Ed, for example. Ed, a large and formidable guy with aggressively bushy hair and a pirate beard, once attempted to rescue a grocery store checkout lady from a crude drunk who was attempting to, shall we say, woo her. Ed tolerated the situation as long as he could and then said to the drunk, "Why don't you just pay the lady and move on?" or words to that effect. He figured the young lady needed some help. The drunk, in turn, asked Ed, "Who are you to criticize me?" To which Ed answered, "I'm just a guy standing in line behind an asshole." In the ensuing battle he received a throbbing knot on his head from a sucker punch and was rewarded with the undying indifference of the checkout lady. Chivalry at the checkout stand is not dead, but it does appear to be somewhat anemic.

Other examples abound, of course. I imagine you could come up with a bunch from your own experiences. Just about anyone could. There's something particularly distressing about having your good deeds flung back in your face. What would happen, say, if you stopped every morning on the way to work and gave a panhandler a ten-dollar bill? Day after day, you hand over the sawbuck and go on about your business. Then one day, you happen to be a little short and give the fellow a five. How's he going to react? There's a pretty good chance he's going to demand to know where his other five bucks are.

Business situations can be the same. The client for whom you generously shaved your writing fee will probably be the client who gives you the hardest time in the approval stage. I've seen it happen lots of times. In fact, I recommend that you avoid lowering your price for that very reason. Also, you should demand a 50 percent deposit on any commercial writing job before beginning work. My feeling is that if they can't pay the deposit then they probably can't (or aren't intending to) pay the whole bill.

If this sounds overly pessimistic, I apologize. I don't want to discourage you from treating your fellow humans with affection and generosity. Just make sure you're braced for what can be disappointing behavior on the part of your neighbors and friends. That said, however, I would hasten to add that some good deeds actually do go unpunished.

Consider, for example, the time I donated five hours of marketing consultation to the local YMCA fund-raising auction. A decidedly "good" deed, I'm sure you will agree. I put a $500 value on my donation and tossed it into the ring with all the free meals, massages, pottery, gift certificates and other assorted gifts the community came up with. I didn't attend the auction, but I'm told that bidding on my donation fell somewhat short of the $500.

At any rate, a few weeks later I got a call from a woman named Betty who had purchased my time—or, as she put it, "I own you." Betty, who has a very well-honed sense of humor, was at the time serving as the president of the local downtown merchants association. The association is dedicated to finding ways to concentrate tourist and shopping dollars in the remarkably snappy downtown section of the little town where I maintain my office.

I put in my five hours interviewing merchants along Main Street about their various sources of business and their opinions regarding the marketing of downtown Hendersonville. Very interesting stuff, actually. No one is quite so passionate about marketing as a small-business owner is. There was quite a mix of stores—an English pub, a high-dollar coffeeshop, a double scoop of antique stores, a nature store, several gift shops, a few restaurants, a bookstore, a picture framing shop and at least one quite interesting art gallery. The observations and opinions I gathered were easily as varied as the stores themselves.

What I deduced from my research was that what the downtown really needed was a professional media-type person to place stories in outlying areas. These would be stories offering up our downtown area as a good day-trip destination or perhaps a weekend shopping venue. One such article in a large metropolitan newspaper would be more valuable than the total of the group's rather modest annual advertising budget.

I presented my findings to the association's steering committee and was met with a collective "Where, oh where, will we ever find such a person?" I just happened to have eight copies of a proposal explaining exactly how I would go about doing the job.

I included plans for story placement and a "value added" section that proposed four free, one-hour marketing sessions per week for the association's membership. And, of course, I attached a fee schedule that provided for a 50 percent down payment, with the balance to be paid over the next twelve months. The steering committee was quite enthusiastic. The budget, however, would not support my proposed fee. I couldn't justify doing all that work for a discounted rate and the negotiations broke down. I didn't get the project, and the association didn't get an experienced media hound like me to represent them. There's no telling how many millionaires I would have created had they only found enough money in the budget.

So at this point, you're probably thinking, "OK, Clausen, you didn't get the job, and you spent your time and effort with no pay. How does that qualify for a good deed going unpunished?" Even leaving aside the fact that I was able to help worthy local organizations earn money, the whole thing was still worth a lot to me. How much it means to me depends on the future, something freelancers are always betting on. Because all of the steering committee members seemed impressed with the proposal I gave them, there is a good chance that one of them may have marketing work for me in the future. Also, I learned some valuable things about working with organizations, a skill that could pay me well in the future. Putting the proposal together was a good exercise for my marketing brain. And lastly, the committee did take my advice to offer free parking downtown during the Christmas holidays, which means that I save a buck or so each day for about a month. OK, so that's not much—but it *is* something.

Even though I didn't get that particular job, the marketing of local associations still represents a great opportunity for freelance writers all over the country. Nearly every town has an organization similar to the one with which I am dealing. Nearly all of them are run by local merchants who have no significant media experience. And nearly all of them are just not getting the job done, at least not as well as they should. You see, in a lot of cases these merchants are getting their marketing advice from people who are trying to sell them print ads or broadcast time. I'm not saying that media salespeople are crooked as a dog's hind leg, but I am prepared to suggest that selling advertising in a small market can be a desperate undertaking. I once sold ad space in my college newspaper to an adult novelty/bookstore/peepshow simply because I had been tossed out by the management of every other business

I'd approached. One guy met me at the door and, without even listening to what I wanted, said, "I don't care what you're selling—get out." Then he put his hand on my chest and pushed me back out of the door. Experience that a few times and you'll understand why a media salesperson can get a little creative when describing the virtues of his or her medium.

Small-business owners and shopkeepers need objective, expert help if they are to make informed, effective media decisions.

I feel this bodes well for any freelancer ambitious enough to pursue the market from a public relations point of view. An article in the local paper is almost always more effective in bringing in business than an advertisement. And who is better qualified to think up and place stories than someone whose whole work life revolves around hunting up story ideas and selling them to publications?

One major caution before we go any further: recall from chapter eleven that submitting stories on behalf of your client as objective, freelance pieces is unwise and unethical. That's not to say that you couldn't write the story as you see it and hand it to the editor (who knows who your client is) as an example of how you and your client see the piece. In the business, that's called a "model press release." Lots of papers, especially small-town weeklies and five-day dailies, will accept the story and run it verbatim—as long as they know the stories are legitimate and you aren't hoodwinking them.

It takes a bit of research to ferret out the really good ideas. Maybe you'll discover a bookstore owner who is also an author. Or a sociology Ph.D. who's running a "politically correct" toy store (no war toys, a minimum of plastic, non-gender specific toys). Maybe the guy who runs the brewing equipment shop can provide some interesting information on beer during Octoberfest. You never know what you'll find when you start poking around in people's lives. I once discovered a blind equestrian who made her living (I swear it's true) exercising polo ponies. Some things—like the blind horsewoman—are just plain naturals. Others you may have to work up a bit. Nevertheless, if you keep talking to people long enough and keep your wits about you, I have no doubt that you'll come up with plenty of stories to position your clients as interesting, worthwhile folks with whom to do business.

If you're marketing small-town businesses, try to emphasize stories that will play in larger, nearby communities. A story in the *Hendersonville Times-News* may reach a few folks who will take a look downtown, but a story in an Atlanta newspaper about Hendersonville as a great day-trip destination will bring in some serious money.

One other caution: If you are a print-oriented freelancer, don't forget to include radio, TV and the Internet in your media plans. Nothing makes the merchant's phone ring like a story on the 6 o'clock news. You owe it to your client to leave no stone unturned. Remember that this sort of thing requires a different kind of pitch. TV, for example, is a visual medium. A client's interesting past history will not play with a TV assignment editor if it doesn't have a visual component. Unusual events with colorful characters work well with TV. I once participated in a Media Milk-Off sponsored by a Sacramento dairy company during the California state fair. Their publicist was short one media celebrity and, knowing that I'm an old farm boy, asked me to sit in. I did—and won the contest, making the 6 P.M. news and bursting a blood vessel in my forearm in the bargain. This was a great promotion on the publicist's part. Everybody there, with the exception of yours truly, ran segments on their participation. The milk company was all over the TV, and lots of people visited their displays at the fair. It was a total home run.

Radio, I think, depends on a news peg more than anything else. They don't have the time to spend on a story that a newspaper or magazine has. And they can't show pictures the way TV can. They need breaking news or short, amusing stories that don't require illustration.

Always have a firm idea of what you wish to accomplish when you launch a publicity campaign. The publicist for the milk company, who happens to be a good friend of mine, once told me that she gets her clients in the newspaper to stroke their egos. But she gets them on the television to make their phones ring. That's not always the case, but after a while you'll learn what works for each medium. It's a matter of studying the client's needs and the individual media outlets.

The same is true if you intend to help your association buy media (as opposed to getting free exposure through public relations). If you don't already know the advertising business, you'll need to study up on cost per thousand (CPM) and other affairs of advertising. Don't jump into media buying and advertising until you've made a thorough study of the field. Then, when you're totally confident in your comprehensive knowledge, offer your services as a consultant.

A serious warning: Never buy the media yourself. Large agencies often buy the media, charge their clients and then receive a 15 percent commission from the media they buy. This can add a nice profit center to the agency's bottom line, but it also entails a considerable financial exposure. I know a publicist in Northern California who signed a billboard media buy and then got stiffed by the client. Her name was on the bill. She had to come up with the money. It took her, if I remember correctly, about five years to recover from the loss. Even very large agencies have trouble surviving a hit like that. It's better to lose the account entirely than take a chance on getting left holding the media bag. A rule of thumb here is that if the client can't front the money to make the buy, then they probably can't afford the media in the first place. Get them to try something equally ambitious but less risky.

A colleague of mine has an interesting way of lowering his risk when buying media. He tells the client that he never fronts the money for the client, but if they will pay the media bill in his agency's name he will split the agency commission with them on a 50-50 basis. This allows him and his client to pick up a nice bit of change while eliminating any risk to his own personal treasury. It's worth a try on your part, but make sure you thoroughly understand the process.

Here's something else to consider when you're dealing with small, local associations: Make sure you are getting paid enough. We've talked about this before, but it bears repeating. Remember that, although you won't be able to charge as much locally as you do nationally, you still have to make a profit. Be brave. Don't worry about losing the job. It's better to lose a high-ball bid than to be trapped in an unprofitable project.

Here's my advice on charging for local jobs. Try to figure out how long the job will take you and then double that figure. Then figure out your hourly rate. Personally, I don't think that should be less than $40 per hour, no matter what the task and your relative depth of experience. Actually, $75 per hour would be closer to the mark.

If at all possible, get a sizable down payment before beginning work. There's a good reason for this, one you can use to explain your demands to your client. The majority of your work will be done early on while you are researching and building relationships with the media folks. This takes time and money if you are to do it right. If you're to get them coverage in the Atlanta market, for example, you are probably going to have to trot down to the city and schmooze with the reporters. You will be buying gas or plane tickets. Lunch will be on you. You will not make reporters, editors and other media types buy their own mint juleps. You'll need collateral material. If the travel editor for a large metro daily asks you for a brochure or a media kit on your clients, you'd better have one. If they ask for photos or videotapes or whatever, you'd better be able to come up with them. This is a campaign, much the same as in a war. You have objectives to reach. You need equipment and resources to meet them.

Don't be discouraged if your clients try to "cheap out" on you. That's just the nature of the business. It's important that you establish yourself as an authority early on. Be a little arrogant. They are hiring you for your expertise. Make sure you don't cave in to their understandable nervousness about spending money. By the same token, make sure that you know what you're talking about. Do your homework and work hard for your money. Don't ever forget that they are paying you for results.

While you're pitching your fee structure and explaining the ways of the media world to your clients, emphasize to them that most of the benefits they will reap will be down the road a ways. Their paydays will occur after you've established your contacts and thoroughly familiarized yourself with your clients and their potential place in the publicity food chain.

I can't emphasize this client/consultant communications too much. Make sure that everyone concerned understands how much your services are going to cost, when the expenditures will be made, what the money will go for and what they can reasonably expect to get for their money. If you blow this, you'll almost certainly have some disgruntled merchants wondering what you're doing with their dough.

Done correctly, this kind of work can easily bring you a medium to high, five-figure income—maybe even more. That's not bad compensation, especially if you get into it by doing a good deed.

CHAPTER TWENTY-THREE

Anticipate Success

Too many of us give up on our dreams. Too many of us, especially in the freelance writing business, let the opinions of others direct our professional and personal lives. We give freelancing a half-hearted shot and then scurry back to the alleged security of a "real" job. There are those who quake at the thought that one's compensation can be absolutely pegged to one's useful output of articles, advertising copy and other forms of writing. Freelancing requires a discipline that is absent in almost all regular jobs. If we don't sell, we don't get paid. The more we sell, the more money we make. It's as simple as that.

And what do our spouses, parents and well-meaning friends advise us? With few exceptions, they tell us to have something to "fall back on." What baloney! How much better it would be if they advised us to make sure we had a good freelance writing business plan. What a relief it would be to have them tell us to make ourselves better writers. If you're working as a self-employed plumber and you have a dry spell, do they tell you that you should have another profession to fall back on? Of course they don't. They'll tell you to get up to speed on the latest plumbing techniques and that you'd better advertise for more customers and you'd better start networking your old customers for referrals. That, my fellow scribes, is good advice—whether you're a plumber, a writer or any other self-employed person trying to stay ahead of your bills. When your business suffers, that's when you need to get serious and "step on the gas." Don't run from freelancing. Run to it. Find out what you're doing wrong and correct it. Don't let anybody scare you away from living your dream.

I heard a great line on an otherwise completely banal TV sitcom one day. "Having something to fall back on," the actor said, "sounds like getting ready to fail."

OK, so maybe freelance writing isn't the safest, most secure route to the world of the BMW and the Rolex watch. So what? I know tons of rich folks who aren't a bit happy. In fact, I know a whole family of rich people whose wealth traces back to an entrepreneur grandfather who got very lucky with a company he started way back. He was a dreamer, and he followed through. His descendents don't have to do a thing to assure their continued wealth, except keep breathing. I've never seen a more miserable bunch of people. They keep trying to justify the fact that they have millions for doing nothing. Of course, you really can't justify such good financial fortune. Nobody really deserves found wealth, no matter how much you try to rationalize it. The best you can do under such circumstances is try to deserve it by your good works and your interaction with your fellow Earthlings. It's much better to be out there chasing a buck and working on your own terms. It's much better to be a dreamer.

The difference between a plain old garden-variety dreamer and a hero is simple. Heroes go for it. They cook up an idea, formulate a plan and then take action. They let nothing and nobody get in their way. They follow through. They have faith in themselves.

How many of us sit around longing for an assignment from *Parade Magazine* or daydreaming about cashing royalty checks from the sale of the novel in our head? How many of us actually send off the necessary query letters or contact a good agent? How many of us have the courage and confidence to follow up on our dreams? The weird part of all this is that it isn't all that hard to "go for it." It's a matter of overcoming inertia, I think. Maybe it's similar to the feeling I get when I sit down to start a large writing project—or even, sometimes, a small project. I feel reluctant to start, so I put it off. Play some hearts on the computer or take a nap or wash the dishes or mow the lawn. Anything to put off the beginning of the work. Then, when time has trickled away to the last minute, I sit down and start banging out the words. The next thing I know, four or five hours have gone by without my noticing and the project is finished or at least well on its way. I've talked to countless writers who have similar stories about sitting down to write. I think it was John Steinbeck who said that he didn't enjoy writing, he enjoyed "having written."

Success in freelancing takes a little tenacity. Don't expect smooth sailing. Don't expect immediate and guaranteed financial success. You'll have to earn your dough. You may have to try hard for a long time. You may have to "continue to begin," as a friend of mine says.

Sometimes this pays off big-time. John McWade, an extremely talented art director with whom I used to work, had a dream of publishing a newsletter for graphic artists. Lots of artists have similar fantasies. The difference is that John went ahead and did it. He made all of the arrangements, devoted his time and energy and money to the project. Eventually he built up a publication that was worth at least a few million bucks. Along the way he risked everything. To say that he used his last buck would not be much of an exaggeration. But he never lost his faith in himself and his vision, and it paid off handsomely for him.

Of course, tenacity does not automatically bring bundles of money. But so what? Life is wonderfully uncertain. Failure is temporary. I've met a lot of talented people who are reluctant to take a stab at success. They are afraid of failure and disappointment. Better not get too optimistic, they figure, or you'll be just that much more pained by defeat.

Go-getters understand that it's better to anticipate success. That way, if they succeed, they'll enjoy both the anticipation and the actual success. If they fail, they have enjoyed the anticipation. There's a saying among poker players that "scared money never wins." Nothing in life is guaranteed, so let's have some fun along the way.

CHAPTER TWENTY-FOUR

In Praise of Sloth

When I was a kid on the family farm, I pretty much considered work to be the enemy.

Not that I didn't work, you understand. I spent many, many days on an ancient John Deere R Series tractor persecuting weeds and turning over soil. Or picking up rocks and piling them on the edge of a field. My mornings and evenings were spent milking cows and feeding (or cleaning up after) a variety of animals.

To be accurate, it wasn't the actual work that I disliked. What I hated was that there seemed to be no end to the stuff, no point at which I could kick back and say, "Well, that takes care of that. Now I'm on my own time." The weeds kept growing back, new rocks continually worked their way to the surface, and the cows would show up twice a day groaning for relief from their swollen udders.

Of course, that is the nature of farming. Actually, that's the nature of life on the planet. There was little I could do to escape. But I tried.

The best part of the day, for me, was right after lunch (we called it dinner) when I could disappear for a few minutes and live life on my own terms. Usually that meant flopping on the grass beneath an old cottonwood tree and letting my mind wander as far away as possible.

To my dad and the other folks working on the farm, this was, no doubt, a clear-cut case of sloth. Fifteen or twenty minutes spent with no hope of tangible accomplishment. A total waste of time. To me, though, those fifteen minutes were what my life was all about. For a quarter of an hour I was my own man, unfettered by tasks or responsibilities.

These days, I like my work a great deal more than I did then. Nevertheless, work stress and other kinds of adult anxieties can build up to dangerous levels if I'm not careful.

I find that I need more than a quarter hour under the cottonwood tree to recharge my batteries. Fortunately, I am now in full charge of my life (IRS, utility companies, credit card payments, etc., notwith-standing), and I can do pretty much whatever I want. That, of course, is one of the great benefits of freelance writing.

I find that tuning out for a short while is more than beneficial to my mental health—it's also very good for my writing. Relaxed minds turn out better ideas. I hope you've worked out your own forms of relax-ation and recuperation. In case you haven't, here are a few that have worked well for me.

1. Declare a mental health day. By this I mean you should shove your keyboard back under the desk, unhand your mouse and march right out of your office with no particular plans and no schedule. Be totally irresponsible. Wander around for a while, look in shops, have a cup of coffee down the street. I like to go over to the local high-dollar toy store and play with the good stuff.

2. Go down to the local mall and find that bench where the old men hang out. Walk right up and sit right down. Ask them how it's going. Be prepared for a deluge of geezer chat. Seriously, you can pick up a lot of interesting information that way, stuff you will never probably use, but interesting.

3. Feed the ducks at the local pond. For the price of a bag of stale Wonder bread and a little shoe leather, you can have an almost God-like experience. You decide which ducks get fed. You decide which ones have to wait their turn. A great chance to organize the world into your version of fairness.

4. Walk in the woods. OK, so this is almost a cliché. But how many of us actually take time to do it? I'm fortunate enough to live next to a National Historical Site (on the farm where Carl Sandburg lived out his golden years, no less) where a sixty-minute stroll will put you in contact with some of the most beautiful scenery in the world. There's even a footpath up to the top of a little mountain old Carl himself used to frequent. No doubt there are some simi-larly tranquil spots near your place.

5. Go to an afternoon movie. I recommend something foreign with subtitles.

6. Go to a shooting range and blast through a few boxes of ammuni-tion. This is particularly rewarding if you are a gun-control advo-cate. Have an NRA member meet you there. Tell him or her that you'd like to see what the big deal is about shooting guns. I guaran-

tee he or she will show up, and you'll have a great time. Plus, it's a great opportunity to be open-minded while indulging your atavistic urges.

I'm sure you will have no trouble coming up with a few more ideas on your own. Just remember, the point is to choose things that require very little, if any, responsibility. The resulting improvement in mental health and inspiration will astound you.

CHAPTER TWENTY-FIVE

"It Ain't the Singer, Darlin', It's the Song."

*My hair is still curly
and my eyes are still
blue. Why don't you
love me like you used
to do?* — HANK WILLIAMS

It's 3 A.M., Thursday morning in Nashville, Tennessee, and I am sitting at a deserted bar in the Opryland Hotel trying to write a country-western song on a cocktail napkin.

Assisting me in this hopelessly clichéd enterprise is the stunningly attractive Naomi Alexander, one of the many singer-songwriters who regularly cruise this town looking for the big break—or at least an open microphone. She knows a thing or two about what success requires in this environment.

"It ain't the singer, darlin,' " she tells me. "It's the song. The words and the phrasing and the tune. That's what sells in this town. Everybody wants a song."

This I find immensely appealing. As a word guy, I figure I can write almost anything. How hard can it be? I mean people have made money—a lot of it—writing lyrics like, "I'm gonna hire a wino to decorate our home" or "She's actin' single and I'm drinkin' doubles."

I actually heard the "wino" song a little while before it was formally released. A friend of mine had something or other to do with a recording studio and somehow got his hands on the tape. Maybe his studio was the outfit that made the recording. I don't know. He just played it for me one day and asked me what I thought of it. It was, I thought, a stupid song. Full of twangy, nasal country-western sounds and having to do with alcoholism, marital discord and all sorts of unpleasantness. I should have known it would be a hit. Instead, I told the guy it was the biggest piece of musical flatulence I'd ever heard and it would probably never see a minute of airtime. A month or more later, I was driving across Nevada and had my radio turned to a country station. Naturally, the song was hovering around the top of the chart and making a fortune for the people who wrote, produced and performed it.

So, considering what gets produced as music these days, I figure it can't be that hard to write a really good country-western song. Thus, with pen in hand and every dredged-up heartbreak and hangover howling for immortality, I begin to write.

As a theme, I settle on a broken relationship, a man trying to get over lost love, and, of course, a cold-hearted woman whose fault it all is. I'm going for a serious, tear-jerking, slow-dancing hillbilly ballad. There won't be a dry eye in the joint when I'm through. An hour or so later I start to realize that maybe this isn't quite as easy as it first seemed. I have written few things in my entire career that are as sickeningly banal as the poetry that stares up at me from that soggy napkin.

This is most discouraging. The sheer poetry I feel in my heart does not seem to flow out the end of my pen. Having been twice married and twice divorced, I feel I should know a thing or two about dysfunction and heartache. I can't believe this isn't working. In fact, I'm about to toss the whole sappy mess into one of Opryland's tastefully arranged trash bins when the ever-optimistic Ms. Alexander takes it out of my hand.

Alternately frowning and lifting her eyebrows, she reads through the first verse and the chorus. Then, with her eyes closed and her head tilted slightly backward she weaves the lyrics into a sad, soft melody.

I feel like I'm witnessing the beginning of something beautiful and important.

As the last note fades, I look at her expectantly. "Yeah, you're right, darlin'," she says. "It pretty much sucks. But let me work on it. I'll send you a tape."

It's been a good experience though. I learned some things about myself and about writing.

First of all, it takes great courage to write for the performing arts. What you hear in your head isn't necessarily what other people are going to hear or produce. You have to be willing to accept that your writing is only a contribution to the end result, not the entire finished product. That's not a bad thing to learn if you're planning to write screenplays, for example.

Second, it's good to step out of your usual genre of writing once in a while. Sort of shake up your approach to the written word, get a new perspective on "writer" as a job description.

If all you're writing is print journalism, for instance, there's a good chance you'll fall into a formula. When I was in the newspaper business, I happened to develop a patented formula for any feature story that I had to write in a hurry. I didn't realize how entrenched that formula was until I started writing for a magazine. I also hadn't realized how nervous the whole daily journalism business had made me. The first magazine assignment I got as a staff writer was supposed to take me the better part of the week to finish. I jumped on it like it was a newspaper beat story and finished it in about three hours. My editor looked me up and down when I handed it in and then told me I needed to "calm down a little." When I look at the piece now I can see that it was a just-the-facts kind of effort one sees in every daily newspaper. It certainly could have used some incubation time—and perhaps a wee bit more research. In time, I learned to pace myself and look for more magazine angles.

Getting out of the newspaper reporter's formula and into a magazine frame of mind was very good for me. It opened my eyes to the abundance of other writing projects (and paydays) that exist beyond the daily grind.

Since then I've tried just about every kind of writing: junk mail (at which I have become disturbingly adept), screenplays (still waiting for my first buck), poetry, TV spots, radio commercials, music videos, greeting card copy, press releases, brochures, advertising of all sorts, e-mail marketing messages, ghostwriting for a motivational speaker, church newsletters, children's science books, nonfiction crime stories, speeches, programs for charity auctions, instruction manuals for computer software and, now, at long last—country-western lyrics.

I encourage you to try to expand your own writing markets, if for no other reason than the perspective it gives you as a writer. I know that writing junk mail has made me a better writer all around. This is because junk mail brings with it the chance to measure your response in a very quantitative sense. You can write the most beautiful and compelling (or so you think) piece of junk mail and have it completely flop. You can see something someone else wrote that fills you with scorn for their lack of skill, and it will pull phenomenal numbers. You'll be forced to look long and hard at what you're writing. You'll realize as never before that people are not obligated to read what you write. Your writing must somehow grab the reader around his brain and drag him in. This sort of introspection is good for any kind of writing. As writers, we're competing with a lot of other mental distractions and stimuli. If we can't get noticed above this cacophony, well, then we're not going to sell what we write, whether it be junk mail, short stories, novels or country-western lyrics.

The experience of doing something different can have a beneficial effect on your skills as a writer. The more experience you gain, the more confident you'll become. Courage breeds courage.

Just because you've never written a stage play doesn't mean you can't do it. And in the process of writing it, you may find a new approach to dialogue in your magazine writing or in your novel.

Just as writing direct mail copy can help you "get to the point" in your other writing, presenting advertising copy to a difficult, demanding client can help you develop a "tough skin" when it comes to criticism. Also, as an ad copywriter, you'll have to learn to look for the unique selling proposition, the thing that makes the product or service in question unique (or at least close to unique). Translate this kind of scrutiny to magazine journalism or any other kind of writing and you'll find that your stories will have a lot more depth and purpose. As a commercial advertising writer, you have to sort of force yourself on your readers in a way that makes your message irresistible. Believe me, it's an acquired skill and a valuable one no matter what kind of writing you end up doing.

Working as a daily newspaper reporter teaches you to write quickly and accurately no matter what's going on around you. My job at a daily newspaper had me sitting at a cluster of three desks near a constantly ringing phone and a never-silent Associated Press wire service machine in a room full of clacking Royal manual typewriters. After a couple of weeks, I was so used to ignoring the noise that if you wanted to talk to me you'd have to tap my shoulder as if I were deaf. The one exception was the managing editor's voice. He could make himself heard in any situation.

Writing poetry, even if it's really bad poetry, forces you to think symbolically, open yourself up emotionally and write with an economy of words. Not everyone is good at this. There are books, I'm told, filled with truly bad stuff. I have a friend who's been writing poetry his whole life. He holds a Ph.D. from Yale, teaches in a private academy and is one of the world's great conversationalists. I've read his poetry and not really recognized it as anything exceptional—that is, I didn't realize it until he read it to me out loud. That's when I realized that reading poetry to yourself, especially if you're as unschooled in it as I am, may not reveal its true essence. When he reads his own stuff, it comes magically alive. This happened to me once before in Sacramento. A friend of mine roped me into attending a poetry reading in which his longtime girlfriend, Olivia, was set to perform. I snoozed through an awful parade of bad writing and poor performances until Olivia took the floor. She recited a poem about being a little Chicano girl in Texas. The poem, if I remember correctly, was about her uncle. The topic really isn't that important. What was important was the performance. She read most of it looking straight at the audience and then turned her head to the right and sang the little girl's words in a childlike a cappella voice. It was downright chilling and gave me a wonderful perspective on poetry and performance. I've heard Olivia several times since then, and her performances always give me a rush of emotion.

What I've learned from all of this is that we, as writers, need to keep experiencing new kinds of writing. Even if you never make an extra nickel from it, the experience alone is worth the effort. It's part of living as a writer. And, of course, there's always the chance that Randy Travis will actually like your song and somebody in a suit will offer you big bucks for it. Or maybe that screenplay will get optioned. Hey, it happens. I know of a screenwriting duo who split $600,000 for writing a truly mediocre script that was actually filmed and made lots of money for its producers.

So, no matter what kind of writing opportunity presents itself, give it a shot. Remember, you can't catch fish if you don't bait the hook. (Hey, does that sound like a Randy Travis lyric or what?)

Index